THRESHOLDS OF ILLITERACY

just ideas

transformative ideals of justice in ethical and political thought

series editors

Drucilla Cornell

Roger Berkowitz

THRESHOLDS OF ILLITERACY

THEORY, LATIN AMERICA, AND THE
CRISIS OF RESISTANCE

Abraham Acosta

FORDHAM UNIVERSITY PRESS

NEW YORK 2014

Fordham University Press has no responsibility for the persistence or accuracy of
URLs for external or third-party Internet websites referred to in this publication
and does not guarantee that any content on such websites is, or will remain,
accurate or appropriate.

Fordham University Press also publishes its books in a variety of electronic
formats. Some content that appears in print may not be available in electronic
books.

Library of Congress Cataloging-in-Publication Data
is available from the publisher.

Printed in the United States of America

16 15 14 5 4 3 2 1

First edition

THE
AMERICAN
LITERATURES
INITIATIVE

A book in the American Literatures Initiative (ALI), a collaborative
publishing project of NYU Press, Fordham University Press, Rutgers
University Press, Temple University Press, and the University of Virginia
Press. The Initiative is supported by The Andrew W. Mellon Foundation.
For more information, please visit www.americanliteratures.org.

To my wife, my son, and those we have lost along the way

Contents

Acknowledgments

In this case, it took a village. Maybe more than one. Okay, perhaps something like three whole villages for this book to come to fruition. What I mean by this, of course, is that this book would not have been possible without the timely and fortuitous interventions from countless individuals, communities, and institutions throughout my life. First and foremost I need to thank Gareth Williams, without whose guidance, direction, and patience this project would never have gotten off the ground. Gareth has been there at each stage of the project, pushing me forward and upward. He is a mentor, a colleague, and most of all a friend to whom I owe a great deal. Alongside him I wish to express my indebtedness to Anton Shammas for his warm and delicate counsel in both good and bad times, Gustavo Verdesio for his insistence that I turn it off every now and again and listen to some jazz, and Javier Sanjinés for his candor, passion, and unwavering encouragement. A special thanks to Joshua Lund, Patrick Dove, Bruno Bosteels, Justin Read, Laura Gutiérrez, Alberto Moreiras, Charles Hatfield, Jon Beasley-Murray, Ivonne del Valle, Oscar Ariel Cabezas, David Johnson, Javier Durán, Sam Steinberg, Nicole Guidotti-Hernández, Isis Sadek, Meredith Martin, Ignacio Sánchez Prado, Brett Levinson, and Sergio Villalobos for their insight, friendship, and support over the past six years; they often devoted their precious time and energy exchanging ideas with me, discussing this project, and generously reading drafts of the manuscript. I cannot thank them enough. Thank you to Andrés Guzmán, Olimpia Rosenthal, Eva Romero, and Andrew Rajca, who made our first seminar together a productive, meaningful, and pivotal rehearsal for the book's central claims.

Many others, with a question here or an observation there, have immeasurably impacted the development of the book: individuals such as Anne Garland Mahler, Santiago Colás, Luis Martín-Cabrera, Graciela Montaldo, Sean Cotter, María del Pilar Blanco, John Kraniauskas, Erin Graff Zivin, Jaime Rodríguez Matos, Nhora Serrano, Ximena Briceño, Robert Wells, Claire Solomon, Mariana Amato, Vanessa Pérez, and Stephenie Young.

This project began at the University of Michigan, where, through the support of numerous faculty, students, and various programs and fellowships, it was able to first see the light of day. I owe a debt of gratitude to Simon Gikandi, Tobin Siebers, and Yopie Prins for their generous support through the Department of Comparative Literature; to the Rackham Graduate School; and to Louis Cicciarelli and the Sweetland Center for Writing. A warm thank you to my cohort Jonah Johnson, Stanton McManus, and Sylwia Ejmont, as well as to Sarah Scott, Chris Luebbe, Megan Saltzman, Asli Igsiz, Meg Cotter-Lynch, Beatriz Ramírez Betances, Charles Sabatos, Madeline Hron, Nicholas Theisen, Ramon Stern, Michael Kicey, Fernando Velásquez, Alana Reid, Orlando Betancor, Sebastián Díaz, Eduardo Matos, Andrea Leigh, and Constanza Svidler.

This book could not have been completed without the financial support of various institutions and foundations. I would like to extend my thanks and enormous appreciation to Malcolm Compitello, Charles Tatum, and the Department of Spanish and Portuguese and the College of Humanities at the University of Arizona for taking me on and for their unyielding support of my professional and intellectual development. I am thankful to the Andrew W. Mellon Foundation and the Woodrow Wilson National Fellowship Program for their generous support of this project, and to Mary Wildner-Bassett, Ken McAllister, and Tom Miller for making it as easy as possible to make the most of that fellowship year.

I would also like to recognize my colleagues here at the University of Arizona, each of whom, in unique ways, provided a most welcome, reassuring, and truly positive environment; they are Yadira Berigan, Sarah Beaudrie, Miquel Simonet, Jaime Fatas, Mónica Morales, Melissa Fitch, Katia Bezerra, Eliud Chuffe, Ana Carvalho, Antxon, Olarrea, Judy Nantell, Dick Kinkade, Lanin Gyurko, Bob Fiore, and Sonia Colina. A special thank you to Mary Portillo, Mercy Valente, Isela González, and Nichole Guard for their tireless efforts in the office. No less significantly, I am grateful to the following colleagues I have come to know and befriend over the course of my time in Tucson: Lyn Duran, Adela Licona, David Gramling, Chantelle Warner, Damián Baca, Adam Geary, Frank Galarte, Maribel Alvarez, Miranda Joseph, Sandy Soto, Brigitta Lee, Rachel Srubas, and Alain-Philippe Durand. A very special thank you as well to JR and Maureen Reid for their friendship, support, and encouragement over the years.

Allow me to end by acknowledging the beginning. I am indebted to the Mellon Mays Undergraduate Fellowship and the Ronald E. McNair's Scholars Program, two minority undergraduate fellowship programs responsible for making the academy visible as a profession to minority students and for providing the means to gain entry and access to it. Without such institutional programs, I simply would not be here. At the University of Southern California, I am beholden to Kadri Vihvelin, Jack Crossley, Daniel Tiffany, Peggy Kamuf, and Jim Kincaid, who saw enough potential in me to work me even harder. I thank them for their mentorship and direction.

A few added words of appreciation are needed here for Helen Tartar, Thomas Lay, Tim Roberts, Judith Hoover, and everyone at Fordham University Press and the American Literatures Initiative. Helen was among the very few editors who truly understood this book, what it wants to say and what it seeks to accomplish; I am grateful it found its way to her careful and discerning hands. Tom and Tim, with whom communications were always timely, efficient, and transparent, were nothing but a pleasure to work with during the entire process. A special thank you to Judith for her patient and delicate work in preparing this manuscript for publication.

I offer my immeasurable appreciation and affection to my family, Rosa Estela and Ignacio Acosta, Claudia Acosta, Diane and Sven Barzanallana, Rose and Jerry Serna. To my nephews and nieces Nicholas, Britanee, Alek, and Katie: whose youth continues to inspire and motivate my work as an educator and scholar. Finally, to Maritza and Ellison, whom I love more than anything else and to whom I dedicate this book: you are both my reason for living and the source for my belief that fighting for the betterment of everyone's life is a precondition for your own.

A section of chapter 1 originally appeared in *CR: New Centennial Review* 13.2 (2013), 203–22; it is reprinted with permission from Michigan State

University Press. An earlier version of chapter 5 was published previously in *Social Text* 30.4 (2012), 103–23; it is reprinted with permission from Duke University Press. A section of chapter 4 was published in the *Journal of Latin American Cultural Studies* 19.2 (2010), 203–23; it is reprinted with permission from Taylor and Francis Ltd.

Introduction

Literary and cultural debates in Latin America have for some time now given way to the assumption that resistance to the West (to colonization, to modernization, etc.) has always been a formative element of Latin American social discourse and continues to be actively woven into cultural representations and practices. This notion has seeped into scholarly production, where it has become commonplace to suggest, among other things, that indigenous resistance to the West began the day the "New World" was discovered, that *mestizaje* as a phenomenon is exclusive only to the Americas, or that resistant, emancipatory thought in Latin America is best served by not going "outside" of its own intellectual tradition and historical specificities. So much has this assumption of resistance taken hold that many have begun to see an uninterrupted, historically and culturally specific legacy of antagonism that, beginning more than five hundred years ago, has become constitutive of Latin American identity and, in many ways, Latin America itself. However, and despite its increasing prevalence, this

notion of Latin America as a primordial cultural antagonism is proving less
and less satisfactory as a principle of analysis and can now be seen working
against its own aims. It seems that in recent years the idea of resistance has
become saturated through hasty, imprecise, and often contradictory usage,
leaving a concept that retains little of its true political meaning, function,
and force. One could even argue that today resistance in Latin America has
become "resistant" to itself.

The present volume inquires into the notion of resistance at work in this
assumption as well as the image of Latin America that emerges through
it. *Thresholds of Illiteracy* is a critical examination of the politics of reading resistance in contemporary Latin America. It posits that predominant
theories of Latin American culture have been and continue to be insufficiently conceived to account for the critical and heterogeneous realities of
modernization in the region. Specifically I argue that prevailing theories
have brought the study of Latin America to a methodological impasse—a
"deadlock of resistance"—that demands serious revision to the concept if
it is to continue to be analytically useful and continue to inspire people's
struggle for freedom. I offer a critical remapping of the form, function, and
effects of resistance within Latin American cultural production and political discourse. Challenging the narrow and limited framework in which representations of social antagonism in Latin America are read and imagined,
I advance the notion of illiteracy as a means to interrogate and rehabilitate
the concept of resistance for contemporary political reflection.

Thresholds of Illiteracy is an exploration into the predominance and inner
workings of certain narratives of cultural resistance within Latin America
and the economies of reading that sustain them. It comprises a series of discrete critical engagements with some of contemporary Latin America's most
widely recognized and politically charged cultural emplotments: *indigenista* narrative in modern Peru and the young protagonist Ernesto from *Deep
Rivers,* caught with the impossible task of preserving meaning between
creole and indigenous cultures; *testimonio* narrative and the promise (and
withholding) of subaltern knowledge; the declarations of "silence" from the
Lacandon jungle by the Zapatista Army of National Liberation (Ejército
Zapatista de Liberación Nacional; EZLN); and the narrative of countless
immigrants, arriving daily at the U.S.-Mexico border, through whose (often
posthumous) narration of their journey north by writers, critics, and activ-
ists bring their experiences of abandonment and exploitation at the border

to light. In each case the analyses contained in this volume foreground the geopolitical, economic, and social conditions that both generate and reveal this crisis of resistance. This book is written with the hope that through a persistent and critical interrogation of the problems (epistemological and political) still inhering in methods used in the interpretation of marginalized voices and texts in Latin America, one may begin the arduous work of accounting for them on more egalitarian grounds. Unfortunately critics and scholars still remain unconvinced of this disciplinary problem's pervasiveness; they remain unconvinced, in effect, that these methods actually reproduce the very conditions of global and structural inequality they were designed to overcome. As such, the analysis contained in this volume is not simply an analysis and critique of the ideologies of reading that inform the discipline today but one that also advances the possibility of a truly democratic reading practice.

This crisis of resistance emerges from the convergence of certain historical and disciplinary conditions. Contemporary Latin America emerges historically as an uneven and ongoing effect of overwhelming political and economic demands on the continent—a withering nation-state; insertion into the transnational market; dictatorships, Dirty Wars, *Contras*—a confused and contradictory social field that today still obtains as an intellectual limit to those demands. Disciplinary reading practices in Latin America bear witness to this postnational torsion, having shifted away, many years ago, from a unitary, homogeneous model of analysis predicated on the national appropriation of previously excluded, subordinated social classes to an interpretive approach based now on affirming their originary and foundational cultural difference from it. For example, if in the previous era Latin American intellectuals were enlisted in the promotion and institutionalization of certain "grand" narratives of cultural nationalism—mestizaje, transculturation—by which to integrate and suture nonliterate, "popular" classes and cultures into the common populace of the nation, today, and perhaps as a result (and a historical effect) of the failure of these projects, one can now see the reverse at work: that forms of resistance (*from the assumed perspective* of those popular classes) against state-sponsored forms of sociocultural mediation have emerged as the principal subject of scholarly work. Conceived within an increasingly expansive disciplinarily matrix that includes (but is not limited to) literature, popular culture, history, philosophy, and anthropology, "resistance" has been ascribed by Latinamericanist scholars to innumerable texts, objects, historical processes, and even entire (sub)cultures, in short, to all manner of cultural artifact or practice found to be exhibiting—performing/signifying—opposition or subversion to the regional, national, and global fields of social ordering in which they are inscribed.

Unfortunately, the conceptual framework behind this disciplinary shift is unable to provide a sufficiently complex understanding of the political field within which these sociocultural phenomena now appear. With very few exceptions, political reflection on or about Latin America continues to draw upon assumed notions of cultural essence and authenticity as a means of identifying and theorizing groups that have traditionally been excluded from official narratives of nationhood. Critics such as Jon Beasley-Murray (2010) have traced this problem to the emergence of cultural studies as a paradigm, which, by inaugurating a hegemonic/popular economy, that is, by cleaving the field of culture between institutionalized (state) and popular ("the people") forms, resulted, according to Beasley-Murray, in the formation of an interpretive model with an implicit populist tendency and a particularly lax, and ultimately unworkable, understanding of state power. Cultural studies' insistence on these popular cultural practices is due to the assumption that, emerging from the people, they are objects of analysis more in touch with the actual life of the community. As a result, popular culture became the privileged mode of analysis, particularly for practices that do not fit into or actively contest the larger, official narratives from which they are often excluded or marginalized. This is where (and how) the people became marked as resistant. This condition is further compounded by another effect of this conceptual partition: the infusing of the subordinate, resistant term (in this case, the people) with the (more often desired) characteristics and attributes that the dominant term is often understood *not* to have. In other words, it is through the notion of the popular or the people wherein is ascribed the essential and desired attributes that make the people a People, that is, an imagined community constituted by its cultural opposition to a state that oppresses the populations that make it up. These terms are each differentially defined through the other; that is, neither of the two results in any positive designation. It is for such reasons that Beasley-Murray (2000) calls instead for an "unpopular" cultural studies. In the meantime the notion of "the people" is still a deeply held assumption,

even among scholars, yet critically it is one that simply does not follow
and is constitutive of the crisis we are tracing. Examining the (unanticipated) effects generated by this conceptual slippage is precisely the focus
of this book.

As a critical intervention into debates on culture and politics in Latin
America, theories of cultural difference take on central importance in this
project. Transculturation emerges in this study as the still predominant
field of intelligibility within which questions of culture, power, and representation are posed. Coined in the early twentieth century as an originary,
cohesive principle of racial and cultural mixedness and assimilation, transculturation has been established as the grand narrative of cultural nationalism in many parts of Latin America and continues to function today as the
predominant disciplinary episteme, promoting mixedness as both an inherently resistant practice (again, to the West, the United States, etc.) and a
defining, historically specific, "Latin American" characteristic. There is no
question that transculturation continues to serve as the primary ideological
process by which cultural difference in Latin America is both conceived (as
different) and reduced (as resistant). In fact its seemingly limitless jurisdic-
tion and subsumptive legislation is exactly what animates (and underwrites)
the very assumption of primordial resistance described in the opening.

If, however, following recent critical work on the concept, a critical genealogy of transculturation reveals itself instead to be a regulatory practice
that appropriates and homogenizes excluded and subordinated forms of
alterity into the field of cultural intelligibility, then there is simply no position "outside" this field, and this appeal to cultural difference turns out to
be constructed by, and therefore the naturalized and concealed effect of,
the very discursive structures that it is purported to resist.[1] In other words,
what if the underlying assumption of a position outside the sphere of Western hegemony as a space from which to critique it actually does nothing to
upset the rationality of the normative ordering of society in the first place?
What if, precisely because it shares in the same assumptions (and problems),
the affirmation of difference ultimately fulfills an integral aspect of capitalist reproduction? Consequently, and this is the wager of the book, if such
a condition is an actual possibility within the field of culture, then the disciplinary appropriation of resistant objects is not only thwarted in advance
but entirely counterproductive as either a cultural politics or a politics of
reading. This book aims to show, in quite critical and salient ways, that

theories of cultural difference simply cannot account for the social contradictions of neoliberal rationality that one confronts today. In fact, such is
the state of this theoretico-political impasse that their enlistment will only
further the promotion of nativist, reverse-ethnocentric, and/or other neocolonial agendas and, as such, form part of the very crisis for which this book
is a critical intervention. A new critical approach must emerge, specifically
one that reconceives and regrounds the relationship between antagonism
and resistance in the contemporary social text.

   Thresholds of Illiteracy thus poses the question of Latin America and theoretico-political reflection in neoliberal times. I aim to offer a sustained
critical examination of the historical and disciplinary conditions by which
this deadlock of resistance and the resultant politics of reading in Latin
America emerges as a dispute over the account that is made of speech. Specifically I analyze the cultural effects and political implications that surface
when this confused critical economy is then used to provide the ontological guarantee for resistant forms of speech, such as orality. Orality is not
only the name used to refer to nonlettered, indigenous speech; it also serves
today to invoke the idea of an alternative, primarily indigenous mode of
consciousness radically incommensurate with Western modes of knowledge
and governance. Employed mainly to mark alternative, culturally resistant
forms of signification ascribed to historically marginalized subjects in Latin
American writing, orality has been used to posit cultural and political representation to subjugated groups and classes and has become the primary
rhetorical means by which to counter hegemonic narratives of nationhood
and modernization. Today representations of oral speech in Latin American literary and cultural production figure as tropes of cultural difference,
serving not only as a linguistic marker of historical ethnoracial subordination to modern, lettered culture but simultaneously as a metonym for alternative (again, primarily indigenous) modes of being persisting in external
relation to, and therefore uncontaminated by, Western categories and reason. Such ideological recuperations of alterity have featured prominently in
contemporary Latin American criticism, most often as explicit references in
the elaboration of a theory or narrative of cultural resistance. However, this
methodological approach to the subaltern voice has been, and continues to
be, underwritten by largely assumed and uninterrogated notions of speech
that in effect confounds its own theoretical promise as cultural critique.
Conceptually what we are presented with is the positing of an identity of

otherness, understood through the category of speech, by which subordinated, alternative, and therefore radically resistant political expressions are
conceived as emerging from a sphere outside Western influence. Such a construct, however, discloses an insufficiently grounded relation to capital, the
state, and neoliberal political rationalities, for in critical terms, this figure
of otherness emerges as a result of a tacit conflation of certain ontological
and logocentric guarantees that confuses assertions of heterogeneity $(A = -(-A))$ with a promise of a positive, substantive, and differential identity with
which to not only critique hegemony but to challenge for it $(A = B)$.

It is beyond doubt that the narrow and limited framework in which
resistance has been understood up until today has become constitutive
of the very crisis it was deployed to resolve and which needs a new analytic approach. It is furthermore quite obvious now that the social, cultural, and disciplinary contradictions that facilitated the current crisis of
resistance were there all along but were simply hidden from view until jos-
tled free by heterogeneous and contingent cultural phenomena for which
current methods could not, and still cannot, account. *Thresholds of Illiteracy* is born from, and therefore is a sustained meditation on, the ruins
of previously established orders of knowledge in Latin America, as well as
on the historical and cultural contradictions—specifically the incursion of
neoliberal rationality and its unanticipated social effects—that ultimately
brought it about. Among the many contradictions that have materialized
is the irreducible gap—or parallax—between Latinamericanist discourse
and its object. If, as Alberto Moreiras (2001: 1) contends, Latin American-
ism constitutes "the sum total of academic discourse on Latin America,
whether carried out in Latin America, in the United States, in Europe, or
elsewhere," then what the present moment bears witness to is the extent to
which Latinamericanist discourse has been revealed to be (unreconceal-
ably) a regime of knowledge fundamentally unmoored from itself, geopolit-
ically and disciplinarily. Moreiras's claim, in other words, is a recognition of
this discourse's always already constitutive relationship to its object, and it
demonstrates an awareness that that onto-epistemic gap was there all along.
It is not, by any means, evidence of an epochal change in the object's status: where, sometime between a before and an after, a once whole, undifferentiated, and homogeneous Latin America lost its ability to speak for
itself, is now only spoken for by foreign, nonrightful entities—including
institutions of interpretation within Europe, and the United States—and

must now be reclaimed. Restoration to a previous state of being, unified and self-identical to itself, that can "know and speak its conditions," what Spivak (1988) calls a "pure form of consciousness," appeals precisely to the same Eurocentric civilizational myth that underwrites the colonial project to begin with and which continues to guarantee neocolonial institutions like anthropology an object of study. In other words, reversion to a state previous to the present is not possible, because that state is simply unavailable except as a key founding myth of Western modernity. Consequently it has become imperative that we understand that when it comes to Latin America, as is true in any other part of the world, claims made by local intellectuals regarding their own geopolitical sphere of influence provide neither the guarantee nor the possibility of an unmediated (non-ideological) relation to the region from/about which they speak. Far from it. Furthermore, evaluating competing claims about Latin America based on an intellectual's proximity to the area only compounds the confusion. As such, appealing to a proper, rightful, and therefore more direct relationship between native Latin American discourse—whether creole, mestizo, or indigenous—and Latin America itself provides nothing that would challenge or resist the pervasive ideological agendas against which it is defined, for they ultimately share in the same assumptions of belonging and exclusion. Unfortunately, appeals to property or properness as grounds upon which to assert the right to speak ultimately and quite easily lend themselves to conservative, antidemocratic interests (colonial and/or indigenous elite, fundamentalist nationalist groups, etc.), and pose no real threat to the naturalized order of domination.

As a result, given the ways speech and cultural difference have served as the overarching categories through which resistance is both theorized and articulated in the cultural field, it is to an exploration of the "deep grammar" of this dynamic—the seat of certain pervasive and deeply entrenched biopolitical assumptions—that we must now direct our attention. For it is in the context of recent debates over the politics of representation, language, and culture in Latin America that such an analysis is to be carried out. *Thresholds of Illiteracy* challenges contemporary understandings of culture, power, and resistance with an explicit and systematic interrogation of the tropes of subaltern speech. Drawing primarily from recent debates on the controversial rise of theory in Latin America, on the indigenista and testimonio narrative traditions, the declarations and communiqués by the

EZLN, and U.S.-Mexico border writing, I offer an analysis and critique of the historical, theoretical, and disciplinary conditions that regulate the category of speech in the Latin American cultural field and govern its outermost expressional limits. I take as my objects of study not only the formalized, textual presentation of speech-acts by various subordinated groups but the unwieldy, radically unpredictable social forces that are unleashed when resistant readings fall prey to the same onto-epistemic assumptions as their traditional counterparts. Together my analyses sketch the contours of the unpredictable and tenuous relationship between inherited systems of representation and the sheer heterogeneity of decolonized space in diverse Latin American contexts, in each case bringing to light the contingencies of modernization that hegemonic and counterhegemonic ideological practices can no longer keep hidden from view.

To this theoretical impossibility to both invoke and substantiate subaltern speech I advance the term *illiteracy*, which I employ as both a critical concept and a mode of analysis that renders visible and intervenes in this crisis of resistance. By *illiteracy* I do not mean just the inability to read and write, nor am I appealing to the voice's primacy over writing; illiteracy as I am developing it should not be confused with the characteristic—individual or cultural—defined by a lack or deficiency of lettered culture and practices. Illiteracy is not the property, characteristic, or identity of those who cannot read. Rather I use the term to express the condition of semiological excess and ungovernability that emerges from the critical disruption of the field of intelligibility within which traditional and resistant modes of reading are defined and positioned. Illiteracy is not a thing nor in itself an object of study, but rather an unreconcealment. I read illiteracy as tracing the critical contradictions at play between ideologically opposed reading strategies, contradictions that, in effect, nullify that very opposition. In other words, illiteracy names irreducibly ambiguous semiosis that, through its active indeterminacy and critically destabilizing effects, at once reveals the ultimately contingent and arbitrary nature of the political order, vacates the very terms of dispute over which competing ideological claims are made, and collapses the field of intelligibility within which the debate is inscribed. I therefore read illiteracy as textual anomalies that emerge between and amid competing ideological appropriations of cultural texts, subverting the very economy of reading that serves as their normative, interpretive matrix. As such, this study is concerned less with the *illegibility* of particular, culturally distinct signs, objects, or practices than with the political conditions that obtain when a given field of intelligibility misreads—proves *incapable of reading*—the zone of indistinction between identity and difference opened up by such phenomena.

The critical value promised by illiteracy as a concept for theoretical reflection in contemporary Latinamericanist debates is secured through what one can call, for lack of a better term, its polyvalence. Indeed, as I hope to express with this term, illiteracy signals and engages simultaneously with a wide range of cultural models and theoretical debates regarding reading, writing, and the political. On the one hand, and most significantly, illiteracy refers to the classical ethnographic duality of writing and orality, which is frequently deployed in making distinctions between modern and premodern or Western and non-Western peoples and societies. If writing is considered a watershed leap in the world-historical development of the human intellect and civilization, it is because the idea of orality was developed as a way to understand why, for European observers, recently encountered non-Western cultures appeared to lack history and social order. In recent years Latinamericanist scholars and thinkers have sought to establish either that Latin American indigenous groups did (or do) in fact have writing or that oral traditions generate their own historical and political potentiality. In some cases these scholars have even sought to reverse the writing/speech hierarchy by asserting that orality constitutes a cultural "authenticity" that must be recovered and preserved against colonial and imperial domination. I aim not to pit writing against orality but instead develop illiteracy as a way of talking about what cannot be subsumed within this cultural economy. I demonstrate the ways in which illiteracy reveals the gap that exists between orality and writing, a condition of excess and subordination that cannot be understood adequately within the framework of writing (Spanish colonial or creole postindependence societies) versus orality (traditional indigenous communities), or modernity versus tradition. In short, illiteracy foregrounds the social contradictions—subalternity and deculturation—that are themselves produced by modernization but that cannot be accounted for by writing versus orality, nor are they assimilable to modernity's structures and institutions. It is in this capacity and context that illiteracy can be read as working against literacy writ large, understood both as a cultural paradigm of modernization, assimilation, or transculturation and as a trope of knowledge and understanding that implies transcending and/or reducing cultural and ethnic boundaries.

Illiteracy thus also represents an intimate engagement with and a critical refashioning of reading as a trope of understanding, comprehension, and commensurability. Illiteracy is what emerges when a regime of sensibility encounters "zones of indistinguishability" between identity and difference, inside and outside, proper and improper, truth and error, and so on. If reading functions as the predominant figure for interpretation, insight, and knowledge production in Western thought, illiteracy names what must be excluded—disqualified or forgotten ahead of time—in order for reading to happen. This unreconcealment, then, is the return of the constitutive repression that makes knowledge possible. This illiterate trace refers primarily not to determinate entities or people but to the points and zones of contact, exposure, and indeterminacy that are at once constitutive of determinate spaces and, at the same time, irreducible to them. As such, these sites of illiteracy are neither proper nor improper, neither inside nor outside, but rather are the unassimilable and uncanny cuts, delineations, displacements, misrecognitions, and openings that make space possible in the first place. Further, illiteracy allows us to understand cultural contact and social conflict in Latin America as a reflected relation in which positions, identities, sensibilities, and differences are generated through relationality itself.

Perhaps most important is illiteracy's relationship with legibility, legality, and law. Illiteracy signals not only a critical upending or subversion of historically established tropes of semiological coherence in Latin America, between writing or orality, the literary and the literal, noise and discourse, silence and speech; it ultimately amounts to a disruption of an existing social order. It is in this sense that illiteracy works to both complement and reinscribe Jacques Rancière's notion of police as well as the antagonistic function of politics that reveals the social order's very lack of foundation. In *Disagreement* (1999: 29), Rancière reserves the name *police* for a certain "configuration of the perceptible" that constitutes the social field, "an order of bodies that defines the allocation of ways of doing, ways of being, and ways of saying, and sees that those bodies are assigned by name to a particular place and task; it is an order of the visible and the sayable that sees that a particular activity is visible and another is not, that this speech is understood as discourse and another as noise." It is this "distribution of the sensible," the assignment and allocation of already recognized groups to properly designated spaces, argues Rancière, that both confirms and conceals the fundamental miscount, the impossible equation between the people and the whole of the political community

("the part of no part"). Illiteracy should be understood as featuring prominently in this miscount, for it lies at the core of the people's (mis)taking for
itself, as its proper lot, the freedom (as speaking beings) that is not proper to
them because freedom, like illiteracy, is not a positive property but merely a
lack of position and indifferentiation (14). All this means nothing, of course,
while the "symbolic distribution of speaking bodies" continues undisturbed.
However it is precisely upon this primordial miscount that any sudden and
unanticipated assertion of equality from the demos conditions the upheaval
of the social field and a redistribution of parts and parties, "the introduction
of an incommensurable at the heart of the distribution of speaking bodies"
(19). This he calls politics. So if, for Rancière, "politics exists when the natural
order of domination is interrupted by the institution of a part of those who
have no part" (11), illiteracy, as the semiological expression of the part of no
part, becomes the specific textual modality through which this interruption
takes place. This illiterate, short-circuiting of the social field makes visible
the possibility of an other social ordering, a democratic reconditioning of the
terms defining speaking bodies, belonging, and community, what Rancière
designates as "the simple counting of the uncounted, the difference between
an inegalitarian distribution of social bodies and the equality of speaking
beings" (38).

Inseparable therefore as a mode of reading contemporary cultural production,   illiteracy is a critical category that foregrounds the irreducible
heterogeneity of the social field and makes visible a beyond to the ideological determinations of theories of cultural difference. Whereas Rancière
emphasizes the visual dimension (appearance, theater, etc.) in such political conflicts, illiteracy engages with the ethnographic debates mentioned
earlier, while also touching on the question of understanding or comprehension that is at the heart of Latinamericanist reflection on epistemology
and alterity. This study draws from various sites of critical conjuncture
wherein narratives of cultural difference/otherness as well as competing—foundationalist and developmentalist—ideological practices align
to establish a field of ethnosocial identity positions. Forestalling hasty
and imprecise claims of difference, otherness, and resistance to otherwise
incorporated social groups with competing ideological agendas, illiteracy instead comes to register heterogeneous, literally unidentifiable, and
hence unassignable speech—as attributed to such figures as *el hombre natural, aclimatados, colonos, monolingües,* and *los que nunca llegarán*—that

unseats not only conventional notions of identity, otherness, and difference but in effect reveals the breakdown in the very signifying structures that govern the intelligibility of speech (i.e., What counts as speech?), political identity (Who counts as a speaking being?), and the "noise" of popular resistance (and On what grounds?). Or, as Rancière (1999: 40) suggests, "a decomposing and recomposing [of] the relationships between the ways of *doing*, of *being*, and of *saying* that define the perceptible organization of the community, the relationships between the places where one does one thing and those where one does something else, the capacities associated with this particular *doing* and those required for another." As such, illiteracy generates the semiological condition of possibility for a reconfiguration of life bound by something else altogether, what Moreiras (2001: 133) wagers as "another lease of life . . . so as to change life itself."

Thresholds of Illiteracy thus serves as a sustained meditation on the terms and limits of reading cultural practices, the notion of the political that can be ascribed to them, and the ways the political can be thought through in contemporary Latin America. It is a calling into question of the grounds of state-culture relations in modern Latin America and of institutionalized forms of knowledge production that maintain established conventions of semiological, racial, and class-based coherence and social ordering. At once a critique and a reinscription of antagonism in the Latin American cultural field, this study offers an accounting of the democratic effects arising from conditions of unforeseeable, and unintended, semiological liberation (a semiosis set free by accident) and advances the possibility of a politics of reading underwritten by their egalitarian and heterogeneous implications. While this book's itinerary is to trace and map the unanticipated, irruptive effects that emerge from the illiterate suspension of the naturalized order, its objective is urgent and precise: to advance a radically democratic, life-affirming determination of resistance within which *any one* can form a part and can speak beyond the field of competing interpretations that constitute the present.

The larger critical agenda I aim to establish both draws from and shares in certain theoretical aspects of Slavoj Žižek's recent work. In *The Parallax View* (2006), Žižek advances a critical rearticulation of the foundational antagonism that lies at the heart of modern philosophical thought. For Žižek, it is an antagonism no longer conceived as between the polarity of opposites (thought and being, identity and difference) but rather one of an "inherent tension, gap, noncoincidence, of the One itself" (7). In other words, the irreducible antinomy upon which modern thought is now confronted is not between, say, Self and Other, but between the Self and itself: "at the very point at which pure difference emerges—a difference which is no longer a difference between two positively existing objects, but a minimal difference which divides one and the same object from itself" (18). This irreducible gap between the thing and itself Žižek calls "minimal difference" or "parallax," and it becomes visible only through a shift between competing epistemological perspectives. The present study and my notion of illiteracy work in compelling ways very similar to this notion of parallax as I trace the point of indistinction between competing theories of culture in Latin America that reveals that the source of resistance one encounters in the cultural field is not the Self's confrontation with Otherness as a positive being but is rather the symptomatic and unpredictable effect of the Self's ultimately vacuous core, for which Otherness (and the like) remain always inadequate and catachrestic representations. Furthermore, and perhaps more fundamentally, *Thresholds of Illiteracy* also shares in Žižek's insistence that this intellectual project not be read as leading simply to a negative, ultimately empty determination.[2] There is a reason why philosophical work moved away from positive designations and properties of things in the first place, for the distinction is ideologically irreducible and no longer tenable. In fact the deployment of this distinction by critics as a means to ascribe greater significance to particular kinds of intellectual labor merely confirms the logocentrism from which they seek to escape. As such, deconstruction as a mode of reading is under no obligation to justify itself—by demonstrating either its affirmative value and function or how it gives new meaning to affirmation—within an economy (affirmative/negative) that it has already put under question. There is simply no such thing as positive or negative intellectual labor but merely contemporary reflection (addressing the most pressing political and epistemological questions) that either attends or does not attend to the problem of meaning and referentiality for which they are both causes and effects. In other words, like all others, this distinction is a trap, and when used as a means to categorically reject certain kinds of intellectual work it further compounds the crisis we are facing. For it is only through an uncovering of the discursive limitations governing cultural intelligibility that creates the conditions for radical—neither affirmative nor negative—political work to take hold. *Thresholds of Illiteracy* is a contribution toward this possibility.

Indeed, and perhaps for these reasons, *Thresholds of Illiteracy* offers an unbound and rather offset mode of cultural engagement than that seen in recent scholarship. Aside from the numerous other studies that I engage directly in the discussions that follow, there are two specific cases with which I would like to juxtapose the present work. The first is Doris Sommer's *Proceed with Caution* (1999), which is a particularly illustrative case that both provides an effective demonstration of the crisis of resistance I am describing as well as insists on the question of reading/literacy upon which my and her studies are based. In her book, which aims to counter what she sees as specific reductive tendencies in contemporary modes of reading, Sommer posits a duality between a certain pervasive, "universalist" ideology of reading and what she calls "particularist" authors and texts. Against a universalist hermeneutic which she conceives as a mode of reading that, through rather aggressive, reductive, and subsumptive, interpretive engagement, disregards and overrides more nuanced inscriptions of resistance, Sommer advances "particularist" texts written by "minority" and/or "ethnically colored" authors that resist such facile appropriations (x–xi). For Sommer, universalist readers, compelled by assumptions of analytic prowess and mastery, who "think they can know more and interpret better than the particularist authors they target" (xii), constitute an undesirable and pernicious form of literacy, a violently appropriative mode of reading that "reduces otherness to sameness" and "eliminates particularity for the sake of unity" (19, 27). Universalist readers, whom Sommer characterizes as "monocultural" (17) and activated by the quest for complete commensurability and understanding, become known through their disregard for a particularist author's marking of cultural distance and difference and an inability therefore to acknowledge the interpretive limits rhetorically imposed on them by that author. These readers thus heed no warning to respect the difference and limits established between themselves and the author and take on the form of a totalizing Self that subsumes the Other into itself as One, "with no remainder" (28). In short, universalist literacy is defined by the indiscriminate way it handles assertions of difference; in this case it names the reduction of difference into the ideological field of cultural intelligibility.

The particularist text, on the other hand, actively resists such efforts at appropriation by universalist readers, offering "opacity" in lieu of transparency "to mark difference" (1999: 17). As Sommer notes, "Particularist texts draw a different map of restrictions. . . . It is a walled city that announces no trespassing. Readers can enter only if they accept unfamiliar invitations that reach out in order to keep us at arm's length" (10). In effect, with particularist writing, Sommer tells us, it is the author who is in control, not the reader; within this inverted dynamic it is now the universalist reader who is forced to contend with the particularist terms of reading. What is more, particularist authors are assumed to be in complete control not only of their subject but also of their writing, as writing is understood by Sommer to unambiguously obey authorial meaning and intentions, including a refusal to allow identification between reader and text either through the calculated production of frustrated desire or through "purposeful incomprehensibility" (15). In short, with particularist writing the roles of meaning production, including the way cultural difference is inscribed and deployed, are reversed. It is the "monocultural," universalist readers now who must accommodate themselves to the text, who must unlearn how they have been conditioned to read in order to be taught anew by a savvy, "multicultural" author. However, according to Sommer, particularist writing doesn't exist merely to challenge universalist readers for its own sake, and it would be a mistake to conceive of such works as highly sophisticated language games, labyrinths, or riddles, for this would only reinforce the universalist ideology of mastery she seeks to displace. No, particularist writing accomplishes a much more sociopolitical objective. For it is only through such texts that a reader can come in contact with and experience forms of culturally resistant writing where the author imposes restrictions and invitations to dialogue. Specifically it is through this engagement between particularist author and universalist reader that the "socially circumscribed limits of interpretation" (9) emerge and are put into play.

However, as conceived by Sommer, particularist writing suffers from some conceptual inconsistency. In the first breath, and in the name of respecting difference and otherness, Sommer defines particularist writing as a formal antagonistic designation, that is, as a strategically obstructive, rhetorically nuanced engagement with a predominant, all-encompassing, universalist ideology of reading. Yet in the next breath she betrays this formal structure by assigning ethnoracial identifications to these categories: the universalist reader is characterized as "monocultural" and the particularist is "ethnically colored," "ethnically marked," "minority," and so on. These two figures are simply incongruous. Whereas the first figure characterizes the writing itself (its formal structure, its discourse, etc.) as the source of the cultural resistance, irrespective of its author, the second figure privileges the author's ethnoracial identification as the source of the resistance, irrespective of the writing. Sommer's choice of the latter figure proves unfortunate, as the implications that stem from it put the entire theory into doubt. This is to say that while monocultural universalists can come from any (literate) segment of society, such is not the case with particularist writing, which, in order to be particularist, *must necessarily* come from an author of a specific ethnoracial—"minority"—identification. Taken one step further this proposition disintegrates entirely, implying that *anything* written by an author of a specific ethnoracial identification is automatically considered particularist writing as well. This statement of course is invalid, which means, consequently, that the figure itself is untenable and irrevocably compromises the integrity of the very relation Sommer posits between universalist and particularist literacies. With this figure, she has succumbed to essentialist appeals of cultural and racial authenticity as a means to substantiate the otherwise purely formal difference between particularist and universalist ideologies of reading. Not unlike the discourse of orality and literacy discussed earlier, particularists and universalists are ultimately stand-ins for a narrative of cultural resistance that is conditioned by the very assumption of primordial antagonism described in the opening.

But that is not all. While Sommer (1999: xi) positions the indiscriminate and voracious interpretive disposition of the universalist reader as against a particularist, "ethnically marked literature," the challenge represented, she insists, is "more hermeneutical than ethical." Which is to say that it is not a society's politics that determines its reading habits but perhaps that the latter ultimately determines the former, that is, that it is not about *what* we are reading but *how* we are reading. In other words, Sommer seems to suggest that it is not just that we need to read more particularist writing, but that reading particularist writing will help rid us of our universalist tendencies. Universalist reading, she asserts, has had the undesired effect of producing confused and ultimately counterproductive (read: monocultural) forms of democratic thinking. Universalism, for Sommer, represents the wrong ideological model; it is simply the wrong kind of reading: "Learning and teaching to read literature in ways that acknowledge difference can be the most basic training for the democratic imagination" (6). As such, what therefore seems to be at stake for Sommer between universalism and particularism is not only to reveal an economy of reading between a hegemonic compulsion to absorb difference into the field of cultural intelligibility and a particularist resistance that obstructs this subsumption, but also what ultimately appears to be for her the main objective of the book: namely, the establishing of particularism as an oppositional and competing ideology of reading. As she argues, "To read particularist fictions in *their* ideal terms needs a paradigm shift" (31). In staking her claim on the consolidation of particularism as an interpretive framework that is both defined against and will compete with universalist reading practices, Sommer thus urges, in effect, not a decentering of hegemonic models of interpretation but the promotion of another.

Toward this, Sommer advances a "rhetoric of particularism" with which to bring together the tropes, "artful maneuvers," and "rhetorical moves" of particularist resistance into an interpretive framework where, instead of overrunning assertions of cultural distance (as in universalist reading), it actually privileges them. For Sommer, becoming sensitive to articulations of resistance and refusal by particularist authors amounts to a new pedagogical method: a "program of training in the modesty and respect that make engagement possible," a "learn[ing] to step differently, to respect distances and explore the socially enabling possibilities of acknowledging our own limits," as well as "invitations to engage, to delay, and possibly redirect the hermeneutical impulse to cross barriers and fuse horizons" (1999: xi, xiii, xv). Further, particularist reading constitutes not only an upending of "underexamined hermeneutical habits" and an "unlearning" of such habits but also the establishment of yet another model of interpretation that requires its own "recognizable and shared rhetorical system" (24). That is, and this needs to be emphasized, the "paradigm shift" that Sommer announces in the name of a particularist hermeneutic of resistance inevitably leads to the founding of yet another paradigm that will itself seek to overtake the current one.

Sommer's institutional aspirations for particularist interpretive ideology contains a serious contradiction here, for it reads both particularism and universalism as simply competing ideological models of interpretation and ultimately calls for the unseating of universalist reading as hegemonic model and the installing of a particularist ideology in its place. The very question of hegemony itself goes unremarked. What Sommer offers is no less than the institutionalization of a race-based, identitarian particularism as hegemonic interpretive model. Consequently if her principal objective is to lay out an alternative hermeneutical model for the reading and interpretation of resistance, and if her principal critique against universalist ideology is precisely its institutionalization as hegemonic interpretive model—that it is the wrong kind of ideology—then her theory of resistance results in no political effect whatsoever, as the very question of hegemony was relinquished in the first instant and given over to particularism as simply the superior form of ideology. While her study is significant to the extent that it also focuses on questions of cultural literacy and modes of reading and interpretation, it ultimately succumbs to the obligation (either/or) to choose between her own binary of universalist and particularist ideology, it continues in the tradition of appealing to essentialized notions of cultural authenticity as grounds of resistance, and it fails to account for how, irrespective of authorship, writing itself can bring about its own form of incommensurability, resistance, and indeterminacy. *Thresholds of Illiteracy*, for its part, aims to account specifically for these limitations.

The second context in which I would like to position the present volume involves two recently published books, Beasley-Murray's *Posthegemony* (2010) and John Beverley's *Latinamericanism after 9/11* (2011), which, having been published within months of each other, have garnered attention for their critiques of current paradigms and their bold diagnoses of the future of Latin American studies. Furthermore, and no doubt due to their nearly simultaneous publication—and therefore the tacit marking of the present historico-disciplinary moment as a specific and crucial vantage point—these two books are already being used to establish the terms and grounds of cultural debate in Latin America for the next several years.

Nevertheless the mutual inextricability of these books extends far beyond the historical proximity of their publication. What we have here are two simultaneously issued critiques of cultural studies and Latin America. Both books in fact provide critical reflections on cultural studies' implicitly contradictory and self-defeating understandings of power and political action. While they are by no means harmonious or congruent projects, one can admit a certain symmetry underwriting the relation between them. *Posthegemony* and *Latinamericanism after 9/11* are deeply and intricately related studies grounded via a set of oppositions and mutually exclusive hypotheses whose claims about the state of critical reflection in Latin America are so widely divergent that their simultaneous appearance quite unintentionally, though dramatically, reconditions the field of cultural intelligibility wherein they themselves are inscribed as limits.

In other words, what we see between the two is the fashioning of competing models and the formation of a new economy of reading. While for Beasley-Murray the problem resides in populism's insufficiently analyzed relation in hegemony theory, for Beverley the problem is that cultural studies as a whole is no longer able, due to its excessive reliance on theoretical discourse, to provide proper political analysis of contemporary popular struggles throughout the continent. *Latinamericanism after 9/11* cites a marked shift in the Latin American political field—specifically the emergence of a cluster of left-leaning governments throughout the continent that have become known as *la marea rosada* (the pink tide)—that has dramatically changed the nature and demand of cultural analysis in the area. One such effect, he argues, has been the revealing of theoretical discourse's limitations as well as its waning critical influence within cultural analysis, in particular, deconstruction and subaltern studies, which he identifies specifically as the theoretical discourses under question. Contending that Latin America has now entered a "postsubalternist" phase, he provides several remarks on what he sees as the end of theory, and the end of deconstruction and subalternity in particular, in the production of thought on or about Latin America: "I have become aware that this identification of subalternism, leftism, and deconstruction has become problematic for me. My sense is that deconstruction is yielding diminishing and politically ambiguous returns" (2011: 9); "The golden age of academic theory is rapidly fading" (9); and "Theory that has become outdated or missed its mark, as I have come to think is the case with deconstruction, can also lead to errors or impasses in political practice" (10). I will have more to say about *Latinamericanism after 9/11* in chapter 1, but for the moment it is sufficient to acknowledge Beverley's categorical—and, based on his previous work, retreating—distinction between politics and theory as well as his attempt to refound a cultural model unhampered by the formal restraints of the latter.

While for Beverley cultural studies became too theoretical, for Beasley-Murray cultural studies has demonstrated that is not theoretical enough. Curiously, as mutually exclusive as these positions appear to be, these projects both depart from a profound dissatisfaction with current theoretical methods, or rather dissatisfaction with the same method. Like Beverley, Beasley-Murray (2010: xiv) also identifies and conflates deconstruction and

subaltern studies within the sphere of his critique of cultural studies, asserting, "I am not content with deconstruction . . . as permanent critique or
labor of the negative. . . . Subalternism holds on to a distinction between
inside and outside, and so perpetuates the fundamental binarism of both
hegemony and civil society." In this passage Beasley-Murray makes quick
(perhaps even hasty) use of the trope that assigns negative (not equal) value
to deconstructive analysis as well as of the premise that subalternism simply sustains the binaries it is enlisted to challenge. In effect, he argues,
it is deconstruction's (and subaltern studies') ultimately negative determination and its reliance on "false dichotomies" that renders it unable to
serve as grounds for positive and productive political practice that he sees
in his competing concept of the multitude: "Subalternity is defined nega-
tively. . . . The multitude, by contrast, is defined positively" (234).

What should be slowly coming into view are the ways in which *Posthegemony* and *Latinamericanism after 9/11* are actually deeply bound to each
other by a tightly contained, though ambiguously related set of political,
disciplinary, and ideological claims. While both develop otherwise largely
antithetical analytical projects related to the study of Latin America, both
do so by first critiquing cultural studies' inability to be sufficiently and
properly theoretical to itself. Moreover whereas Beasley-Murray identifies
hegemony as the specific concept of inquiry in his study, Beverley posits
subalternism as the concept with which to name this particular historico-disciplinary shift. In other words, and as a further demonstration of
their inextricable relation, both projects culminate in critical reevaluations
(and a rebranding) of critically complementary (and inextricable) terms:
post-hegemony and *post*-subalternism.

But that is not all. While one critiques cultural studies for being insufficiently theoretical (and calls it *posthegemony*) and the other for being exces-
sively so (and calls it *postsubalternism*), the source of the problem is the same
for both: deconstruction. In other words, both Beverley and Beasley-Murray explicitly name deconstruction and subaltern studies as modes of analysis that are no longer adequate for contemporary reflection and from which
one must now move away. While both name deconstruction as the larger
underlying problem for political reflection today, neither, it could safely
be said, offers any serious critical engagement with it at all; in each case,
they appear as offhand, casual dismissals (i.e., "deconstruction has become
problematic for me"; "I am not content with deconstruction"). In short, not

only are their critiques of deconstruction identical and equally unsubstantiated, but they each lead to complementary, mutually exclusive formulations: *posthegemony* and *postsubalternism*. Yet the question remains: How do two mutually exclusive political projects develop from the same disciplinary premise: the rejection or presumed exhaustion of deconstruction as a critical practice? What is revealed by this occurrence? And how are we thus to understand the absolute distance that ultimately separates *posthegemony* from *postsubalternism*?

If, in other words, Beasley-Murray's and Beverley's critical projects are determined by their positions against deconstruction, and if both of their (rather thin) rejections of deconstruction are ultimately indistinguishable from each other as well, then not only do both projects rest on precarious and unstable ground, but the fate of one is inevitably tied to the fate of the other. Therefore, as projects identifying deconstruction as the primary antagonism against which they take shape, and despite their seemingly exclusive claims, *posthegemony* and *postsubalternism* are nevertheless remarkably congruent. Of course, and this is yet another instance of the crisis of resistance my notion of illiteracy aims to trace, the foundational antagonism against which Beasley-Murray's and Beverley's projects define themselves is at bottom not between two competing and opposed discourses—that is, *posthegemony* (affirmative) versus deconstruction (negative); *postsubalternism* (politics) versus deconstruction (theory)—but rather the threshold of illiteracy between these discourses and themselves. In other words, deconstruction does not inhabit any discursive sphere of its own; it refers to a condition (and process) of meaning always already at work within discursivity itself, one that makes visible the contradictions of signification and referentiality inscribed at the core of any pronouncement of knowledge or authority. Which is why, therefore, one cannot avoid the pitfalls of logocentrism when attempting to position oneself against deconstruction, because, and despite one's dissatisfaction with the latter's results, the source of antagonism is never with deconstruction as such but with discourse itself. Deconstruction is instead the means by which this irreducible semiological gap is made to appear in the first place. So when, for instance, Beasley-Murray asserts that posthegemony offers a way out of deconstruction's and subaltern studies' "false dichotomies," he misses the point. Quite simply, these modes of analysis neither suggest that such dichotomies are "true" nor claim that one cannot do without them; on the contrary, deconstruction and subaltern studies disclose that *all* dichotomies are contingent and arbitrary—including positivity versus negativity—and thus posit that the historical constitution of the social text can therefore always be otherwise. This proposition occupies the critical core of my notion of illiteracy; it both foregrounds and affirms the politics of heterogeneity activated by the confirmation of such breaches in the social order.

Thus far I have characterized the general character of this study, including its disciplinary rationale, theoretical implications, political stakes, and critical contributions. The aim of this book, including my concept of illiteracy, is to offer a sustained critical reflection on the historical and disciplinary conditions by which this deadlock of resistance in Latin America emerges as a dispute over language itself. While the discussions contained in this study are grounded in specific, contemporary cultural and historical contexts in Latin America, and while each chapter is focused on exploring and interrogating the nature of the particular disciplinary disputes arising from their respective sites of inquiry, all are shown to be intimately linked and bound together by a gap in the fabric of intelligibility, a threshold of illiteracy that manifests the unstable and unpredictable effects of the contemporary crisis of meaning. With this, I now move on to a brief discussion of the chapters composing this study.

Chapter 1 is an extension and detailed elaboration of the theoretical and disciplinary debates broached here in the introduction. Specifically it traces the emergence of postcolonial theory in Latin American studies during the 1990s, a disciplinary shift that sparked a serious and hotly contested debate over the terms and conditions of intellectual exchange between metropolitan institutions of interpretation in Europe and the United States and those in Latin America. Latin American scholars opposed to this disciplinary trend drew attention to the foundational singularity and irreducibility of Latin American history and identity, asserted the categorical impropriety of drawing from European theoretical models—as well as postcolonial intellectual production from former British colonies—to reflect on Latin America, and appealed to Latin America's own intellectual tradition as a means to counter and resist what are perceived as homogenizing and subordinating globalized narratives. While these debates went on (without resolution) well into the next decade, the state of the dispute itself points to a persistent and pervasive crisis of understanding over the relationship between speech and resistance in the social field—that is, What counts as resistant speech, and who counts as a resistant being? This chapter returns to these debates in order to trace the political implications and cultural effects of this disciplinary deadlock. This discussion introduces my central thesis and lays the necessary theoretical and critical groundwork for establishing the relation between these larger claims and the claims I make in subsequent chapters.

Chapter 2 advances a critical rereading of José María Arguedas's celebrated novel, *Deep Rivers*. Arguedas (1911–69) is considered to be the one of the most influential Latin American writers of the twentieth century, and his literary and ethnological work on the indigenous communities in the highlands of Peru remains a central and indispensable touchstone in discussions relating to indigenista narrative and politics. To date, however, most interpretations of this novel continue to promote homogeneous readings of the narrator-protagonist Ernesto as the quintessentially resistant, mestizo figure of modern Peru. This chapter examines the ways such conventional readings of this novel offer increasingly conservative ideological returns for Peru, modes of reading that advance no real threat or challenge to predominant notions of national culture. My reading of *Deep Rivers* thus not only examines the narrow framework by which Arguedas's novel has been and continues to be read in Latin America but also interrogates the terms of indigenista nationalism as a vehicle for articulating alternative and progressive forms of sociopolitical organization.

Chapter 3 proposes a critical genealogy of the testimonio form as crystallized through the controversy surrounding *I, Rigoberta Menchú*. Testimonio emerged in the 1960s as an alternative narrative form that proposed a new mode of social articulation in Latin America for marginalized and oppressed communities in the wake of the success of the Cuban Revolution. Defined explicitly in opposition to the novel, the testimonio form facilitated the direct expression of insurgent and subordinated voices and was heralded as the genre prefiguring a revolutionary age in the Americas. However, current scholarship fails to account for the fact that there are actually two competing theories of testimonio, and though similar in many ways, in certain areas they are critically at odds, even mutually exclusive. This chapter critically juxtaposes these competing theories of testimonio and reads them against one other. In light of this analysis, I turn to a critical rereading of *I, Rigoberta Menchú* that highlights the testimonio genre's confused and often contradictory formalization as a vehicle for narrating subaltern revolutionary history.

If in chapters 2 and 3 I emphasize the ways illiteracy destabilizes the biopolitical terrain of the oral and the literate in Latin American literature, in the subsequent chapters I demonstrate the extent to which illiteracy also manages to configure current and actual political realities. Chapter 4 examines the political implications and cultural effects of the Ejercito Zapatista de Liberación Nacional in Mexico. It is a critical discussion of the extent to which the EZLN's emergence in 1994 has fundamentally altered the political landscape in Mexico and, in many ways, the Mexican political system itself. Specifically this chapter illustrates how the EZLN's public discourse represents a far more radical presentation of democratic, subaltern politics than previously understood. I read from the EZLN's various "Declarations" and other official proclamations in order to analyze the critical ground of their discourse. While current scholarship concludes that the EZLN's discourse is essentially a translation of indigenous "silence" into Western speech, I argue that the EZLN instead incites a direct challenge against such transcultural interpretive conventions, provoking a condition of semiological ungovernability that makes it possible to ask What counts as speech? Who counts as a speaking being? and On what grounds?

Chapter 5 examines the U.S.-Mexico border as the site of a contemporary and unprecedented crisis of global immigration. Drawing from recent critical discussions on sovereignty and the state of exception in political theory, this chapter reflects on critical questions of the border in neoliberal times and explores the "bare life" that inhabits it. In this chapter I read *The Devil's Highway* (2005), Luis Alberto Urrea's documentary narrative account of a failed expedition across the border in 2001 that killed fourteen migrants. I read Urrea's narrative reconstruction of the Wellton 26, a case that remains the single worst migrant death event in Arizona border history, as unconcealing the existence of a negative territoriality and community of migrants, without which this border ceases to be. Thus I argue that the U.S.-Mexico border, along with the heterogeneous figure of the contemporary migrant itself, disallows any attempt to serve as the ground for any culturally resistant claims. I conclude with an afterword reflecting on the social and political impact of Arizona's recent anti-immigrant legislation, SB1070 and HB2281.

Thresholds of Illiteracy, or the Deadlock
of Resistance in Latin America

The emergence of postcolonial theory in Latin American studies during
the 1990s sparked a serious and hotly contested debate over the terms and
conditions of intellectual exchange between Europe and the United States
and those in Latin America. Many speculate that this debate was initially
sparked in 1991 by Patricia Seed's review essay "Colonial and Postcolonial
Discourse," wherein she outlines, with absolute prescience and clarity, the
significance that this "emergent interdisciplinary critique of colonial discourse" would have for Latin American studies (182). It wouldn't be until
two years later, through the publication of a special issue of *Latin American
Research Review* (1993) on this very issue, with contributions by Seed, Her-
nan Vidal, Walter Mignolo, and Rolena Adorno, that it became a fieldwide
point of discussion and controversy. In addition to the numerous books
and articles published throughout the decade, edited volumes also appeared
with such titles as *The Postmodernism Debate in Latin America* (Beverley, Aronna, and Oviedo 1995), *Teorías sin disciplina* (Castro-Gómez and

Mendieta 1998), and *El debate de la postcolonialidad en Latinoamérica* (Toro and Toro 1999), all reflecting on the same questions: What does it mean to be "postcolonial"?, To what extent is Latin America "postcolonial"?, Has Latin America been "postcolonial" this whole time?, and Is Latin America "postcolonial" at all? Nevertheless many Latin American critics voiced opposition to this disciplinary trend. Such scholars pointed to the foundational singularity and irreducibility of Latin American history and identity, asserted the categorical impropriety of drawing from European theoretical models—and further, those from former British and French colonies—to reflect on Latin America, and appealed to Latin America's own cultural specificity as a means to counter and resist what are perceived as homogenizing and subordinating globalized narratives.

Curiously, however, the very critiques issued against postcolonial theory as a homogenizing narrative have themselves fashioned a remarkably consistent rhetoric that asserts Latin America's difference from the rest of the postcolonial world. One of the first critiques of this kind, if not the first, comes from J. Jorge Klor de Alva (1992: 3) in his essay "Colonialism and Postcolonialism as (Latin) American Mirages" wherein he states, "It is misleading to characterize the Americas, following the civil wars of separation, as postcolonial. In short, the Americas were neither Asia nor Africa; Mexico is not India, Peru is not Indonesia, and Latinos in the U.S. . . . are not Algerians." Another iteration of this position can be found in Hugo Achugar's (1997: 381) piece, "Leones, cazadores e historiadores": "To a large extent, thought originating from the 'Commonwealth' of postcolonial theory often ignores production from Latin America, or, in the best of cases, it proceeds to analyze it as part of a homogeneous entity that assumes a shared colonial history with India, Africa, and other regions of the world" (my translation).

As we know, these debates went on (without resolution) well into the next decade. However, while this particular position against postcolonial theory has never really been abandoned, its on-again/off-again rehearsal over the years coincides with certain ebbs and flows in theoretical debate in Latin America. So while it is not surprising to see that this position has once again been taken up by a new group of Latin American scholars and critics, it is disappointing to see that neither the terms nor the tone of this argument has changed since its earliest articulation. Notably, Central American critic Mario Roberto Morales (2008: 501) asserts:

Our problem consists in defining our modernity and what we want
it to be from now on, which implies explaining our intercultural
dynamic and, with it, the character of our differential and plural mestizajes. . . . In fulfilling this task there is no space for notions such as
those of postcoloniality, postcolonialism, or subalternism as they are
used in North American academia to refer to a homogenized subaltern subject, manipulating the contributions of Said, Guha, and others, claiming it to be universal, and idealizing it. . . . The postcolonial
dilemma of the Middle East, Asia, and Africa is not ours.

And most recently we have Ignacio Sanchez Prado from a paper given at the
2011 MLA convention on a panel titled "Is the Postcolonial South Asian?":

Even though postcolonialism has allowed for areas like South Asia and
the non-European Francophone world to claim their rightful place
in English and French departments and academic practices, and even
though the dialogue with postcolonialist scholars in those traditions has
been highly productive for Latin Americanists, the fact is that the only
way in which the postcolonial is South Asian comes from the assertion
of English as the central language of thinking and that the thinking
that emerges from the histories and struggles of regions like Latin
America and of languages like Spanish, Portuguese, Aymara or Nahuatl
can be ignored, brushed off or cast aside.[1]

One could go on citing example after example of this discursive positioning
against postcolonial theory's seemingly unwarranted incursion into the
field, but for now it is sufficient to acknowledge that in each of these
pronouncements, spanning almost twenty years, identically formulated
rejections of postcolonial theory as a framework for reading Latin America
are infused with claims of specificity, difference, and exclusivity from other
formerly colonized groups and spaces, that is, "we" are not Africa, Asia,
or India. In each of these pronouncements there is an explicit desire for
the consolidation of a "we" that can serve as the guarantee of a cultural
identity that resists being homogenized into the otherwise African, Asian,
and Indian—that is, postcolonial—milieu. In essence what one sees in
this reaction to postcolonial theory in Latin America—a mode of reading
that critically brings to bear the irreducible heterogeneity and contingency
of the social text and remains an as yet unsurpassed critique of Western

epistemological and historical models—is a refounding of originary narratives of regional and cultural difference as grounds for resistance against other, either European or postcolonial, theories of resistance perceived as both foreign and hegemonic.[2] In other words, what we are bearing witness to in these times is the manifestation of a critical impasse in Latin American thought, a deadlock of resistance, a breach of unintelligibility within which even theories of resistance are being met with resistance. Nevertheless what this deadlock of resistance—this retreat from European and postcolonial theoretical models and an insistence on disciplinary and geopolitical specificity—keeps hidden from view, however poorly, are the hegemonic and subordinating effects inhering in its affirmation of a Latin American identity, in this case a resistant Latin American identity defined in opposition to not only the West but the entirety of the Global South as well.

Ultimately the persistence and irresolvability of this debate itself points to a pervasive crisis of understanding over the relationship between speech and resistance in the social field: What counts as resistant speech? Who counts as a resistant being? and On what grounds? This chapter turns to these debates in order to trace the political implications and cultural effects of this disciplinary deadlock. In particular I demonstrate the ways this crisis of understanding is of such pivotal, generative significance in Latin America today and, most important, how the form and terms through which this dispute arises provides insight into heretofore unperceivable social realities for which a new critical model is needed. To be clear, I am less interested in establishing, once and for all, whether or not Latin America is indeed postcolonial than in the political form through which this dispute arises in the first place. The reason for this is straightforward: postcolonialism is not a historical category but a historiographical one. To conceive of the postcolonial literally, as quite simply the historical period that proceeds from colonialism, is to fundamentally misapprehend it. Postcolonialism does not signify independence, autonomy, or even emancipation, though it is often confused as such when understood as a historical event. In other words, postcolonialism is not a point in time signaling a nation's independence or transition to a nondependent condition but rather the critical perspective that emerges from the realization that it has failed to do so, that it will always fail to do so, what Ranajit Guha diagnosed as the "historic failure of the nation to come to its own" (Guha and Spivak 1988: 43). Instead I read postcolonialism less as an object or event that can be plotted along a time-line than as an interrogation of Western philosophy of history itself and a critical rewriting of the very historical and epistemological narratives one takes as normative, specifically the narrative that upholds emancipation as the historical realization of the transition from feudalism to capitalism, colony to nation-state. Therefore, as a critical reevaluation of temporality itself and what time within capital ultimately signifies, postcolonialism is a historiographical resituating of History itself (as the narrative of development and progress) as read against precisely those failed historical junctures, or as Spivak (1988a: 16) posits, "the absolute limit of the place where history is narrativized into logic."

Such is the confusion with this concept that critics of postcolonialism often appeal to the very narrative of history that postcolonialism displaces. This is the case with Klor de Alva (1992: 3), who, while advancing a compelling postcolonial critique of Latin American history, continues to understand postcolonialism as a historical period yet to come: "It is misguided to present the pre-independence *non-native* sectors as colonized, it is inconsistent to explain the wars of independence as anti-colonial struggles, and it is misleading to characterize the Americas, following the civil wars of separation as postcolonial." This passage begins well enough. As we can see, Klor de Alva is correct to acknowledge that independence in Latin America was the result essentially of a civil war fought between Spain and Spanish creole elites, as opposed to, say, a native bourgeois class. He is therefore right in recognizing that this mere transfer of power between Spanish elites does not constitute an "anti-colonial struggle" and deducing that therefore no such struggle ever took place, and as such, Latin American never ceased being colonial. The problem here is that while Klor de Alva draws from postcolonial critique to assert that colonialism has actually not been superseded, despite the legacy of independence, he nevertheless employs these premises to conclude that because no real decolonization (indigenous independence) ever took place, no real period of postcoloniality obtains in Latin America. Unfortunately what he fails to see is that the same postcolonial perspective that enabled him to see that Latin American independence did not signal any real form of emancipation should not only also warn him against relying upon traditional forms of historical periodization (like pre- and post-) but should also make him suspicious of anticipating any historical events of cultural purification such as decolonization, which are ultimately not available as programs. As such, my insistence on postcolonialism does not constitute a dismissal of Latin American history or the historical differences between Spanish on the one hand and English, French, and Dutch colonies on the other. This is not a case of theoretical stakes overriding regard for historical specificity; it is about recognizing the historical as itself bound to its own theoretical assumptions that can no longer be ignored. Ultimately postcolonial theory obliges us to account for the ways the displacement of traditional historical models fundamentally unsettles and reconfigures the nature and disposition of the historical specificities that constitute our narrative of reality. *Postcoloniality* is the name for this unsettling and tenuous reconfiguration. The following chapters aim to demonstrate the effects of such displacement, unsettling, and reconfiguration in the anticipation of another historical modeling.

I therefore suggest that the very rationales given for rejecting the idea of postcolonial theory in Latin America instead provide the best evidence for it; they provide a critical illustration of how postcolonialism continues to be misunderstood in the field; why, consequently, it needs to be taken more seriously; and what effects this has for critical reflection in the region. In short, despite assertions to the contrary, it might not be that theory in Latin America has gone too far, extended too far beyond itself, thereby spurring a nationalist impulse to invert this economy and privilege Latin American over non–Latin American thought, but rather the reverse: that insofar as Latin American critics continue to foster the desire for cultural specificity and identity, the forced (and false) opposition between Latin American and non–Latin American thought itself reveals that theoretical reflection in the region has quite simply not gone far enough.

José Martí's canonical essay, "Nuestra America," often serves as the ideological ground upon which claims to this kind of intellectual properness and property are made. Published in 1891, Martí's essay, originally published in a New York paper and speaking directly to the heightened tensions in Cuba (and elsewhere in Latin America) between the Ten Years War and the Spanish-American War, sought not only a rhetorical stance to differentiate and distance itself from both Spain and the United States but, more important, to elucidate a cultural and political principle of exclusivity that would bestow upon Cuba, and every other Latin American country, a biopolitically legislated right and obligation to govern itself: "The government must be born from the country. The spirit of governance must be that of the country. The form of government must arise from out of that country's constitution itself. Governance is nothing more than the equilibrium of a country's natural elements" (translation in Ramos 2001: 296; Martí 1977: 33). In other words, one sees in Martí's pronouncements a persistent emphasis on an exclusive notion of a "we" onto which to ascribe the property of being "oneself" and of the capacity to possess one's own characteristics. Other oft-cited phrases from Martí's essay—"Our Greece is preferable to the Greece that is not ours [Nuestra Grecia es preferible a la Grecia que no es nuestra]" and "If our wine is made from bananas, and if its taste turns out bitter, it is still our wine! [El vino, de plátano; y si sale agrio, ¡es nuestro vino!]"—leave no doubt as to his appeal to the proprietary ("nuestra") and therefore tautological terms of Latin American cultural identity, sovereignty, and governance (Ramos 2001: 297, 299; Martí 1977: 34, 37).[3]

This understanding of property also extends to one's intellectual tradition—which Martí called "la Universidad Americana"—as well as to the ultimate subjects of such local knowledge, whom he called "natural man [hombre natural]": "Thus, has the imported book been vanquished by natural man in America. Natural man has vanquished the artificial men of letters. . . . Natural man is good, and he obeys and rewards a superior intelligence; and yet the latter does not obtain his permission to wound him, or offend him by ignoring him—an unpardonable thing for natural man" (Ramos 2001: 296–97; Martí 1977: 33). No doubt this passage was written with the objective of illustrating the absolute impotence of foreign ideas and methods when applied to peoples and contexts for which they are inappropriate. The "imported book" and the "artificial" intellectual are easily defeated by "natural man," Martí argues, not because the "natural man" is averse to all forms of writing and knowledge but because he does not respond favorably to foreign, nonlocal, forms. For Martí, "natural man" recognizes and will always obey "superior intelligence," but only if it comes from within. It is important to keep in mind that in Martí "natural man" does not benefit directly from such knowledge but rather profits from it by being well governed by leaders and intellectuals instructed in such local knowledge. Part of that knowledge consists in knowing how to govern "natural man" in the first place and keep him appeased. To be clear, Martí's audience in "Nuestra América" was never "natural man" but a class of lettered men to whom he has just revealed their legitimate right to govern "natural man." While Martí's essay is heralded for its critical position against nineteenth-century developmentalist discourse ("There is no battle between civilization and barbarism, but between false erudition and nature") and race ("There is no hate among races, because there are no races") a logic of hierarchy and subordination nevertheless permeates "Nuestra América" (Ramos 2001: 297, 301; Martí 1977: 33, 38). In effect Martí's essay is a counterhegemonic assertion of a biopolitically instantiated sovereign identity that demands the rights of governance over one's "own." "Nuestra América" can be no clearer about its biopolitical aspirations: "The uncultured masses are lazy, and timid in matters of the intellect, and they want to be well-governed" (Ramos 2001: 297; Martí 1977: 33).

Seen in this light, Alberto Julián Pérez's essay "El postcolonialismo y la inmadurez de los pensadores Hispanoamericanos" (1999) typifies this position in the discussion of postcoloniality in Latin American criticism. In this essay Pérez urges current Latinamericanists to resist privileging Eurocentric or British or Francophone postcolonial thought as the means by which to read Latin America and to instead embrace Latin America's very own intellectual tradition as a canon of, for, and sufficient unto itself. The problem, as it was with Martí, is that the reason given—"because it is ours"—does not withstand much scrutiny as it promotes an ultimately faulty and groundless appeal to cultural properness. In Pérez's essay U.S.-based postcolonial scholars take the brunt of the critique: "For one who has not studied Sarmiento, Martí, Rodó, and Kusch, what can Spivak and Bhabha say to them? What do these two have to say that would be relevant for the study of an American thought one does not know nor value? . . . If we still do not yet know or even understand our own tradition, what can we learn from the magnificent writings by Said and Spivak?" (203, 205, my translation). Like Martí, whose essay attempts to effectuate a fundamental redistribution of sovereign rights away from the foreign born and/or educated—the "criollo exótico" or "letrado artificial"—to a locally born and locally educated elite, Pérez here attempts to recuperate the very philosophical tradition ("la Universidad Americana") that Martí was appealing to as the legitimate patrimony of this local elite. Like Martí, Pérez's appeal to "lo nuestro" is also motivated by an ultimately reactionary and misguided intellectual nationalism. Again, however, and various suspicions emerge from this, the primary objects of critique in Pérez's essay are critics and theorists from former (non-Hispanic) colonized regions of the world, such as Gayatri Spivak, Homi Bhabha, and Edward Said, non–Latin American critics that Pérez argues have been given critical priority to reflect upon Latin America's most pressing cultural issues. Pérez goes on: "Anyone who has ever read Said and Bhabha immediately realizes that the problems they pose, while interesting, remain relatively external to our most pressing problems. Our own thinkers (Rama, Cornejo Polar) have been working through, using their own critical methods, many of the same questions posed by them [Said and Bhabha]. The question is which tradition, of the two, to privilege. From a methodological standpoint, it should be ours. Our path passes through ourselves" (210–11). Several claims are expressed in this passage, the most significant of which is the assertion that Latin American thought *prefers* to exist in an oppositional form of relation with not only Europe but the rest of the formerly colonized world. And again no intellectual grounds are offered here, save only the insistence that to read non–Latin American thinkers perpetuates Latin America's inability to think and know itself. Of course, this claim is unsustainable, for one does not necessarily lead to the other, and the latter—"thinking and knowing" oneself—is in itself a direct appeal to a traditional and uncomplicated Cartesian consciousness that is no longer valid or binding in any serious kind of way. In fact the second half of the passage is particularly illustrative in its willful misrecognition, for while Pérez continues to suggest throughout the essay that postcolonial theory has virtually no bearing on Latin America's most imminent problems, he then asserts that Latin American critics like Angel Rama and Antonio Cornejo Polar have themselves already engaged with and reflected on many of the same questions posed by them. So which one is it? Is it that Latin American and postcolonial critics have nothing in common, or is it that they have too much in common? It simply cannot be both.

Joshua Lund provides further critical insight into the formal aspects of this deadlock. In *Impure Imagination* (2006) Lund advances a critical reevaluation of theories of racial and cultural miscegenation in modern Latin America; his study posits hybridity as the central—though ambivalent—concept around which Latin American identity is conceived and narrated. In this critical genealogy, Lund acknowledges that hybridity has worked to become the single defining ideological feature of Latin American culture, enabling, once again, certain tacit claims of ownership over the concept and resulting in a very complicated relationship between Latin American critics and other theoretical articulations of hybridity coming from other global spaces and times, such as the work of Bhabha (1994) and

Mikhail Bakhtin (1981). In each case, Lund (2006: 48) outlines, the primary argument issued against them is that Latin Americans were theorizing hybridity first and thus have no need to seek out or draw from extraneous sources. Consequently, such reasoning goes, since Latin America has such a long-standing and unrivaled history of hybridity, and since hybridity has been the object of reflection since that history began more than five hundred years ago, it is therefore sufficiently and properly understood in its Latin American context, and other postcolonial elaborations of hybridity hailing from other places will yield little if anything novel or relevant that contributes to the idea of Latin America, the narrative of its origins, or the form of its cultural identity and resistance.

Of course, as Lund himself demonstrates, serious flaws invade such a rationale. One does not so easily avert the contradictions of postcoloniality by claiming a hybrid origin. Subscribing to the logic underwriting hybridity is itself one of modern Latin America's many contradictions. For Lund (2006: 48) in particular, this strategy is suspect as it reveals a racialized undercurrent and an ultimately conservative agenda:

> What seems unacceptable, however, is to use this assertion [that Latin Americans theorized hybridity first] as an excuse to wall off Latin American hybridity from geoepistemologically disparate theories that go by the same name and that can perhaps be appropriated for the productive analysis of aspects of Latin American cultural, social, and artistic phenomena. . . . If hybridity is critical at all, its critique stems from its incessant disruption of authoritative legitimacy (e.g., pure race, pure genre, pure canon, pure reason). As such, if Latin American hybridity is a theory that only works in Latin America, and if Latin America is a geoepistemological space that will only accept a hybridity as theorized within Latin Americanist fields, then what Latin Americanism calls hybridity is not really hybridity at all, but rather a new purity.

If Lund is right, and I think that he is, what we see at work among these kinds of critiques is a tacit desire for a Latin American thought constituted via a self-authorized exclusion from—and fundamental opposition to—all (other) postcolonial contexts. As we can see, however, such a strategy would also have the effect of unconcealing the extent to which Latin American thought is also grounded upon a foundational exclusion from itself.

In other words, the self-attribution of hybridity as Latin America's foremost defining characteristic can ever and only prove more ideological than real, for, as Lund amply demonstrates, hybridity as a concept in Latin America is inextricably bound to notions of race and, as such, relies on many unfounded assumptions about cultural and biological reproduction that are simply impossible to confirm. From the rationale to the perceived (though always already desired) results, there is nothing nonideological about these cultural narratives of hybridity. Nevertheless they continue to operate as the dominant and most pervasive narrative of origins in Latin America, such that they have become the institutionalizing force they were designed to displace. Given the innumerable contradictions and critiques adhering to this family of concepts, it is hard to understand the continuing vitality of such narratives, particularly their current resurgence in Latin America as a mode of cultural and geopolitical resistance against postcolonial theory. What is clear is that mestizaje's ideological core has proven much more powerful and affective than previously estimated, in particular for the critics themselves who continue to promote it as an irrevocably resistant position.

In a move that can therefore be described as *doubly* questionable, the myth of mestizaje has been resurrected to fuel the debate against postcolonialism. Mario Roberto Morales develops this argument in an essay titled "Peripheral Modernity and Differential *Mestizaje* in Latin America: Outside Subalternist Postcolonialism" (2008). Once again the argument turns on the assumption of Latin America's key—hybridic—difference from the rest of the Global South:

> If in Africa and the Middle East a subaltern colonial subject that can be
> binarily opposed to the colonizer emerges, this is due to the fact that,
> in the colonizing adventure of the countries of the North of Europe,
> biological mestizaje was the exception and not the rule, whereas in
> the case of Spain and Portugal, it was the rule and not the exception.
> This was due above all to the well-known fact that these two countries
> were conformed by one of the most intense processes of mestizaje that
> Europe had experienced. This fact explains why a colonial subject who
> is neither unique nor uniform but rather plural and differentiated (in
> class and ethnicity) emerges in Latin America. This complicates the
> colonial landscape and forces us to think the colonial, postcolonial,

and neocolonial realities of Latin America with notions that should
go beyond the binary dichotomies, bipolar essentialisms (strategic or
fundamentalist, it doesn't matter), and oppositional contradictions
between hegemony and subalternity, elitist domination and popular
resistance, hegemonic and counterhegemonic practices, and so on that
animate all postcolonial and subalternist methodologies. (488–89)

Beyond the trajectory elaborated by Klor de Alva and Achugar—appealing
to Latin America's specific colonial history as the reason for postcolonial
theory's categorical impropriety—in this essay Morales bases his argument
on one further assertion of difference: Latin America's specific history of
miscegenation. However, as is quite evident in the excerpt, this is not to
suggest that among other histories of miscegenation in the Global South,
Latin America's was simply different. No. Morales's claim is stronger: that
Latin America's history is different *because* it is a history of miscegenation.
Here Morales describes the exclusive, totalizing, though nevertheless still
resistant legacy of mestizaje in Latin America: "This axis is originated by
the concrete historical facts that determined the formation and development of the intricate differential and differentiated *mestizajes* that constituted the colonial and postcolonial history of Latin America, and which
produced a pluralistic mestizo subject who is located in all social classes
and who is ethnoculturally differentiated by his or her respective mestizaje"
(480). Morales's elaboration here easily confirms Lund's thesis that hybridity in Latin America functions as an assertion of purity. For if mestizaje in
Latin America were so complete, so total, so all-encompassing as to produce a whole though nevertheless heterogeneous—*differential* and *pluralistic*—population, as Morales argues, then mestizaje itself loses from the
start all referential power to, by definition, distinguish and identify among
the parts of the community from which it springs. What we see instead in
Morales is mestizaje itself installed as the name for a whole, as the name
for everyone and everything, as the name that conditions the fundamental and absolute homogeneity of the community. Through such claims of
difference that ultimately work to reestablish forms of hegemony, Gareth
Williams's (2002: 24) discussion of transculturation as a master language
for populist nation-state consolidation projects in twentieth-century Latin
America immediately comes to mind; a critique in which he uncovers its
form as an "intellectual desire" that "establishes the fictive relation between

the state and the notion of the people that constitutes collectivities as particular represented populations." Morales's elaboration of mestizaje as an inherent and originary form of immunity against postcolonialism is a very accurate rehearsal of the national-popular discourse discussed by Williams, down even to its mobilization as a defense against the "foreign." Unfortunately Morales asserts as resistant a principle of racial and cultural mestizaje that had previously been deployed in the service of populist state agendas throughout Latin America (notably in Mexico, Peru, Brazil) in the previous century.

But this is not all that is wrong with Morales's position. According to him, mestizaje is not only unique to Latin America (against all other formerly colonized regions of the world), but it is also all-encompassing within and throughout Latin America (where there are no nonmestizos left). Consequently because all Latin American societies are always already (i.e., at least) mestizo and therefore racially indistinguishable, postcolonial and subaltern theory—conceived by Morales as a strict colonized-colonizer economy—does not apply. The following passage summarizes his understanding: "In the case of India, and the Middle East, strategic binarism may have been the only way possible in which to move forward, given the recent and nonmestizo character of their colonization. But this is certainly not the case of Latin America" (2008: 486). From these passages one gathers that Morales's position against postcolonial theory is based on three interrelated though faulty premises: (1) that postcoloniality is theorized to operate only in settings with clear, definable, colonizer-colonized identity positions (his assumption here is that this includes former British colonies), (2) that mestizaje constitutes the unique, historicocultural loophole through which Latin America emancipated itself from this binary, and (3) that it is inherently resistant to any postcolonial affiliation to anywhere else in the Global South.

Both of these premises rely on a complete misapprehension of postcoloniality and subalternity themselves, which, because they are grounded on the recognition of the relationality and heterogeneity of decolonized space, aim at the displacement of the colonized-colonizer binary, not its retrenchment. Unfortunately this confusion is not limited to Morales's essay; it serves as the very guiding principle of the edited volume in which it appears, Coloniality at Large (Moraña, Dussel, and Jáuregui 2008). The editors, in their introduction to this volume, make it a special point to stress the "uninterrupted" workings of colonialism in Latin America, that, through-out its existence, Latin America has never not been colonial (10). And this is precisely why, their reasoning goes, a critical concept such as postcolo-nialism is approached with skepticism if not resistance. They argue, "It could be said, that by exposing the perpetuation and metaphoric strategies utilized over the centuries by colonial and neocolonial domination, Latin American history challenges the concept of *post*coloniality from within. This is particularly true when the prefix is used to connote the cancellation or overcoming of political, cultural, and ideological conditions imposed by foreign powers in societies that existed under colonial rule" (110). Based on the implications in this passage, Moraña et al.'s problem is clear: they have reduced a historiographical concept to a historical moment. In effect the primary flaw in their understanding (and rejection) of postcolonial-ism is confusing a mode of reading and analysis that critically challenges the normative historical narrative with the overcoming of coloniality itself as a historical event that *hasn't happened yet*. In other words, postcolonial thought reads and traces the critical contradictions inhabiting the coloniz-er-colonized binary, revealing how it was *never* about a simple relationship between the colonizer and the colonized but was rather, and was all along, a cultural context within which power is negotiated and distributed among an array or social positions. It is precisely the splintering of colonized-col-onizer identity positions that marks the rupture not from colonialism to postcolonialism but from colonial to postcolonial discourse. It constitutes a fundamental reconfiguration of the colonial text and its actors, not a pro-nouncement of emancipation from colonialism. Consequently, organized and premised as it is on such a crudely defined understanding of postcolo-nialism, *Coloniality at Large* (as well as Morales's essay) ultimately provides an unreliable mapping of the stakes and terms of postcolonial critique and its relationship to Latin America.

Thus if narratives of mestizaje or decolonization are here offered as grounds upon which Latin America defines itself against the rest of the postcolonial (and hence "nonmestizo") world, and if mestizaje is there-fore advanced as the proper name and the genetic source of Latin Amer-ica's inherently "differential" and "pluralistic" nature, then mestizaje, as an ideology of property, properness, and identity, is not only not resistant but an utterly reactionary and conservative retreat from critical thought that reproduces that which it claims to supersede: binary thinking (i.e., "us"/"them"; "foreign"/"local"; "colonizer"/"colonized"). Neither mestizaje nor the assumptions of decolonization signify, in any way, a beyond or an outside to postcoloniality, for which neither are available as programs; their active and uncomplicated promotion in this case only further testifies to their persistent and fundamental (even if undesired) inextricability from it.

Nevertheless these critical implications do not prevent critics from reading mestizaje as an inherently resistant form. Attempts even by scholars seeking to salvage the mestizo by unmooring it from its predominant race-based inscription fail to escape the latter's ideological and conceptual grasp. In her essay "Are *Mestizos* Hybrids?" (2005), Marisol de la Cadena advances a genealogical analysis of the terms *mestizo* and *mestizaje* as used in the Andean region of Latin America. In an attempt to, in her words, "rescue mestizos from *mestizaje*," de la Cadena reveals a history of the term *mestizo* that goes beyond its conventional understanding as the empirical result of biological or culture mixture (262). According to de la Cadena, the ideology of mestizaje has all too simplistically reduced this concept to a race-based whitening process, a "transitional teleology . . . [that] purifies mestizos *away* from indigeneity" (262). She challenges this convention by suggesting that the term *mestizo* houses a "doubly hybrid" nature based not only on racial and cultural mixture but also on an ambiguous ideological conflation of Christian and scientific regimes of knowledge and classification (264). In other words, de la Cadena explains, the term *mestizo* is not simply a concept denoting biological, empirically observable instances of miscegenation but one that is also ideologically determined by other cultural and religious factors not tied to race. For de la Cadena, this "culturalist" coding of race explains why, in certain social contexts, an indigenous individual or family would be considered mestizo, and why therefore this conceptual plane of mestizo-ness offers the possibility of an alternative social ordering that challenges predominant racial and cultural categories (264, 272).

Unfortunately de la Cadena's genealogy of the mestizo does not signal the move away from mestizaje that she promises. Her otherwise productive assertion of the ideological—religious and scientific—component in *mestizaje* is undermined precisely when defined *against* the process of real, empirical, biological hybridization of discrete racial entities that she concedes as its nonideological core. I am suggesting that as a discursive formation, there is no such (nonideological) space to mestizaje; every aspect of it, including its reactionary, biological, and even revolutionary articulations, constitutes the field of intelligibility within which every theory, assumption, and calculation about mestizaje are predetermined and rendered thinkable. For instance, the discourse of mestizaje takes the following abstractions as foundational conditions of possibility: that there is race, that there are races, that those races are not equal, that those unequal races can mix, and that the resultant mixture constitutes an entity of homogeneous though debatable—culturally sanctioned—quality. De la Cadena (2005: 264) ultimately takes no course against these propositions as equally ideological components as the ones she identifies in her work but instead limits herself simply to the suggestion that "biological or cultural hybridity does not exhaust the semantic field of the mestizo." Consequently, to posit the "epistemologically hybrid" nature of the term *mestizo*, as de la Cadena does here, particularly as the means by which to reveal and explore its other, more ideological—"culturalist"—form, is to admit as real and as primary the racial and biological trademarks of miscegenation that she sought to displace.

For de la Cadena (2005: 268), *mestizaje's* multilayered and "heteroglossic" nature not only reflects this concept's inherent epistemological hybridity but is also what gives it a transgressive sociopolitical character. Nevertheless her analysis ultimately accomplishes very little in upsetting the hegemonic notions of hybridity and miscegenation she was working against. In fact one may argue that after her attempt at "rescu[ing] the mestizo from mestizaje," matters are even more confused. Toward the end of her essay, de la Cadena identifies the ways indigenous communities have embraced and appropriated the "culturalist" form of being mestizo for themselves, particularly as a means by which to negotiate and secure social, political, and economic advancement *without* abandoning their indigenous identity. She attributes this indigenous manner of understanding as "resting on a conceptualization of indigeneity that comfortably allowed for the 'mixture of orders' . . . and disregards the purity that the empirical mixture implied in mestizaje demands" (281). Most important, however, for de la Cadena is that this social dynamic has led to the development of a specifically indigenous form of hybridity which, unlike its hegemonic articulation under mestizaje, does not rely on pure categories and does not result in the production of a third entity: "The indigenous strategy implies the relentless mixture of things 'foreign' and 'local' in such a way that, rather than producing a third set of things—a hybrid in the dominant sense of the word—the 'foreign' becomes indistinguishable from the 'local'. . . . Indigenous hybridities ignore purified categories" (281). This passage raises a number of questions: If by categorically distinguishing between indigenous and Western forms of hybridity, based exclusively on their requirement for pure categories, has she not just reproduced the conditions of purity/impurity that "indigenous hybridity" claims to be able to do without? In other words, despite the still arguable assertion that indigenous hybridities can indeed ignore purified categories, isn't indigenous hybridity itself already a purified category? Isn't indigenous hybridity itself the irrevocable result of the foreign and local that de la Cadena insists does not result in further hybridization? And if so, how exactly does indigenous hybridity actually come to challenge hegemonic theories of hybridity? If, ultimately, a strategy that seeks to challenge Western theories of hybridity has been *identified* with and *attributed* to a specifically indigenous population that wishes to remain so, how can one argue that this identity-based premise constitutes the "ignoring [of] purified categories" when it is actively promoting it? And what better way to accomplish this than to suggest the originary and inherently hybridic nature of the concept of hybridity itself?

Needless to say, de la Cadena's critical though ultimately uneven and contradictory approach to mestizaje demonstrates that this discourse is inescapably bound to identitarian and binary positions, even though—or perhaps because—the stated activity is miscegenation. Ideologically, it seems, the most direct way to promote culturally specific—that is, "pure"—identities and cultures is to actively encourage their mixture. De la Cadena (2005: 268) admits as much in a footnote: "The trick is that translation (mixture or hybridity) enables purification—there is nothing to separate if things are not mixed." In short, as might be the case in all theories of hybridity, *the assumption of mixture is primary.* It should be clear now why even critical appeals to mestizaje in the name of resistance and emancipation actually, and tautologically, reproduce the very hegemonic rationale of purity and mixture from which it springs. Mestizaje, or any other rationale of miscegenation, for that matter (including de la Cadena's), does not lead to the end of the idea of race; it leads to its further compounding and perpetuation. A sustainable, progressive politics in Latin America cannot emerge from among these principles of race and mixture.

Consequently if one takes these assertions of originary miscegenation as direct appeals to established configurations of power and sovereignty rather than as forms of resistance against uncomplicated notions of purity, as we now should, a field of intelligibility opens up that would condition and enable another mode of reading the social text. The lesson here is that while claims of hybridity (or any other articulation of originary miscegenation) appear to function by appealing to historically verifiable and empirically observed scenes of genetic mixture from previously isolated and homogeneous groups, they do not. Rather, and as de la Cadena concedes, claims of hybridity ideologically function by *retroactively* framing and constituting—as distinct, homogeneous, *and* preexisting—the genetic sources that one takes as a legacy. In other words, the presumed homogeneous source entities do not preexist the claim of hybridity to which they are identified as origin but rather are posited and inscribed as such at the moment an appeal to hybrid origins is announced. This modality clearly renders visible the inextricability of ideology from any historical and empirical claims of racial and cultural miscegenation at work in the former. Given this revelation, the question would no longer concern from what originary cultures and races one is constituted. Instead the question is: What genetic and cultural sources have been imagined, developed, and deployed to serve as the referential guarantee of that originary claim to hybridity? The difference between these two results is irreducible, and the latter cannot simply be disproven by persistent, hasty, and frustrated identitarian appeals to the former. In fact the latter function already resides deep within mestizaje's discursive core as its foundational, and therefore irrevocable, condition of possibility.

To be clear, this is not to suggest that by resolving hybridity's many formal contradictions one solves Latin America's; far from it. The problem that many critics like Morales and de la Cadena fail to see is that hybridity is itself one of those contradictions. The deadlock of resistance I am tracing in this discussion is the result of this confrontation between assumptions of hybridity as a self-evident, naturally occurring (and yet still resistant) process of social and cultural reproduction in Latin America, and critiques of hybridity (and transculturation) as a pernicious biopolitics grounding claims to hegemony, sovereignty, and exclusion.

By *biopolitics* I am referring specifically to the discursive mechanisms through which a society and its ordering come into being, are made to exist, via a foundational demarcation between distinctly characterized forms of life. I am referring to Giorgio Agamben's notion of sovereign power and his understanding of the division, constitutive of the city, between *zoë* and *bios*, natural life and politically qualified life. That being said, however, one does not simply invoke the concept of biopolitics without also bringing to bear Michel Foucault's social theory of biopower, which conceptualizes the development and instrumentalization of a rationalized, disciplinary approach to the administration and management—governance—of the social body. As outlined in his lectures at the Collège de France as well as in *The History of Sexuality*, biopolitics emerges from a fundamental transformation in the systems of state power whose task has now become the monitoring and optimizing of the biological health of its populations.[4] Nevertheless while my study does not directly engage with the "regulatory and corrective mechanisms" and explicit calculations of state power over birth and mortality rates, rates of reproduction and fertility, immunization, and so on, it does in fact rely on these processes as the principal means through which inclusion and exclusion within a given community is confirmed (Foucault 1978: 144). But the processes Foucault discusses in his work do not, in and of themselves, establish inclusion or exclusion within the social body; something else is constitutive of this. Agamben calls this the sovereign exception. If, as he argues, the polis—"the city of men," politically qualified life—is founded on the exclusion of natural, "bare life," then not only is bare life excluded from belonging to the community, and not only is the exclusion itself the condition that brings the community into being, but the bare life that resides at the borders thus becomes the very thing against which biopolitics emerges as a preemptive social defense. It is in this way that I see Agamben's and Foucault's theorizations of biopolitics as complementary and not mutually exclusive. What is more, it is also in this way that I see Agamben's and Rancière's conceptualizations of speech and exclusion as demonstrative of a shared political agenda. For Rancière, the police order is constituted as a symbolic distribution of bodies, within which there are those who can be seen, who have names, who have logos, and those one doesn't see, who are nameless and without logos, "the part of no part." In Agamben the structure of inclusive-exclusion is the mechanism through which the bare life that is excluded from the social must first (and also) be included as an exception. This exception takes the figure, as in Rancière, of beings without the capacity for language: "The living being has logos by taking away and conserving its own voice in it, even as it dwells in the polis by letting its own bare life be excluded, as an exception, within it. . . . There is politics because man is the living being who, in language, separates and opposes himself to his own bare life and, at the same time, maintains himself in relation to that bare life in an inclusive-exclusion" (Agamben 1998: 8). It is the capacity for speech that obtains in both Agamben and Rancière as the central biopolitical designation through which politically qualified life is demarcated and opposed against bare life.

Ciro Alegría's *The Golden Serpent* provides a perfect narrative illustration of these biopolitical stakes. Originally published in 1935 as *La serpiente de oro*, the novel centers on the village of Calemar, Peru, which lies in the deep valleys of western Cajamarca along the banks of the large and treacherous Marañon River, serving as a ferrying site across the river. The narrative focuses on the community of ferrymen whose livelihood and survival are determined not only by their use of this river but through their cultural and political relationship with it: "We, *cholos* (half-breeds) of the Marañon, listen to its voice with an alert ear. We know not of where it rises or where it ends . . . but [it] tells us plainly of its immensity" (1943: 7; 1993: 11). While the novel's central narrative revolves around the appearance and subsequent death of a Creole engineer from Lima, Osvaldo Martinez, whose intent it was to survey the valleys surrounding Calemar for potential economic development, it is Alegría's extended figuration of the Marañon River itself in this novel, the river as biopolitical ground for the *cholos* (urbanized indigenous communities, i.e. "cultural mestizos") of Calemar, that is of interest to us in this discussion.

"The Golden Serpent" was the name Osvaldo Martinez was to give to his development company upon return to Lima, because, "seen from above, from the Campana Ridge, the river looks like a great serpent. And as it is so rich!" (1943: 149; 1993: 125). For Martinez, the river itself signifies its value in cartographic and developmentalist terms, that is, as uncharted and undeveloped territory, in an era of modernization. Though Martinez would never return to Lima to found this company—he would ironically be killed by a venomous snakebite while surveying the valley—the Calemarinos themselves would later appropriate his designation of "La serpiente de oro" as a figure for the Marañon. Don Matías, the elder Calemarino, attempts to explain why Martinez's metaphor actually works for them too:

Don Oshva knew what he was saying, although he was talking about it from a different point of view, when he called this river a golden serpent. That's right: a serpent of gold it is. Look how well all of us live here. We want for nothing and it is all thanks to the river. This valley belongs to it, the water we row across belongs to it. It never stops flowing and the only bad thing about it is the danger . . . but it comes when we least expect it, and the beautiful river kills us in its own beautiful valleys, and it kills us suddenly, like a golden serpent. (1943: 174; 1993: 146)

As distinct from Martinez's vision of regional modernization and development, for Matías and the rest of the Calemarino community, the river signifies not simply Calemar's natural life but its very *bios*, the source and foundation of social order and cosmic equilibrium. Throughout the narrative the valleys and river figure anthropomorphically as the principal source of cultural understanding for the racially and ethnically marked characters of the novel: "But we cholos belong to the river more than to the land and we stay because we are men and we have to live on the terms life offers" (1943: 171; 1993: 144). This proclamation of river-based life and purpose in the Marañon Valley is determinant not only of the Calemarino community itself; for the foreigner, the non-Calemarino, it is also an announcement of the river's inscription as this community's political foundation.

Thus it can be argued that the Marañon River, "the golden serpent," is constitutive of Alegría's Calemar and its residents to the extent that the river also functions as the sovereign exception that establishes this community's cognitive topological map, from the river *outward* to land. The following passage, for instance, positions the Marañon River not in some idyllic, natural, out-of-the-way corner of the Andean universe but rather in a crucially centralized position with national implications: "We will probably die without remembering how many there were. Life is like the river for those who live beside it: always the same and always different. And in a rhythm of rising and falling waters, there we are, the boatmen, steadfastly crossing the river, joining the regions it separates, binding them together [Moriremos sin recordar, acaso, cuántos fueron. Junto al río la vida es como él: siempre la misma y distinta. Y entre un ritmo de creciente y vaciante, los balseros estamos tercamente sobre las aguas, apuntalando las regiones que separan, anudando la vida]" (1943: 181; 1993: 151). In this passage the Marañon River is understood as representing a natural, cultural, and political scission in Peru; Calemar and the river itself constitute the threshold between two Perus, the sierra and the coast (yet another duality of indigenista critique). The Calemarinos are articulated as not only acknowledging this schism but accepting the role of bridging this gap: "there we are, the boatmen, steadfastly crossing the river, joining the regions it separates, binding them together." To bridge the two sides of the river is to bridge (*apuntalar*) the two sides of Peru and therefore to somehow bind (*anudar*) Peru's racial, ethnic, and cultural life. This doubly metonymical scheme functions in a very straightforward and conventional manner, albeit allegorically: *The Golden Serpent* positions Calemar and its cholo residents in a strategically centralized cultural frame. Ideologically it suggests that it is the mestizo, the cholos from Calemar, who can unify the Peruvian interior with the coast; they alone can render the Sierra commensurable with the coast. Alegría's Calemar ultimately posits an alternative nationalist topography conceptualized neither from the grid of the "Lettered City" nor from the vectors of Tahuantinsuyo but from the banks and currents of the Marañon River and its point of traversal, or at the axis of the Golden Serpent. The paradox, of course, is that the Calemarinos are articulated as both the river's flow and its crossing, this is to say, *at* the threshold serving as the point of traversal between the two sides of Peru, and *as* the threshold that would unite them. *The Golden Serpent* is not mapped in conventional oppositional terms; Osvaldo Martinez and don Matías do not represent mutually exclusive, geocultural imaginaries. Rather Calemar and its cholo residents are placed at the intersection of an even larger social text wherein their protagonism is determined by their topographical and ethnocultural centrality with regard to both the *criollo* from the coast and the *indio* of the highlands.

The opening pages of *The Golden Serpent* make the narrative's identitarian positioning abundantly clear: "We, the cholos of the Marañon [Nosotros, los cholos de Marañon]" (1943: 7; 1993: 11) as well as "We cholos whose story this is live in Calemar [Los cholos de esta historia vivimos en Calemar]" (1943: 8; 1993: 12) announce a discursive politico-narratological emplotment at the cross-section between the criollo/indio economy, at the intersection of both the highlands and the coast (the Marañon Valley) and orality and literacy (Quechua and Spanish)—this is to say, at the thresholds of criollo and indigenista cultural discourse. The fact that the narrator (later revealed as a cholo resident of Calemar named Lucas Vilca) articulates both himself and his community as cholo is significant because, as in Peruvian cultural politics, the cholo serves not only as a distinct identificatory marker whose main function is to immediately distinguish him socially and culturally (but not racially) from the rural indigenous populations but also represents part of a politically crucial demographic in Peruvian state consolidation.

And this is where *The Golden Serpent*'s critical value lies: in the installation of the figure of exclusion and marginalization that is produced in the attempt to supplant criollo and indigenista cultural discourse with the Marañon Valley and the cholos of Calemar. The following passage renders visible the form and terms through which cholo protagonism is imagined.

> They do not eat mangos, plums or guavas, because they think they
> give them malaria. In spite of this, and though they merely come here
> and go right back, they get the chills and fevers and die shivering
> like dogs in the wind in their huts which tremble at the blasts of the
> highland gales. This is not a land of Indians, and only a few managed
> to acclimate themselves. To the Indians the valley is like a feverish
> agitation and to us half-breeds (mestizos), the loneliness and the silence
> of the highlands make our breasts ache. Here we flourish like a green
> bay tree. (1943: 9–10)

> Ellos [indios] no comen mangos porque creen que les dan tercianas, y
> lo mismo pasa con las ciruelas y guayabas. A pesar de esto y de que no
> están aquí sino de pasada, los cogen las fiebres y se mueren tiritando
> como perros friolentos en sus chocitas que estremece el bravo viento
> jalquino. Esta no es tierra de indios y solamente hay unos cuantos
> aclimatados. Los indios sienten el valle como febril jadeo y los mestizos
> la soledad y el silencio de la puna nos duelen en el pecho. (1993: 13)

While these statements seem to lay the groundwork for the novel's precise, localized, narratological perspective, it is plain to see that, narratologically, the deployment of cholo protagonism in *The Golden Serpent* both posits and circumscribes indigeneity under the erasure of cholo signification. When Vilca states, "Esta no es tierra de indios, y solamente hay unos cuantos aclimatados [This is not a land of Indians, and only a few managed to acclimate themselves]," he is suggesting that this narrative will not be about indios and that when they do appear within this narrative space— they are few—they shall be marked as "aclimatados" to the Marañon Valley and consequently rendered nameless and voiceless to the course of the narrative. But this statement also suggests that the natives, being not from this territory, do not therefore hold any compelling relationship to the valleys and the river, as the cholos of Calemar do. Or further, that these "aclimatados" might not have the same relationship to the river as the Calemareños would. Both of these possibilities resonate given the narrator's terms, "solamente hay unos cuantos aclimatados," and given the need, not only by *The Golden Serpent* but also by the Peruvian state, to maintain the crucial but fragile distinction between cholo and indio. In this instance, we can see that the interests of both, the novel and the state, coalesce onto one strategy: the maintenance of *cholaje.*

However, it might also be the case that cholaje can come into visibility only through subordination of indigeneity. *The Golden Serpent's* narratological structure dictates not only that cholaje be constituted within simultaneous discursive processes—distinction from yet continual coevality with indigeneity—but that this derivative indigeneity be reproduced in deterritorialized and expropriated terms, that is, of an indigeneity inhabiting a space that is not indigenous. Here Vilca's statement "Esta no es tierra de indios, y solamente hay unos cuantos aclimatados" takes on added dimension in that it manifests the tension that cholaje needs in order to be sustained: the reproduction of the Marañon Valley by those expropriated from the highlands. In other words, the aclimatado, indigenous nonindigeneity, is deployed in the reproduction of cholaje; the former is constitutive as always already displaced yet always menacing by proximity.

Consequently the aclimatado in *The Golden Serpent* is a narratological problem but also its condition of possibility. If we continue to reflect on the assumptions that inhere in aclimatado, we will do better at arriving at the novel's discursive core. One can posit that, in this instance, the aclimatado is a cholo articulation for the subjects of migrational and assimilationist effects on indigenous populations in nineteenth-century Peruvian developmentalist policy. It could be further asserted that, being a cholo ascription for displaced rural Indians, Calemar's current population would have called their own village's founding families aclimatados as well, since by definition every cholo was once an aclimatado. In concise terms, the aclimatado is a historiographical category. So it might not be the existence of the cholo that determines this novel's contemporariness; neither would it be the "presencing" of mere displaced natives in the Andean valleys. Rather it is their very inscription as aclimatados, which is to say, the already manifest displacement and incorporation—the primitive accumulation—of indigenous populations into capitalist relations of expropriation and labor in Peru. In short, and in ironic fashion, it is the biopoliticized indigenous laborer, the aclimat-ado, that provides a narrative of cholaje protagonism with its centrality and historical relevance: registering both the narrative and its nationalist struc-ture within the time horizon of capital.

The aclimatado in *The Golden Serpent* is therefore not some inconse-quential name for these otherwise displaced and subordinated indigenous subjects who find themselves in Calemar; in effect, it is the aclimatado, more so than the cholo, who is constitutive of *The Golden Serpent*'s regis-ter of signification. Looking yet again at Vilca's statement "Esta no es tierra de indios, y solamente hay unos cuantos aclimatados," this premise does not simply suggest that the Indians *do not* have a compelling relationship to the river because they are not from there, nor does it imply that they *should not*, by necessity, have a compelling relationship to it because they are not from there; rather it implies that the aclimatados cannot have a compelling relationship to the Marañón because their cosmology would be missing the most necessary constituent element in Alegría's Calemar: the aclimatado itself, or the cultural articulation and presentation of their own displaced "bare life"-ness onto the Marañon Valley. In other words, Cale-mar would not be Calemar without the specter of the aclimatado as already incorporated (as excluded) into its social order. The desired narratological grounding here is cholo, but only because the identification and incorpora-tion of the aclimatado into the Marañon region makes the cholo visible to itself. Consequently the aclimatado, who neither belongs (by not belong-ing) anywhere else nor exists to anyone else (as excluded) but to the cholos of Calemar, comes to function biopolitically as the necessarily excluded and subordinated element within the Peruvian social text that makes national unification even imaginable.

As the privileged figure of exclusion and displacement, the aclimat-ado is constituted as doubly subordinated and doubly silenced: indig-enous within a cholo socius and expropriated from the traditional high-lands to the Marañon Valley. In the *Golden Serpent* the aclimatados do not speak; they are simply only spoken of and spoken to. Yet without their inscribed exclusion, Calemar and its cholo residents would cease to exist as such. While Latin American cultural and critical history is replete with moments such as these, no clearer demonstration of subalternization exists to serve as an allegory for the deadlock of resistance at work today in Latin American fields. However, it would do absolutely no good to simply (and hypothetically) turn to the aclimatados themselves and ask what they think of their conditions, for this would only further entrench what is already an irreducibly ideological proposition. Again, the aclimatado doesn't exist as such; it exists by and for the cholos of Calemar exclusively to name and signify those who have been expropriated from other lands and displaced onto the Marañon Valley seeking work. Though they belong to a *bios* that calls them aclimatados, one can be sure that those who have been ascribed as such would not use such a name. It is remarkably easy to see how marks of subalternization will appear even in the most strident emancipatory declarations: "We, the cholos of the Marañon." And as I am attempting to show in this discussion, the contemporary deadlock of resistance at work today is the inevitable result when the intellectual becomes unable to distinguish (or confuses the relation) between a truly progressive political agenda and populist nationalisms.

Twenty-five years ago, at around the same time these critiques against postcolonial theory were being launched, Gayatri Spivak produced an essay of no small influence to literary and cultural studies in the academy. Through a Marx-inflected form of deconstructionist critique, Spivak's essay forged into relief the critical pitfalls associated with the intellectual practice of solidarity-based politics and representation, the kind that *The Golden Serpent* most clearly and aptly foregrounds. The essay I am speaking of is "Can the Subaltern Speak?" (1988a), and while many would argue that this piece marked a watershed moment in critical thought and that its impact can be seen in numerous disciplines within the humanities and the social sciences, its reception everywhere has not always proved felicitous. Such is the case in Latin American studies, for which this essay provokes a certain ambivalent and contradictory relation.

In somewhat paradoxical fashion, though no Latinamericanist would dispute this essay's critical import to the field—as an intervention in the positing, reading, and limits of the social text—it is nevertheless an essay that has been systematically and repeatedly misread. There are exceptions, of course; in the years since its publication a handful of notable works have appeared that draw meaningfully from Spivak's intervention in order to critically reflect on the state of the field.[5] Far more often, however, the essay, which to this day continues to be referenced as a pivotal essay for critical literary and cultural studies in Latin America, is invoked by title only and with an accompanying yes or no response. In short, twenty-five years after this essay's publication, the predominant Latinamericanist response continues to be "The subaltern may indeed be speaking, but no one is bothering to listen."[6]

Again, I am not suggesting that Latin American studies has neglected or resisted incorporating this essay into its critical canon. What I am suggesting is that, by and large, the terms by which this essay has been appropriated or dismissed in the field stems from a fundamentally (and doubly) metaleptic reading, for while "Can the subaltern speak?" persists as the *only* question that elicits a response, the more critical intervention the essay actually invokes ("Are we [intellectuals] assuming a pure of form of consciousness?") continues to go overlooked and dis-acknowledged.

In many ways, the response noted earlier—yes (the subaltern can speak) *and* no (we just don't listen)—crystallizes the field's relationship to Spivak's essay. On the one hand, the formal structure of this reply accomplishes two things simultaneously: it marks an acceptance of the terms (the subaltern can speak) but a rejection of the question (we just don't listen) in which these terms are conceived and posed. In other words, it grants the subaltern an identity within the Latin American scene of cultural intelligibility, but as a positive entity completely devoid of its relational, structural, and ultimately heterogeneous, critical import. As such, this reply signals not only an adherence to ontological assumptions vis-à-vis the subaltern (understood in positive terms: i.e., "flesh and blood") but also a certain unproblematic expectation of a direct, unmediated political relation of solidarity with or through them. More specifically what this reply reveals is that it has misperceived the question of the subaltern—and whether or not it can speak—as the impetus for the political relation rather than as the discursive effect of the discipline's "complicit[y] in the persistent constitution of Other as the Self's shadow," which serves as the epistemological terrain by which subalternity emerges in the first place (Spivak 1998a: 280). The results of this metalepsis are obvious: in taking the figure of the subaltern as the cause and not the effect of the question "Can the subaltern speak?," the reply reproduces a critically hampered, even inverted understanding of what subalternity means in this discussion. This further highlights the fact that "Can the subaltern speak?," though it is the question this essay is most known for, is *not* the primary question Spivak's essay ultimately poses.

In effect this reply functions by retaining the use of the subaltern while simultaneously seeking to extricate it from the neoliberal critical realities—the complicity between Western intellectual production and globalized economic interests—that both condition it and for which it is a name. This includes the tacit excision of the very specific, intimate, and unwitting role the intellectual assumes in its reproduction. This is the second metalepsis. Consequently the form this reply has taken obscures, from the start, the critique of the "sanctioned ignorance" that Spivak presents as an obligation to attend to within our own disciplinary practice (1988a: 291). Her critique serves as an injunction to guard against disciplinary representational tendencies through which "the intellectual within socialized capital, brandishing concrete experience, can help consolidate the international division of labor" and wherein, "representing [the subaltern], the intellectuals represent themselves as transparent" (275). Again, this reply (yes *and* no) misperceives that the critical force of "Can the Subaltern Speak?" lies not with *the* subaltern and whether (or not) *it* can speak, but rather as an interrogation of the postrepresentationalist intellectual disposition that is revealed by it, where, from the assumption of "a pure form of consciousness," the subaltern is inscribed as a subject that "can speak and know [its] conditions" (283, 286).

This very limited (I argue, metaleptic) understanding of subalternity and speech, the very forms against which Spivak cautions, serves nevertheless as the ground of dispute between both subalternist and nonsubalternist critics in Latin America. This condition emerges at the outset, in the Latin American Subaltern Studies Group's (LASS) "Founding Statement" (1994). This document constitutes, if not the earliest then at least the most widely recognized attempt at conceiving and elaborating upon subalternity's critical role in Latin American disciplinary practice.[7] However, even from within its form as a programmatic disciplinary intervention—acknowledging the limitations in conventional models of interpretation to account for subalternity's elusiveness and resistance—the subaltern is nevertheless presented in the Founding Statement as a subject that "can speak and know [its] conditions":

> To represent subalternity in Latin America, in whatever form it
> takes wherever it appears—nation, hacienda, work place, home,
> informal sector, black market—to find the blank space where it
> *speaks* as a sociopolitical subject, requires us to explore the margins
> of the state. . . . Our project, in which a team of researchers

and their collaborators in elite metropolitan universities, want
to extricate from documents and practices the *oral* world of the
subaltern, the structural presence of the unavoidable, indestructible,
and effective subject who has proven us wrong—she/he who has
demonstrated that we did not know them—must itself confront
the dilemma of subaltern resistance to and insurgency against
elite conceptualizations. Clearly, it is a question not only of new
ways of looking at the subaltern, new and more powerful forms of
information retrieval, but also of building new relations between
ourselves and those human contemporaries whom we posit as
objects of study. (10, emphasis mine)

In this passage one reads the group's insistence that the subaltern, despite
"demonstrating that we do not know them," continues to be theorized as
one who can speak and one who speaks from an alternative ("oral") and
resistant cultural formation (that is, yes *and* no). As such, the Founding
Statement innocently, though no less problematically, reiterates the very
assertions of subaltern consciousness that incited Spivak (1988a: 274) to critique in her essay as "disavowing the role of ideology in reproducing the
social relations of production." A juxtaposition of this statement's assumptions of subaltern consciousness with the one Spivak ascribes to Foucault—"The masses know perfectly well, clearly, they know far better than
[the intellectual] and they certainly say it very well" (qtd. in Spivak 1988a:
274)—reveals in the former a self-imposed retreat from subalternity's more
critical stakes. Instead, and as a result, the Founding Statement defaults to
an onto-epistemological guarantee of a sovereign subject, foreclosed to us
in/as the subaltern, and installed as/within Latinamericanism's hegemonic
exteriority. This gesture of simultaneously positing a "pure form of consciousness" existing outside of Western thought and therefore our very fore-
closure from it is what Alberto Moreiras (2001: 135) calls "restitution," or the
foundational Latinamericanist practice of reducing and preserving alterity as a disciplinary condition of possibility. In this discussion, restitution
works as the intellectual desire for an assumed commensurability of speech
(an epistemo-ontological guarantee) that both the Latinamericanist and the
subaltern can, and do, and should share.

    In addition, this metalepsis is further compounded by the implications
the Founding Statement seeks to draw from this assumed commensurability

with the subaltern. Though the Founding Statement attempts to problematize a direct and unmediated access to the subaltern by acknowledging the
latter's success in "prov[ing] us wrong," it nevertheless also posits the disciplinary potential of eventually getting it right, where, through the appeal
to "build new relations" with the subaltern, "new and more powerful forms
of information retrieval" are both implied and warranted. Once again,
when the subaltern is posited as the cause and not the negative constitutive
effect of the politico-intellectual relation, the line between "Can the subaltern speak?" and "[How] can the subaltern [be made to] speak?" becomes
indistinguishable.

In the introduction to a special issue of *Dispositio/n* on LASS, "Latin
American Subaltern Studies Revisited" (2005), Gustavo Verdesio addresses
the now defunct status of the group, and, reflecting on the various narratives given explaining its demise, seeks to provide some kind of "post-mor-
tem" that might be instructive for future intellectual projects. Among the
various explanations entertained, most of which involved professional or
conceptual differences among it members, one in particular stands out for
its resonance with the present discussion: that certain members of the group
privileged the work of South Asian subalternists over scholars and critics
working in Latin America. Verdesio asserts, "This is why I have been always
mystified by the violence of the debate between Latin America–based and
North America–based Latin Americanists, and by the worship some members of LASS showed for intellectuals so far removed from their more
immediate intellectual and professional ties. I am referring, of course, to the
admiration shown by some members of LASS for intellectuals like Ranajit
Guha and other members of the South Asian Subaltern Studies group" (20).
Quite succinctly, this passage advances that one of the reasons, if not the
main reason, for the "violence" between Latin American and North American Latinamericanists is the latter's preference for drawing from non–Latin
American scholars and critics. It infers further that the main difference
between Latin American and North American Latinamericanists is the latter's preference for not just any theoretical model but a particular kind of
theory. This passage could even be taken one step further to suggest that
were it not for the involvement of non–Latin American intellectuals into
discussions pertaining to Latin America in the first place, there would be
no (need for a) distinction between Latin American and North American
Latinamericanists. I discussed the problems associated with this kind of

reasoning earlier in the chapter. But this is not all; for despite Verdesio's reiteration of this nationalist impulse of containment, he is simultaneously concerned with the lack of recognition and reciprocity given by these South Asian subalternists to the Latin American group: "Why do South Asian subalternists olympically ignore the work by their Latin American peers?" (7). Once again the contradictions surface: Are the South Asian scholars "peers" (from whose work we may draw) or not? One simply cannot have it both ways. One cannot demand, simultaneously, both their noninvolvement in these discussions and their recognition. In exactly the same way, the notion of the subaltern in the Founding Statement demonstrates this disciplinary contradiction lying at the heart of the LASS collective. I am insisting that the predominant Latinamericanist response to "Can the Subaltern Speak?"—yes (the subaltern can speak) *and* no (we just don't listen)—is not arbitrary but rather evinces a formal rhetorical structure in its restitutional practice, that this stems from a metaleptic reading of Spivak's more critical intervention, and that this limited understanding of the subaltern form pervades even its inaugural elaboration in LASS's Founding Statement. From this vantage point, it is not difficult to see why resistance to subaltern studies (and maybe even the demise of the group) may be attributed to its troubled formulation in this document. Nevertheless this form of disciplinary practice is not the only manner in which the subaltern is conceived and dispatched within Latin American critical thought.

One encounters this more nuanced critique in Mabel Moraña's essay "El Boom del Subalterno" (The Boom of the Subaltern) (1997). In this essay, Moraña assesses the globalizing impact of current North American intellectual projects over Latin America, projects she sees as the continuation of the trope of Latin American dependency as a pretheoretical blank page onto which Western thought is inscribed (53). Moraña's concern is over the emergence (the *boom*) of postcolonialism and subalternity in Latin American studies and how exactly this theoretical discourse reconfigures (is a reconfiguration of) the predominance of North American critical influence in literary and cultural debates in the region. More specifically her discussion concerns the status of the Latin American intellectual now that postcolonial and subaltern studies have effectively decentered the local intellectual's role—a displacement of the authority that came with knowing and speaking for the local—as the arbiter of representation. Unlike what we saw earlier in the Founding Statement, which transparently positions the intellectual in subaltern restitution (yes *and* no), for Moraña the problem is reversed: one reads the question of subalternity as leading to the subalternization of the entirety of the non-North, including its local intellectuals, for whose ability to stand (in) as a representative of "the people" has been short-circuited by the very global theoretical agendas they seek to ward off: "How to redefine North/South relations and its ideological space within which one thinks and constructs Latin America as an irreducible space of otherness, and one from within which the I that speaks (that *can* speak, despite Spivak's objections) is neither decentered nor epistemologically and politically destabilized?" (51, my translation).[8] In this passage, three gestures simultaneously run together as one. Taken as a syllogism, Moraña's question reveals an argument that runs something like this: (1) Hegemony/subalternity is a categorically North-South geopolitical relation; (2) *I*, however, an intellectual from the South, am not subaltern; (3) therefore, you cannot call *us* subalterns. In other words, Moraña explains, if *I*, an intellectual located in the periphery, can speak, then no one (here/there at the periphery) is subaltern. These three itineraries, however, brusquely interwoven as they are, function more as a confirmation of Spivak's proposition than as a critique of it. For it is precisely through the collapsing of the *I* (as intellectual) and the *we* (as the people) in representation (proxy/portrait) that this line of reasoning works to preserve as well as conceal the conditions of subordination. In other words, this is precisely how, according to Spivak, the collapsing of the categories of representation (*Vertreten/Darstellen*) leads to "an essentialist and utopian politics" (Spivak 1988a: 276–78).

Many have criticized Moraña's essay, including John Beverley (1999, 2008), who saw in it the reactionary gesture of a "neo-Arielist" and "neo-conservative" impulse. However, I perceive an even more fundamental logic at play in her argument that proves particularly instructive in this discussion. While Beverley's critique of Moraña's argument is ultimately concerned with its premises (hegemony/subalternity = North/South), I am tracing the effects of her conclusion: *I*, a Latin American intellectual, am not subaltern, therefore *we*, Latin Americans, are not subaltern. It is with this latter itinerary that I am most interested, for it is precisely through it that, against this North-hegemonic/South-subaltern polarity, national, regional, and local relations of power are both sutured and sustained. This effect is most clearly illustrated when Moraña (1997: 52) conceives of subalternity as yet another Eurocentric globalizing narrative that betrays the organic function of the local intellectual to articulate resistance and instead irrevocably subalternizes both the intellectual and the people as one and as global Other:

> The current elaboration of the concept violates, somehow, this discontinuous and episodic quality, converting subalternity into a globalizing narrative applied to a great variety of social subjects. In this manner, the political activism that laid the foundations for the texts included in the *Prison Notebooks* [by Antonio Gramsci] is being replaced by an intellectual exercise from which one can read, more than the story of the strategies of resistance of the dominated South, the history of representational hegemony of the North, in its new era of postcolonial re-articulation.

Unlike in the Founding Statement, where the subaltern as sovereign subject is installed (and foreclosed) through the transparent relation between radical exteriority and interiority (the subaltern that knows itself), here we witness a contrapositive relation: subalternity qua postcolonial discourse qua northern representational hegemony is rejected in order to affirm the nontransparent (organic) relation between the intellectual *I* (that *can* speak) and the "Latin American subject" whose alienation prevents the recognition of "his image in the elaborations that objectify him" (that is, *I*, the intellectual that knows better; 53).

Moraña here rehearses the very practice of subalternization she sought to resist. In an attempt to avert the subalternization and de-centering of the local intellectual by North American representational hegemony (i.e., postcolonial studies), she subordinates "the Latin American subject" as the means through which the intellectual's speech (*I* can speak) can retain its representative and authoritative function. These are precisely the consequences that Spivak's essay both cautioned against and rendered visible, and the very reason why I insist that her argument has still not been taken seriously enough. Ultimately what one witnesses here is a critical illustration of how the Latinamericanist intellectual's authority to speak is enacted and preserved precisely by the disavowal of its conditions of production (*I*, the intellectual that knows the "nonsubaltern" *better* than they). In other words, a critic's inability to see his or her own positionality (as an intellectual "that *can* speak, despite Spivak's objections") within socialized capital only further reproduces the subalternity that is being denied. As these observations demonstrate, the categorical rejection of a question that poses an intellectual's complicity in the reproduction of unequal relations of power (hemispherically *and* regionally) is itself a political act, and one that is not so easily dispatched without further subalternization.

Nevertheless, despite these limitations, and including Beverley's (2011: 9) most recent assertion that Latin America has now entered a "postsubalternist" phase, Brett Levinson (2007: 73) quite rightly reminds us that subaltern studies is still the project at hand: "Latin American subalternism's main interest is not subjectivity but heterogeneity: heterogeneity as liberation from a universal Sameness whose name ranges from the West to metaphysics to capitalism to neoliberalism. The Latin American difference, even when presented as a specific alterity or identity, discloses the intrinsic heterogeneity of being, freed from the despotism of the One: a global heterogeneity that names the future liberation of mankind." Levinson's point here is to reemphasize the primary aim of subalternist critique: to unconceal the ultimately baseless and illusory nature of any claim to unity, homogeneity, and consistency, no matter how diverse and inclusive. However, if, as Beverley claims, the *marea rosada* governments are constituted by the inclusion of certain social movements from the popular-subaltern sectors of society—subalterns "becoming the state"—does that mean subalternization is no longer an active, formal function of governance and statehood? Have the conditions of socialized capital changed so dramatically since 9/11 that such a mode of critique is no longer necessary political work? Is it really that difficult to conceive that, while certain groups have managed to acquire the visibility and "voice" necessary for political inclusion, there are always others whose own subordination conditions it?

The answer to these questions is no, yet Beverley nevertheless cites the historical emergence of the *marea rosada* as establishing a "postsubaltern" era, by which he means a subalternism now completely devoid of and unhampered by its critical, theoretical—"deconstructive"—function.[9] One might argue that based on the uneven formalization of subalternity in the LASS Founding Statement and other pronouncements about the group, such an intentionally untheorized articulation of subalternity was exactly what Beverley had in mind all along, and it was precisely the complications of theory to his notion of the subaltern that led him to dissolve the group. In effect, *Latinamericanism after 9/11* may be Beverley's (2011: 59) way of refounding a subaltern studies project in Latin America that for once can

eschew theoretical reflection for direct and unmediated analysis of subalterns and their "*struggle*, both political and military." Once the object of
critique in previous years for representing the most insidious form of theory
in Latin America, particularly by critics such as Morales and Moraña, Beverley's notion of subalternity in *Latinamericanism after 9/11* has been gutted
of the critical purpose ascribed to it by Spivak and assigned the meager task
of identifying counterhegemonic and/or subhegemonic groups in the struggle for power. Beverley's notion of subalternity now conforms to the antitheoretical critiques previously laid against it and aligns itself perfectly as
the latest manifestation in the deadlock of resistance I have been tracing in
this chapter. As I have illustrated throughout this discussion, there may be
no greater act of subalternization imaginable than disavowing the existence
of subalternity, except, of course, declaring the end of it. *Latinamericanism
after 9/11* accomplishes just that. Therefore, when Beverley asserts, "Theory
that has become outdated or missed its mark, as I have come to think is
the case with deconstruction, can also lead to errors or impasses in political
practice" (10), one should remember that theory in Latin America is never
rejected because it is outdated or flawed but because it is simply never Latin
American enough. As such, there is nothing apolitical about this gesture,
and as an antitheoretical theory—a deadlock of resistance—it is itself the
very impasse it seeks to avoid.

Levinson nevertheless allows us to go even further. Seemingly anticipating Beverley's proposition, he advances that not only is Latin America itself
"theory," but Latin America is itself globalization. I cite at length.

> The point is that Latin America offers to its outside regions the
> theories, the models of globalization, to which they recur. Hence,
> efforts by Latin Americanism to theorize the reality of Latin America
> will always fail, will always reduce materiality to speculation, to a
> mere theory, because Latin America cannot be theorized. It is instead
> theory. . . . Latin Americanism is the unfolding of a program that
> it cannot evade, for the design is the immanence of its foundation,
> "prior" to it. Yet the unfolding happens not "in" Latin America for,
> while immanent *to* this area, it is the immanence *of* globalization.
> Latin Americanism is the thought of that immanence, which is
> why Latin America finds its true self only "in theory." The more
> Latin America skirts theory, the more theoretical and speculative

it becomes, and the less able it is to think itself for itself: not as the reality upon which outside paradigms have been dropped, but as an inside theory, as the labyrinthine sketch of a globalization still "under determination." . . . Autotheorization, indeed, is but the greatest of Latin Americanist fictions, since there is no *auto-* without an *alter-* that always already crosses it. This, indeed, is why there is theory at all, theory in the first place, in Latin America. (2007: 81–82)

Levinson quite clearly and simultaneously foregrounds Latin America's irreducible globality and its sheer inextricability from "theory." As he argues, and as I have been at pains to demonstrate, attempts to effectuate either— subtract theory from Latin America or subtract Latin America from the global—"will always fail" because such agendas disavow from the start the heterogeneity that both conditions and marks it. If, then, as Levinson insists, one cannot "do" Latin America without also (and simultaneously) engaging in theory and without thinking globally, then what we "do" here is always already marked (as innermost) by that which is perceived as most external and foreign. This is an irrevocable predicament; it is why epistemic decolonization is not available as a program and why postcolonialism cannot be rejected out of hand. "Latin America" is itself foreign and external; it is its own externality, its own foreignness. Therefore, and despite the many assertions to the contrary, Latin America is always already postcolonial, and most irrevocably so in those moments when it is desired as something unlike itself: as something proper, as something of someone's own. If, in addition to all the other reasons given, postcolonial theory is categorically rejected in Latin America because it would also invalidate such discursive claims of identity, properness, and own(ership), then for once one might see a rationale for its value and necessity as a source for critical reflection. The aclimatado discussed earlier—displaced indigenous nonindigeneity— again serves as the foundational figure in this discussion because the same assumptions and methods that are used to differentiate Latin America from the rest of the postcolonial globe are the same ones used to exclude, and oppose, Latin America from itself. It concerns one of the oldest economies in Latin American thought, and it revolves around the role, form, and function of speech. I am referring to the orality-literacy duality. It is the wager of this chapter, indeed this book, that a critical return to this economy of signification will yield a way out of this deadlock.

The past twenty years have seen the publication of a wealth of material dedicated to studying the emergence, form, and representation of indigenous speech and language within various cultural practices and emplotments, from the colonial era to the present.[10] By and large these debates have turned on the category of orality as the name for and as the means by which to conceptualize the formal, political, and aesthetic properties of indigenous language and its relationship (often antagonistic) to Western, lettered writing. As it stands in these debates, however, orality-literacy has more often been assumed than critically interrogated. For what specifically is the relation between them? How, exactly, do we understand their relation as exclusive and irreducible, foundational semiological forms? Is one simply inconceivable without the other, or must one rely on the ontological guarantee provided by the other? At bottom, does this economy provide us with the insight needed to unconceal the sheer contingency of a social order in Latin America—that these categories are ultimately nothing but empty, formal markers of difference or subordination to otherwise equal speaking beings—or does it smooth over these power relations? In other words, if orality is ultimately advanced here as an authentic, non-Western language form (i.e., orality as a logocentric reversal or substitute for Western literacy and written culture), what exactly is revolutionary or emancipatory about that? In more formal terms, is this binary conceived and deployed as a hegemonic-subaltern or hegemonic-counterhegemonic relation? There is a difference, and though often confused, this distinction is significant and strikes at the core of the notion of the political and contemporary political thought in Latin America.

It goes without saying that the category of orality has never simply been a descriptive category but is a constitutive one burdened with the considerable weight of anthropological discourse whose implicit ethnocentricity cannot be easily dismissed. In a recent article, Galen Brokaw (2010) takes up the question of orality in Latin America and addresses this particular disciplinary problem in the study of alternative "writing" systems in the colonial era. Brokaw's essay foregrounds how the concept of orality within dominant historical and anthropological discourse not only assumes the existence of subjects and communities that persist (or have persisted) without any recognizable or legitimate (read: alphabetic) writing system whatsoever, but also how this concept perfectly accommodates itself to the underlying Western assumption of (its own form of) writing as the necessary condition

for civilization: "Anthropological thought (whether it be expressed by his-
torians, anthropologists, sociologists, or literary critics) has a tendency to
draw a distinction between oral and literate societies based on the presence or absence of writing, which is usually defined in phonographic terms"
(130). The problem with this premise, what Martín Lienhard (1991: 5–11)
has called the "fetishism of the written word," is the series of other interconnected disciplinary conclusions that ultimately places Western writing
and writing cultures at the apex of a long evolutionary curve. According
to Brokaw (2010: 120), because "dominant historical and anthropological
theories have often identified writing as a precondition for the development of complex socio-economic and political systems," orality and literacy
have come to articulate and correspond to different and unequal modes of
thought inextricable from the hierarchical structures they simultaneously
imply. Under this anthropologico-historicist model, Brokaw reminds us,
orality, because it posits a primitive evolutionary state of existence prior to
writing, is simply and always subordinated to it.

Brokaw's essay seeks not only to articulate the contours of an alternative
model for reading indigenous mediatic forms that avoids the many misapprehensions commonly associated with the concepts of orality and literacy;
it offers yet another reminder of just how deeply intertwined our objects of
study and our concepts have become and of the unpredictable disciplinary
effects such conditions produce. By highlighting, in very concise terms, this
implicit and foundational presupposition wherein orality and literacy constitute watershed stages in human perception and cognition, one that therefore warrants and necessitates the very "dichotomization of human society
itself into those that are literate and those that are oral," Brokaw (2010:
121) rightly acknowledges the explicitly teleological and developmentalist
demands of the orality-literacy binary and exemplifies the kind of work
challenging their viability in contemporary thought.

Brokaw's is the latest to insist upon the critical limitations of the concept of orality when employed to articulate discrete, non-Western semiological phenomena in Latin America. However, Brokaw's critique doesn't
go far enough. While this study's primary objective is to clear the ground
of orality and literacy as conventional disciplinary concepts for the articulation of a more precise nomenclature or method for reading Amerindian
"writing" practices, this conceptual shift is nevertheless premised on, and
therefore still reproduces, the very assumption of difference (otherness and

exogeneity) for which such categories were first enlisted. In other words, to the extent that Brokaw insists on the need for a more culturally and historically sensitive model of reading that can account for radically distinct indigenous language forms, another, more crucial presupposition is being missed.

To be clear, what Brokaw's intervention does not do—and in all fairness does not intend to do—is to interrogate the cultural-political use to which these categories have been put in recent years. While his piece draws from colonial Amerindian media such as the Andean *quipu* and Mesoamerican iconography, its primary motivation is to develop a way to move beyond orality and literacy as predominant guiding categories and their inability to sufficiently describe and ascertain such phenomena (and its epistemological implications) in any responsible way. If in Brokaw's critique of the anthropologico-historicist model orality functions not only as a reductive, catch-all term for disparate, Amerindian semiological forms but also as the sign for its naturalized subordination to Western writing, in recent cultural debates orality's role has been completely recast into an onto-epistemic recuperation of alterity from which he cannot entirely escape.

Within such discussions, and in a complete inversion to the early theorists Brokaw himself takes on (Goody 1977, 1987; Havelock 1986; Ong 1982), orality has effectively been reconfigured into the central concept in the elaboration a theory of cultural politics in Latin America. Specifically this model aims to transform the ascribed atavism of alternative, non-Western speech attributed to historically marginalized, primarily indigenous communities into a semiology of resistance. What we've thus come to see in recent scholarship is orality being enlisted to posit cultural authenticity and political representation to subjugated groups and classes and as the conventional rhetorical means by which to counter hegemonic narratives of nationhood, development, and modernization in Latin America. This is not to suggest that representations of orality no longer function nor serve as tropes of cultural difference; they simply no longer mark Amerindian, ethnoracial subordination to modern, lettered culture, but instead constitute the metonymical trace for alternative (again, primarily indigenous) modes of being persisting in external relation to and uncontaminated by Western categories and reason. As such, within such debates orality has been promoted as the guarantee of an alternative, non-Western consciousness radically incommensurate with and resistant to institutionalized modes of knowledge and neoliberal forms of governance.

However, as theoretical grounds for cultural critique, this approach to the subordinated, resistant voice continues to be underwritten and confounded by traditional notions of speech. This disciplinary predicament, which, following Lienhard's figuration, can only be described as a fetishization of the non-Western voice, has been critically addressed in a recent critique of Walter Mignolo's "decolonial" project. In their essay "Rethinking Border Thinking," Scott Michaelsen and Scott Cutler Shershow (2007) demonstrate how Mignolo's propositions on writing and orality, propositions that serve as grounds for his own conceptual framework, reveal a series of misapprehensions and contradictions that instead puts the entire structure into doubt. Not unlike the ways the notion of orality is being refashioned today, one of decoloniality's foundational premises, the notion of colonial difference, affirms the distinct, and always conflicting, nature between Amerindian systems of signification and Western writing culture. Within Mignolo's decolonial model therefore, concepts such as "border thinking" or "double translation" (the latter of which I examine more closely in chapter 4) come to represent the production of radically emancipatory thought articulated from the margins and/or the intersectionality of these oral and literate modes of being. Nevertheless, while the "colonial difference" relies on the now conventional presumption of a cultural difference between the orality of one and the alphabetic literacy of the other, it is still not the only distinction being made. Specifically, according to Mignolo, because Amerindian language systems do not practice scriptural representations of speech but use other forms of recordkeeping (*pace* Brokaw: the Andean quipu and Mesoamerican iconography), they fall outside the realm of, and are thus not bound to, the principles of Western metaphysics, theories of language, and their critique. Among the things Mignolo excludes from consideration when dealing with Amerindian semiological forms is logocentrism and therefore its mode of critique, deconstruction: "Western logocentrism shows its limits when confronted with forms of knowledge and understanding built upon alternative philosophies of language, and alternative speaking practices and writing systems" (qtd. in Michaelsen and Shershow 2007: 42).

If, then, according to Michaelsen and Shershow (2007: 43), Mignolo's "elaborate theoretical machinery depends on a single fundamental claim:

that Amerindian systems of signification were so distinctively different as to escape the problems Derrida described under the term *logocentrism*," it is because Mignolo posits writing itself as an irreducible distinction between speech and orality. Under this model, orality's relationship to writing is seen as completely exogenous, foreign, incommensurate, while speech's relation to writing is seen as congenital, mutually determinant, and therefore fundamentally interlaced. For unlike speech that needs writing to signify, orality does not. According to Mignolo, then, orality, since it bears no writing component, does not engage in representation, and since orality has no need for representation, it therefore doesn't suffer from the irreducible problems (of authorship, presence, and truth) inherent in Western speech and writing. Consequently, Mignolo's reasoning goes, orality is immune from charges of logocentrism since it is not speech that requires a supplement or substitute (i.e., writing) that assumes the function of a necessarily inferior record, and thus nothing *against which* it can be privileged as a source of truth and meaning. In this model orality is categorically distinct from speech. In other words, orality is conceived by Mignolo as whole, undifferentiated, and without any internally constitutive tension or opposition whatsoever that would confuse it with Western speech. The result is an articulation of a mode of language that, because it signifies beyond representation, assumes a dangerously idealized, pre-Babylonian character. Michaelsen and Shershow themselves are quick to point out the flawed and ultimately untenable nature of such a proposition: "One must suspect that Mignolo's claim itself springs from a kind of nostalgia for some unadulterated Amerindian 'voice' imagined as not yet disturbed in the plenitude of its self-presence and self-possession" (43).

Ultimately a contradiction inhabits this distinction between orality and literacy, and this further confuses the discussion at hand. It is important to see that fundamentally the active economy here is not between orality and literacy but between orality and speech—or rather the distinction between orality and writing and speech and writing. If for Mignolo and others orality-literacy expresses a dialectic between two radically different language forms, it is not simply because speech and the representation of speech through writing are semiological phenomena specific to Western language, nor that only alphabetic writing of such form conditions the emergence of logocentricity as an exclusively Western problem, nor that orality partakes of none of these characteristics. Rather orality's assumed difference from speech has been, all along, the latter's inextricable relation to writing.

This premise is significant for two reasons. First, this proposition admits that orality is meaningful only differentially, that is, as vocal semiosis that, specifically because it is unlike speech, harbors no relation to writing. As such, orality, when defined not against writing but against speech, presents no positive property of its own. What therefore first appears as a substantive, world-historical dialectic when opposed to writing is revealed instead to be a critical misapprehension when orality is juxtaposed against speech. In short, the difference between orality and speech is writing itself. Even between such categories as speech and orality, writing remains the indelible, determinant factor; writing thus obtains as the difference that defines them *both*.

This begs the question: Beyond the orality-literacy opposition, is orality really devoid of its own mode of writing? According to Michaelsen and Shershow, the answer is no. Indeed, and as suggested by Brokaw's very program to reread Amerindian mediatic forms, Michaelsen and Shershow (2007: 45) argue that "as soon as there is, in any sense, *record, account,* or *document,* as soon as inscription of any kind offers itself as at once a supplement, and a substitute for a memory that already supplements and substitutes for the trace, one is already . . . within that strange economy of what Derrida calls *différance*." Which is to say that, in formal terms, there can be no vocal semiosis (even Amerindian) without an attendant writing or, in Brokaw's terms, media. As such, and despite the persistent assertions to the contrary, the epistemological distinctiveness attributed to orality and the colonial difference—nonrepresentational, nonlogocentric—is simply unsustainable, and the implicit difference between speech and orality appears ethnocentrically rather than democratically premised.

But that is not all. A second facet to this proposition warrants scrutiny. Further still, and bringing us back full circle, the subordination of speech to orality, using speech's relation to writing as justification, culminates in the exertion of the very logocentrism that Mignolo contends is impossible with orality. That is, what the distinction and privileging of orality over speech seeks to establish is that speech, like writing, is also a poor substitute for orality and thus could never stand in for it (either). The reasoning goes, as writing is a poor substitute for speech because it is distant, impoverished, and representational, so too is speech a poor substitute for orality. In other words, the formal terms that both bind and separate speech and orality are the same ones that are at work with speech and writing as well, and for the same reasons. Orality, far from being the semiological mode that would finally offer a way out of the paradoxes and aporias of Western metaphysics, instead features as its incomparable primordial figuration that signals a retrenchment, not a disruption, of logocentric claims. In effect, with orality logocentrism has been neither averted nor nullified but rather concentrated and recentered, this time in the name of an intellectual project that is ultimately anything but emancipatory.

Amounting therefore as nothing more than an inferior and inadequate accounting of orality, speech (and writing) nevertheless obtain as the only means by which to conceive and explore it. What the present discussion is making amply clear is that the concept of orality is marked by an internal confusion (and continuous slippage) between it as the name for indigenous semiosis (taken to be unmediated subaltern speech overdetermined by the assumption of a non-Western logos) and the inevitable *record* of this oral speech upon which these studies are based. Therefore at one and the same time and without apparent contradiction, orality is affirmed as primordial semiological practice yet posited as radically exogenous phenomena for which no adequate representation is possible. Under these terms one cannot mount a convincing narrative of resistance to lettered Western hegemony through the assumption and promotion of alternative linguistic identity positions when those very positions are grounded within the very logocentrism they claim to escape. Orality, as these pages aim to illustrate, is as irrevocably Western as the literacy (and speech) it opposes itself to, and therefore provides no ontological guarantee of the cultural difference that is ascribed to it. So how best to conceive and engage the inner workings of this hasty idealism as it continues to be used as foundational semiological antagonism for many, if not most, theories of Latin American culture and identity?

The orality-literacy relation, I suggest, beyond its current enlistment as a marker of epochal and epistemological difference, and/or as the basis for cultural resistance, might more productively be conceived today as a biopolitical formalization of exception in Latin America. Giorgio Agamben, discussed earlier, assists in formulating the problem at hand. In *Homo Sacer* (1998), Agamben outlines the originary processes by which sovereignty is both grounded and established in a relation of exception with life itself.

Defined as the "form of relation by which something is included solely through its exclusion," the relation of exception functions as the universalizing principle of exclusion by which political rule is established: between chaos-order, biological life (*zoë*)–political life (*bios*), between inside-outside (18–19). However, the state of exception not only distinguishes between inside-outside—bios and zoë—but indeed constitutes them by both presupposing them and maintaining itself in relation to them. Agamben argues:

> The state of nature and the state of exception are nothing but two
> sides of a single topological process in which what was presupposed as
> external (the state of nature) now reappears, as in a Möbius strip or a
> Leyden jar, in the inside (as state of exception), and the sovereign power
> is this very impossibility of distinguishing between inside and outside,
> nature and exception, *physis* and *nomos*. The state of exception is thus
> not so much a spatiotemporal suspension as a complex topological
> figure in which not only the exception and the rule but also the state of
> nature and law, outside and inside, pass through one another. (37)

Agamben's principal advance here is the realization that sovereignty is not to be conceived as the imposition of a political order onto an already existing, though unguarded, state of things. In other words, at the moment of the sovereign decision both the state of exception and the state of nature are constituted simultaneously, which is to say that sovereignty is founded both on the ground of conditional temporalities (as if there was a before) and conditional spatialities (as if there was an outside). As such, what appears as external to the social order provides no ontological guarantee of difference but merely a manifestation of the sovereign exclusion's innermost and fundamental processes.

For the orality-literacy relation the implications are clear: given the formal logic of exclusion as outlined by Agamben, orality is neither literacy's historical antecedent nor its juridical exteriority, even though it is understood and expressed as both. Constituted simultaneously, and from the same principle of exclusion, orality cannot express anything beyond its formal function as the limits to literate signification and, as such, is both fundamentally and inextricably included within the field of semiological intelligibility that appears to exclude it. My interest lies in critically interrogating the grounds of orality and literacy's very discursive formalization: as categories instrumental to the forging of cultural and racial hierarchies in

Latin American society and as concepts that continue to function as a disciplinary index of cultural, linguistic, and ethnic difference. In Latin American literary and cultural fields, orality and literacy have together enjoyed a certain privileged status as the hegemonic register of signification through which all sociocultural meaning is conceived and generated. This is to say that in contemporary Latin American criticism, dominant and marginal cultural positions have never not been understood through the orality-literacy relation; they have never not been ascribed the qualities of *at least* one (or some mixture) of the two.

Orality and literacy's cultural legacy has been most succinctly presented in Angel Rama's *The Lettered City* ([1984] 1996), a seminal essay that posits writing and written culture as the principal agent in the historical formation of Latin American societies. Originally published in Spanish as *La ciudad letrada*, this book advances a history of the Latin American urban center from within the logic and topographical structure of Western writing systems. As such, it also reveals the systematic nature in which the Lettered City emerged as the site where the processing of knowledge and consolidations of power converged in Latin America. As it hinges upon non-Western speech and the category of orality that is used to render it thinkable, Rama provides very little except for one key passage: "To the degree that this dying cultural universe depended on unwritten traditions and oral communications, one might say that urban letters came to its rescue, but only to hold its funeral services in writing" (62). From this brief passage one gleans a critical view of the Lettered City's formal operations as a reduction and transcoding of orality's alterity into a language homogeneous to and commensurate with the epistemological grounds of its originary lettered positing. Thus the Lettered City represents the site where all endotopic exclusions are conceived, rendered, and deployed as exotopic, which is to say, where orality is conceived, marked, contained, and preserved as literacy's radical exteriority. For Rama, the positions are clearly drawn; orality and literacy function as a state of nature and a state of exception.

Nevertheless Rama's assertion of the Lettered City's effective capture of oral language forms has not gone uncontested; many have taken issue with his depiction of the Lettered City's monolithic accumulation and incorporation of orality into its logic, insisting instead on orality's irreducible difference from literate signification. A crucial instance of this can be seen in Antonio Cornejo Polar's *Escribir en el aire* (1994). Cornejo Polar contests literacy's complete and homogeneous absorption of the Andean oral world within Latin American writing by asserting the inescapably heterogeneous and contradictory nature of its sociocultural makeup and the equally symptomatic nature of its literary tradition, a heterogeneous context which, he argues, cannot be reduced to a monolingual code of letters. Responding to Rama's conception of the Lettered City, Cornejo Polar insists, "It is not about founding a 'linguistic model' that, while 'overcoming the contradictions between two communities and two cultures,' projects itself toward the constitution of a new and presumably homogeneous society, but rather to recognize the impossibility and perhaps even illegitimacy of such a model that unifies what is different, diverse, and discovered" (200, my translation). According to Cornejo Polar, any linguistic model that is based on transculturation and homogeneity misses the point entirely. Instead *Escribir en el aire* represents just such an attempt to break away from the monological structure of the Lettered City and instead urges a consideration of the ways orality not only resists lettered capture but actually affects and transforms *it* in the process. For Cornejo Polar, orality not only resists incorporation into literary networks of signification, but it also short-circuits the literary forms used to appropriate it. And this, according to Cornejo Polar, is its virtue: orality marks literacy's expressional limits; it constitutes the cultural heterogeneity that the Lettered City cannot incorporate into its homogeneous logic. However, affirming the state of nature because it is different from the state of exception does absolutely nothing other than reproduce the originary sovereign claim. For it is possible that, in his insistence on affirming orality's irreducibility and radical exteriority to literate signification, Cornejo Polar is simultaneously reproducing the Lettered City's neocolonial processes. That is, in his attempt to substantiate orality's difference from within Latin American culture, he further entrenches the Lettered City's conceptual sovereignty over all semiotic activity in Latin America.

Furthermore this nativist and reverse-ethnocentric slippage underlying most, if not all, claims to cultural difference continues to go largely unheeded and unacknowledged, even in recent scholarship. For example, in her recent book *The Inner Life of Mestizo Nationalism*, Estelle Tarica (2008: 98) draws upon orality and literacy in order to discuss the representation of the Quechua language in the writings of the Peruvian author and ethnographer José María Arguedas.

> My argument here builds on [Rama's and Cornejo Polar's] observations, but with one substantial revision: orality in this novel is not opposed to writing. It is rather a function of a specific quality of Quechua, its highly developed sound-symbolic resources, specifically onomatopoeia, a quality that is noticeably underdeveloped in Spanish and other European languages. . . . Thus, rather than speaking of "oral culture," I will focus specifically on "Quechua." And Quechua, furthermore, will come to configure a whole socio-geographic sphere and become a way of enframing indigeneity more broadly, as a field of natural belonging that is constructed by language and is organically linked to the Andean landscape.

Three moves are made in this brief passage. Tarica proposes a Quechua-Spanish opposition to displace orality-literacy as master antagonism and to break it apart into autonomous and unopposed attributes available in all languages. No doubt she does this in order to position these languages on more equal analytic terms and therefore to highlight Quechua's "highly developed" onomatopoetic (i.e., oral *and* lettered) qualities vis-à-vis those other European languages. With these criteria in place, Tarica can assert that because Quechua can be as literary as any other Western language, it is therefore equal to any other and cannot not be defined, categorized, and discounted as simply another "oral culture." However, her promising egalitarian impulse is abrogated in the very next sentence, when, in the attempt to articulate what she sees as Quechua's defining characteristics (what distinguishes it from any other Western language), she deploys the tropes of nativism, reverse-ethnocentrism, and logocentricity long associated with premodern cultures—"natural belonging," "organically linked"—to fill out the space. In the attempt to finally wrest the Quechua language from the preestablished hierarchies implicit in the either/or of orality and literacy, Tarica nevertheless ascribes Quechua with the very essentialisms of primitive "oral culture" she sought to avoid in the first place. In much the same way as Cornejo Polar's, Tarica's proposition fails to account for the threshold of illiteracy that inhabits the orality-literacy relation itself: the principle of exclusion that governs the formal, empty nature of their semiological identity and intelligibility.

Consequently the following discussions are attempts at unearthing and rendering visible a conceptual field wherein orality and literacy are conceived not only as oppositional and mutually constituted categories but one in which they have become the *only* categories available to conceptualize the linguistic landscape in Latin America. In this field, orality and literacy have come to function as a hegemonic register of signification for all semiotic activity in Latin America, one that implicitly regulates signification and determines whether a given utterance is lettered, oral, or both *but never not one of the two*. Orality and literacy in Latin America are not just objects of representation; rather their discursive tensions represent a formal, biopolitical engagement that, as a matter pertaining to governance, continues to organize and configure racial, ethnic, and social life. As such, orality and literacy must both be understood in their full biopolitical capacity as their onto-epistemological figurations in culture and criticism constitute the grounds of sovereignty and subalternity simultaneously. Consequently orality's "liberation" from literacy's subordination is neither itself the objective nor the problem; orality cannot serve as grounds upon which to critique or resist the West, for orality already lies at the heart of the former. As Agamben (1998: 50) reminds us, "The nonlinguistic is only ever to be found in language itself": in this case, orality—the nonlettered—is only ever to be found within literacy itself. Orality is therefore not a constitutive outside to literacy but is its founding and innermost sovereign exclusion. Orality can no longer be simply conceived as a subaltern entity resisting literacy's predominance; rather it is orality and literacy *together* that constitute the field of semiological activity in Latin America that establishes and governs the intelligibility of speech. The "problem" of orality and literacy in modern Latin America is therefore no longer which of the two to privilege in cultural criticism (orality *or* literacy) but rather to trace the limits of the inside-outside relation itself (neither/nor) and to exploit the continuous threat of indistinction upon which such dualities are always founded and which are kept hidden from view. Orality and literacy are thus political in the manner understood by Rancière (1999): not in their configuration as an either/or but as the site of contestation over what speaking means in the very rationality of the speech situation. The task of critique, then, is to remain vigilant against reproducing orality as the "nonlinguistic" outside to literacy's "linguistic" inside and to seek and exploit the breaches of illegibility and indistinction from within their systematic semiotic hegemony. As a way out of this deadlock, this book proposes a new site of interrogation, not one found between and among orality and literacy but one that traces orality and literacy's coextensive exclusions—at the conceptual threshold (and limit) of communication and understanding in Latin America—where signification is illegible, incommensurate, and therefore ungovernable. I call it *illiteracy.*

Illiteracy is the name I give to the semiological short-circuiting of orality and literacy in the Latin American social text. I employ the term to trace and articulate discrete, momentary glimpses of aberrant meaning within cultural and historical narratives that reveal—and unwork—the arbitrary and groundless nature of state-sponsored (linguistic, racial, and class-based) categories and the economies of reading that sustain them. Once again, by *illiteracy* I do not simply mean the inability to read and write, nor am I appealing to orality's primacy over Western writing systems; rather I employ *illiteracy* as the name for the disruptive, political effects brought about by the contradictions *between the two.* As such, my notion of illiteracy gives semiological specificity to what Rancière understands as politics. For Rancière, politics occurs when the grounds of a speaking situation are disputed—in the form of a semiotic irruption that emerges from within the logic of an entrenched social order—and which effectively both exploits and transforms the conditions of speaking within that social order. "Politics," he argues, is

> whatever breaks with the tangible configuration whereby parties
> and parts or lack of them are defined by a presupposition that, by
> definition, has no place in that configuration—that of the part of
> those who have no part. This break is manifest in a series of actions
> that reconfigure the space where parties, parts, or lack of parts have
> been defined. Political activity is whatever shifts a body from the
> place assigned to it or changes a place's destination. It makes visible
> what had no business being seen, and makes heard a discourse
> where once there was only place for noise; it makes understood as
> discourse what was once only heard as noise. . . . Political activity
> is always a mode of expression that undoes the perceptible divisions
> of the police order by implementing a basically heterogeneous
> assumption, that of a part of those who have no part, an assumption
> that, at the end of the day, itself demonstrates the sheer contingency

of the order, the equality of any speaking being with any other speaking being. (1999: 29–30)

"Political activity," Rancière notes, is at bottom a "mode of *expression*." Illiteracy is the name for that mode of expression that articulates the contingency of equality of any speaking beings whatsoever. But further, and as a condition of possibility for politics itself, the political sequence "must give rise to a meeting of police logic and egalitarian logic that is never set up in advance" (32). Not only are the conditions for politics unpredictable and precarious, but they also have to actually take place; the egalitarian contingency must be enacted, activated, in performative fashion. My staging of illiteracy in this volume has the same conditions, which is why, specifically, I reflect on moments of linguistic confrontation in the social text, what Gareth Williams (2011: 15) calls "speech scenes," of ambiguous, unassimilable speech whose very heterogeneity threatens the "symbolic distribution of speaking bodies" with indistinction and destabilizes established conventions of cultural and political coherence. I therefore conceive of illiteracy as a critical category that not only demonstrates the contingent and arbitrary nature of the political order in Latin America but also offers itself in the reconfiguration of the field of experience.

Through this notion of illiteracy, the subsequent chapters advance an analysis and critique of the historical and disciplinary conditions that regulate the intelligibility of speech and speaking beings in the Latin American social field, of the irruptive, democratic effects that emerge from the upending of that natural order and the disciplinary economy of reading that sustains it. It is an upending that is also a "disidentification, a removal from the naturalness of a place, the opening up of a subject space where anyone can be counted since it is the space where those of no account are counted, where a connection is made between having a part and having no part" (Rancière 1999: 36). Ultimately illiteracy articulates the textually unreadable condition that obtains in the cultural field from the collapsing of institutionalized conventions governing the intelligibility of speech and political identity that make it possible to ask What counts as speech? Who counts as a speaking being? And on what grounds? Illiteracy is thus advanced as a mode of inquiry that interrogates institutional and disciplinary processes that reproduce the oppositional and hierarchical nature between modern lettered culture and orality as an entirely unmediated, self-present mode of expression. Illiteracy, as Rancière (1999: 42) argues, "produces both new inscriptions of equality within liberty and a fresh sphere of visibility for further demonstrations." As such, illiteracy offers an accounting of the democratic effects arising from these conditions of semiological ungovernability and advances the possibility of a politics of reading underwritten by their egalitarian and heterogeneous implications.

Other Perus: *Colono* Insurrection
and the Limits of *Indigenista* Narrative

Historically *indigenismo* in Latin America emerges as a nationalist political platform grounded on a set of sociohistorical assumptions and literary representations privileging indigenous culture, language, and identity.
And while indigenismo has appeared in numerous ideological forms and
programs throughout the twentieth century in Latin America, it is its discursive formalization in Peru that has become representative of the tradition by Latin American literary and cultural critics. To this day one need
only invoke Clorinda Matto de Turner's *Aves sin Nido* (1889), José Carlos
Mariátegui's *Siete ensayos* (1928), or the literary production of José María
Arguedas to attest to Peru's definitive provenance on indigenismo's historical and cultural form in Latin American studies. Furthermore, recent
work on the subject from María Elena García (2005), Rebecca Earle (2007),
Estelle Tarica (2008), and Jorge Coronado (2009) illustrate Andean indigenismo's continuing vitality and relevance as a source of discussion for
scholars and critics in the field.

However, indigenismo in Peru, as sociopolitical agenda and literary-critical field, has never been immune to criticism. What has made this tradition so pivotal and yet so ripe for contention is the degree to which indigenista cultural production can be said to be representative of Peruvian "reality"; most critiques seem to imply that the symbolic field constituted by indigenista discourse—an economy of dichotomies, the most salient of which are Indio/Criollo, Quechua/Spanish, orality/literacy, modern/traditional, coast/sierra—can very easily be determined to be either a "real" or simply an ideological conceptualization of Peru's sociocultural grounds (see Mariátegui, Sánchez, and Aquézolo Castro 1976). In either case the debate over indigenismo's historical and cultural legacy has never been over its accomplishments but rather over its political and literary "failures," what to do with them, and where exactly to situate them within the study of Latin American culture. One could argue that indigenismo continues to occupy a critical place in Latin American thought precisely because what is at stake in these failures—how to read them and what to do with them—continues under heated and polemical dispute.

In his essay "Sobre la heterogeneidad de la letra" (2003), William Rowe summarizes his position against indigenista criticism by articulating what he sees as the fundamental flaw in its practice: not what indigenistas read but *how* they read and the way in which Peru is misread by them. He argues, "I do not uphold the thesis, absurdly obvious, that the ubiquitous social effects of racism in Peru have been resolved, rather I am proposing that indigenista rhetorical strategies—their way of reading Peru and its languages—have been incorporated by state institutions, most notably by the Velazquista regime, but effectively commencing from the first Belaúnde, without which the problems referred to by their discourse would have been resolved" (249).[1] The key phrase here is "[indigenismo's] way of reading Peru and its languages." The issue for Rowe is not about the persistent social effects of racism in Peru, which he himself acknowledges is a nonideological issue ("absurdly obvious"); the problem that he ascribes to indigenista criticism is that it cannot distinguish between what is ideological and what is nonideological representation in cultural practice. In short, Rowe's comments imply, there are ideologically and nonideologically motivated perspectives on "Peru and its languages," traditional indigenista criticism is based on a confusion between the two, and that the gap between the text and the nonideological position is accessible only through a serious commitment to reading.

According to Rowe (2003: 249), indigenismo's principal flaw, aside from its subsequent appropriation by a populist Peruvian state, has been in its positing of a historicocultural schism in Peru—indigenous orality *versus* Western writing—as the grounds of an interpretive strategy that, he contends, asserts the former's presence despite, and at the expense of, the meaning to be derived from reading, asserting indigenismo's "rejection of the written word for speech." In other words, as a mode of interpretation founded on the "historical fable" of the Lettered City, as the oppressive written word that impedes the expression of the marginalized voice (226), indigenismo's privileging of indigenous speech over the written word amounts to an ideological position that has little to do with the actual practice of reading texts: "Indigenismo appears as an ideological projection of what it wishes to read in words as it obscures the real processes of reading" (251). That is, reading itself is the very process by which the critic distinguishes between ideology (what one wishes to read in words) and the nonideological (what the text actually signifies), and indigenista criticism has suffered from its neglect. For Rowe, there is no confusion between these realms, and he offers no reflection as to whether that which he considers nonideological—text, reading, meaning, truth, and reality—is not the very stuff ideology is made of and the very terms with which ideology naturalizes itself as nonideological in the first place.

This notwithstanding, what is illustrative about Rowe's essay is the degree to which, as an otherwise justifiable critique of indigenismo's inherent phonocentrism, his understanding of reading and writing nevertheless falls prey to the same metaphysics of presence. In this essay Rowe (2003: 245) aims to extricate or even salvage Arguedas from his installation as an indigenista writer, arguing that "Arguedas no . . . es indigenista." However, in order to accomplish such a thing, Rowe wagers, one must mount a reading of Arguedas that displaces orality as the privileged signifier in his work. If indigenista writing's utilization and incorporation of orality is one of its defining stylistic features, it must therefore be shown that Arguedas's work is not based on such concerns. Rowe's reading of Arguedas's *Los ríos profundos* yields the following assertion: "His handling of Quechua words and phrases goes beyond mere folklorism or indigenista appropriation: it acquires the freedom of a new poetics that, thanks to the conquest of a space where sound is silenced, is then inscribed as a scriptural materiality [*material escritural*], and through its play with the visual world, generates images" (244). In this passage Rowe suggests that indigenous speech in Arguedas should not be understood as orality, as speech with no relation to writing. Rather, Arguedas's narrative operationalizes an inscribing of Quechua speech onto material, physical signs that makes it legible, that gives it a "new legibility [*nueva legibilidad*]." While for Rowe this signals a new poetics, in formal terms the contribution is minimal. Rowe's new poetics is merely the inversion of indigenista reading practices that privileges orality over writing into a poetics that privileges orality itself as writing. It stems from a reversion from the economy of reading that conceives of Quechua as orality devoid of writing, and which is now rendered intelligible, legible as writing. In other words, Rowe's new poetics is based upon substituting orality for writing as the means by which to make Quechua legible to a Western audience. If Mignolo and Tarica demonstrate an overdetermined preference for an orality radically unbound to writing, with Rowe we see the reverse tendency. In effect, the invention and development of other modes of literacy to better read cultural phenomena do not engage the critical question of literacy itself, its role as governing principle of analysis and interpretation in Western thought, and its inextricable function in the conceptualization and formalization of signification in Latin America. In both cases (Mignolo and Tarica, and Rowe) we can see these transactions accomplish nothing further than simply reversing the hierarchical torsion of one and the same dichotomy, ultimately leaving untouched and intact the discursive nucleus of all that binds and separates orality and literacy in the first place. What we see in Rowe is that far from proposing a critical reading of indigenismo's founding categories, orality and writing, a practice he rejects as "too abstract, metaphysical, and lacking any connection to real places" (248), his assumptions about the nonideological physical Andean text (the *quipu*, the *waca*, Incan murals) lead to their being ascribed an equally privileged form of self-presence, where the very irreducibility of the material sign serves as logos's enduring guarantee.

Rowe's essay puts into relief, and in a very symptomatic way, my point of departure for this chapter and its critical direction. It reproduces a now conventional logic within indigenista criticism that takes up the binary of orality and literacy and posits its relationship as a substantive—ideological or nonideological—choice. But as I show in following pages, these tropes of indigenista criticism are not arbitrary; the discourse of indigenismo is grounded on these tropes and cannot dispense with them.

Rowe's essay is but one example of the critical tensions and discursive contradictions that, to this day, constitute indigenismo and its criticism. The problem is, however, that as orality and literacy have become institutionally conceptualized *together* as the scope of and limits to communication and understanding in Peru and Latin America, we are simply not dealing with an antagonistic duality wherein Western and non-Western forms of consciousness compete for prominence, as Rowe (and others) would suggest, but rather with one inscribed entirely within Western reason (Self/ Other, identity/difference).[2] In other words, it has been precisely in orality's difference where one can see Western writing understanding and reading itself against its own imagined differentiation from speech and indigenous speakings. As such, orality—as Self's shadow—is no less "Western" than writing, and to either affirm or reject one in the name of the presence of the other only further reproduces their systematicity as a logocentric assumption that delimits the realm of speaking beings in Latin America: what, from now on, shall count as speech, and who shall thus count as a speaking being.

To argue that the binary of orality and literacy is only meant to signal the totality and multiplicity of linguistically expressive forms in Latin America or to claim that they represent the bookends of a far larger spectrum of transculturated possibilities does little to displace the binary as an epistemological framing of linguistic and cognitive assumptions between Western and non-Western languages, traditional and modern culture, fetishistic and scientific thought. The question is not about the choice between orality and literacy; it is about how the critic cannot but confront them *together* as the parameters constituting the field of semiological intelligibility and the means by which one might interrogate its very sustainability as an analytic assumption.

The aim of the present discussion is to analyze how this either/or was established in the first place and whether, by revealing and examining some of its many discursive tensions, one can trace the implications of its inherently unstable and ultimately unsustainable character. As such, I will not deviate far form these critical tropes, nor will I presume a critical positionality exterior to it. However, I will suggest that when representations of different language forms and purportedly exclusive cognitive states (orality and literacy) interact—when, as in indigenista narrative, they are placed in confrontation with one another, ideologically, linguistically, and textually—traces of unaccountable expressional modes nevertheless and uncontrollably present themselves as obstacles to communication and understanding. A critical effect is produced by this interaction, and though contingent, unpredictable, and radically incommensurate to assumptions about orality and literacy, it is nevertheless constitutive of this binary. I use the term *illiteracy* to signify such abject forms of narrative aberrancies that breach the conceptual limits imposed by orality and literacy and as the critical trace through which their effects reveal the sheer contingency of the social order that delimits communication and understanding in Latin America and the unhinging of orality and literacy as the history of that social order. I propose such an "illiterate" analysis of one of the more representative—and widely read—indigenista novels, José María Arguedas's *Los ríos profundos* (1958). But I will first begin with a critical examination of the discourse of indigenismo as conceptualized by Mario Vargas Llosa and the Peruvian literary critic Antonio Cornejo Polar, as I seek to show how the trace of illiteracy is revealed by and through their readings of the indigenista narrative form.

By the 1960s, with the emergence of the Latin American "boom" authors into the global literary market and their insertion into the networks of international publishing, in particular with the success of the author Mario Vargas Llosa (1936–), literary production in Peru succumbed to the new literary standards established by its incorporation into the noted ranks of world literature (Cornejo Polar 1984: 181). Before the end of the decade, Vargas Llosa published "Novela primitiva y la novela de creación en America Latina" (1969a), an essay that at first sight signals an attempt to reconfigure the Latin American literary map by placing himself, the rest of the boom authors, and their narratological innovations at the apex of a long and, according to him, rather poor literary genealogy. Here we see his compartmentalization of Latin American novelists into "creationary" and "primitive" authors: "The creationary novel ceases to be 'Latin American,' it is now free from this servitude. It no longer serves reality; reality now is in the service of it. In distinction to what happened with the 'primitives,' there is no common denominator among these new novelists, neither of issues, style nor technique: their commonality is their diversity. These writers no longer struggle to express 'one' reality, but rather, multiple, personal visions and obsessions: 'their' reality" (31). Against the "novela de creación," Vargas Llosa opposes the "novela primitiva," or the traditional novel form, which, in the Latin American context, signifies almost every novelistic practice preceding the boom's emergence, in particular, "la novela de la tierra," "novela regionalista," and "novela costumbrista." Not surprisingly, the indigenista narrative tradition is also included in the genealogy of primitive novels due to its use of conventional narrative forms and, according to Vargas Llosa, its politically committed quality (29–30). Nevertheless this categorical distinction between primitive and creationary novelists is not without its notable exceptions. Spared from Vargas Llosa's list of primitive novelists is Peru's most successful indigenista novelist, ethnographer, and anthropologist, José María Arguedas (1911–69), upon whom he bestows unique praise.[3] However, the terms of Vargas Llosa's appreciation for Arguedas is limited to him as a fiction writer and, as we shall see, is of little value since this seemingly positive critique results in a critically ambivalent rendering of his legacy.

Though Vargas Llosa's discussion of primitive and creationary literature is essentially a conventional piece of literary critique, it is difficult to overlook that this discussion grounds a significantly larger cultural stake than simply the primitive quality of literary production in Latin America prior to the boom. What we can also see here, through this aesthetic dichotomization of primitive and creationary literary production, is Vargas Llosa's initial attempt to lay claim to literary indigenismo's (and Arguedas's) historical and cultural legacy at a time in Peruvian history when the indigenista movement, headed by organizations like the Alianza Popular Revolucionaria Americana, began losing much of its social momentum and political force. In particular Vargas Llosa's manifesto of the new literary vanguard might have more to do with a newly conceived understanding—a postboom reading—of the social functionality of the novel form, of its relationship toward oppositional cultural discursive formations like indigenismo, and of emerging and sudden economic and political changes in Latin America. In short, it might not be accidental that Vargas Llosa launches the first of many critiques against indigenismo at the moment when mestizo nationalism begins to overtake the former culturally and politically. Much more criticism of Arguedas will follow from this moment onward, and it will emerge paratextually to Arguedas's own work.

To attempt now to read the work of Arguedas without the textual presence of Vargas Llosa might be an impossible task. Since "Novela primitiva y la novela de creación," Vargas Llosa has written numerous essays on Arguedas's work, including an essay on his most successful novel, *Los ríos profundos* (1958), which appears thereafter almost permanently in subsequent editions and translations of the novel. The essay "Ensoñación y magia en José María Arguedas" first appeared as a prologue to a Chilean publication of *Los ríos profundos* in 1967 and then as an afterword under the title "Dreams and Magic in José María Arguedas" in the English translation eleven years later (1978). Another essay by Vargas Llosa, entitled *"El sexto* de José María Arguedas: La condición marginal," first appeared in the prologue to a Spanish publication of Arguedas's *El Sexto* in 1974. What I wish to emphasize here is the nature, care, and degree of Vargas Llosa's self-appointed charge over Arguedas's work and his legacy for Peru. Vargas Llosa is not an arbitrary critic in this discussion; rather, and by some design, he has emerged as the predominant figure through which Arguedas is read. This charge culminates almost thirty years later in his publication of *La utopía arcaica: José María Arguedas y las ficciones del indigenismo* (1996).

In what amounts to a crystallization of Vargas Llosa's (1969a, 1969b) earliest critiques of indigenismo and Arguedas's novels, in *La utopía arcaica* we also sense an urgent shift in Vargas Llosa's literary charge of Arguedas. Like his initial assessment of Arguedas's creationary qualities, it presents Arguedas in a unique and exceptional relationship to his own life, to indigenista literary production, and to Peruvian cultural politics at large. However, unlike his earlier writings, Vargas Llosa now reads Arguedas, who is now deceased, in a postindigenista context, a context presuming the emergence of a "new" Peru freed from ethnic and cultural conflicts between indigenous, mestizo, and criollo social groups. Though his postindigenista contextualization of Peru represents more of an ideological position than an expression of historical affairs, tactically it appears as a way for Vargas Llosa to read Arguedas by extricating him from the larger cultural context in which he wrote. One of the more critical implications we can draw from this claim is whether or not, in this postindigenista context, the role and reading of literature (reading Arguedas in this case) changes.[4] Vargas Llosa urges the need for such a shift, and his reading of Arguedas's work amounts to a reconstitution of indigenismo's historical legacy from within the parameters of predominant mestizo and neoliberal discourse. This results in the simultaneous forging of a postboom register of literacy that reads indigenismo no longer as a radicalized and politically charged literary project but rather as historically anecdotal, individually experienced, subjectively imagined, and socially innocuous. In *La utopía arcaica*, Vargas Llosa accomplishes this by attempting to shed any and all ideological attachments between indigenismo and Arguedas's work.

Vargas Llosa's critique of indigenismo—that politically committed literary writing amounts to poor literature[5]—has remained consistent since his earlier piece, but this time Vargas Llosa uses this critique against indigenismo as a positive attribute in Arguedas. Positive not in that Arguedas was able to produce exceptional politically committed literature but rather that Arguedas was able to produce exceptional literature *because* he was not committed politically. According to Vargas Llosa, Arguedas's decision to write about the Andes and the indigenous groups was not because he was committed to rectifying their social and political disenfranchisement in Peru but because his youth was spent in those parts and his writing about those areas served a more therapeutic, autobiographical, that is, creationary interest:

José María Arguedas experienced this terrible dilemma, leaving traces of this fragmentation in his work and daily life. He was born in the Andes, in spite of being the son of a middle-class lawyer. Due to his disaffection for his step-mother he spent long periods of time with Indian servants, peasants and tribes, and was, until he was eight, according to his testimony, by the language he spoke, the things he felt, and his view of the world, one of them. Later in life, in adolescence, he was converted into a Peruvian living on the coast, belonging to the middle class, speaking and writing in Spanish. His life oscillated between these two cultural worlds; they fought over his spirit, at times sleepily, at times stormily. Writing literature signified for him both an impetuous and melancholy way to return to those times and places of his youth, to the tenderness, the fears, the sexual fantasies and the horrors it induced, to the village of San Juan de Lucanas, the town of Puquio or the city of Abancay, but above all, to the pastures and the men of the highlands, to his flora and fauna, which he was able to mythically re-create in happy prose. (1996: 29)

According to Vargas Llosa, Arguedas and the rest of the indigenista narrative tradition occupy seemingly mutually exclusive positions; that is, what the rest of the indigenista tradition lacks and what Arguedas has are identical: to not only be in possession of creationary attributes but also to have the necessary lack of political commitment to produce "good" literature. Vargas Llosa depicts Arguedas as having both, and consequently, within Vargas Llosa's framework, constructs a figure of Arguedas that is not an indigenista author at all, or perhaps an indigenista by accident alone.[6] Thus to read Arguedas as an indigenista would not only amount to a misreading of him but would constitute a depreciation of his otherwise exceptional literary work. However, given the care taken by Vargas Llosa to establish himself as the contemporary interpreter for Arguedas and indigenismo, a discursive strategy that seems to have taken hold, one might ask whether the simple de-indigenization of Arguedas is his only objective. That is, beyond Arguedas's reconstitution as simply a troubled and conflicted figure with an accidental relationship to indigenista cultural politics, what else is at stake in Arguedas for Vargas Llosa?

This will not be Vargas Llosa's final word on Arguedas; in fact what follows will seemingly contradict almost everything Vargas Llosa has asserted up to this point. At the conclusion of *La utopía arcaica*, wherein Vargas Llosa lays out Arguedas's historical and cultural legacy for Peru, he concludes, most paradoxically, that Arguedas plays no role whatsoever in the construction of the new, postindigenista Peru:

> Peruvians of all races, languages, economic conditions and political per-
> suasions agree that the Peru of the future will not, and should not be
> a revival of Tahuatinsuyo. It should not be an ethnically defined col-
> lectivist society, a country at odds with the "bourgeois" values of com-
> merce and wealth. It should not be closed off to the world in defense of
> its immutable identity. Neither Indian, nor White, neither "indigenista,"
> nor "hispanist," the Peru that is emerging and that is here to stay is still
> an unknown quantity. However, we can assure with utmost certainty
> that it will not correspond in the slightest to the images with which it was
> described—through which it was invented—in the works of José María
> Arguedas. . . . Needless to say, this discrepancy does not impoverish these
> works. On the contrary, it allows for their literary nature. It highlights
> their inventiveness and consecrates them as fictions that, thanks to the
> skill of the creator who intertwined personal experience, the avatars of the
> society in which he lived, together with the generous and violent desires
> that inspired him, appeared to portray the real Peru when they really con-
> structed a dream. (Translation in Williams 2002: 229)

After all the prologues to his novels, after all the praise bestowed upon him for his creationary attributes, for Vargas Llosa, Arguedas's legacy in

Peru will be one ultimately of infamy and one hostile to him. Here Vargas Llosa asserts, rather explicitly, that Arguedas, regardless of his previous exemption as an indigenista author, is nevertheless ideologically representative of indigenismo and that *he* and *their* conservative, reactionary stances against state-led assimilationist projects explain and justify indigenismo's political and cultural decline. In other words, Vargas Llosa argues, history has proven Arguedas wrong as Peru has opted for the neoliberal mestizo state, because "that Andean society which Arguedas privileges is unrecognizable, and no longer in existence" (translation in Williams 2002: 327). Hence the only value left to Arguedas is as a literary and historical reminder of how close Peru came to being otherwise. In his reading of *La utopía arcaica*, Gareth Williams (2002: 227) calls this gesture the "impaling" of José María Arguedas, wherein "Vargas Llosa resurrects the figure of José María Arguedas (almost thirty years after his suicide), only to reinter him finally as no longer of this world, as no longer of the now." The impaling of Arguedas seems a necessary component of a larger objective to reconstitute the new Peruvian literary canon by the removal of all previous evidence of cultural opposition from it, in this case indigenista discourse, and curtail any further commensurability between Peruvian literature and the historically political, in what Williams calls "the end of History" (229).

Here we are seeing a critical effect of Vargas Llosa's own ambivalence with regard to Arguedas—to not read him as an indigenista but to nevertheless deploy him as one—which leads us to certain contradictions. For instance, was not the reason Arguedas was designated a creationary novelist because he was *not* politically committed? If he in fact was not, as Vargas Llosa indicated earlier, why was he categorically dismissed along with the rest of the indigenista writers? In other words, even Vargas Llosa himself is unsure as to whether or not Arguedas was politically committed. One thing he is certain of, however, is that whatever Arguedas's tacit affirmations were, they will have been complete and utter fictions that have absolutely no bearing on contemporary Peruvian life. Vargas Llosa (1996: 84–85) insists:

> Arguedas's work, to the extent that it is literature, constitutes a
> radical and total negation of the world that inspires it: a lovely lie.
> His vision of that world, his lie, was more persuasive and imposed
> itself as artistic truth. Arguedas's narratives are not "veritable" in

the sense of the word of those who see the value of literature as measured by its capacity to reproduce the real, to duplicate the already existent. Literature expresses a truth that is neither historical, sociological, nor ethnological; it is not determined by its semblance to preexisting models. It is a slippery truth manufactured from *lies*, profound modifications of reality, disrespectful subjects of the world, corrections to the real that pretend to be its representation. Discrete catastrophe, audacious contraband, an accomplished piece of fiction destroys reality and supplants another, fictitious one, whose elements have been already named, ordered and disposed in such a way that essentially betrays what they appear to re-create.

Up to this moment Vargas Llosa has never hesitated to praise Arguedas's inventive use of his creationary capacity. He insistently returns to Arguedas's depictions of subjective (that is, irrational) experience in the face of objective reality as examples of him at his best; Arguedas's representation of such fantastical, magical disavowals is precisely what Vargas Llosa seems to appreciate the most in him: an outright failure to accurately connect language to reality, but a beautiful failure nevertheless. It is only by reading Arguedas's work as complete fantasy, as radical fiction, that one can find and appreciate his creationary attributes. However, the very attributes that consigned Arguedas as a creationary novelist, his ability to create a literary world "which negates and destroys the real world," is precisely what, according to Vargas Llosa, warrants Peru's historical wrath upon him; that is, the present world will also never forgive the beautiful lie that never came to pass.

The consequence of this is that any political thought inscribed in Arguedas's work and the indigenista movement is now placed under erasure, rendered meaningless through its noncorrespondence to a fictional reality that no longer exists anyway. Far from simply de-indigenizing Arguedas's work, which was Vargas Llosa's initial effect, he ultimately renders it radically, incommensurably fantastic in relation to the new, postindigenist Peru. Ironically, neither of these de-politicizing gestures proved sufficient to spare Arguedas from impalement. Rather it seems Vargas Llosa's ambivalent, irresolvable reading of him expedited the need for it. More than presenting a program for the expunging of oppositional cultural discourse from the new Peruvian canon, *La utopía arcaica* also illustrates the need to expunge any and all traces of ambiguity from it as well. Paradoxically, however, Vargas Llosa all but conceded Arguedas's critical and inextricable role in the Peruvian and Latin American canon at the moment of his impalement, that is, from this posthumous and unequivocal exclusion.

Besides the necessity to contextualize the larger political discussion of indigenismo in Peru through an analysis of Vargas Llosa's vision for a postindigenista Latin America, what I want to stress in his reading of Arguedas and literary indigenismo are aspects of his analysis that will arise in dialogue with Antonio Cornejo Polar's theory of indigenista narrative. Of principal interest is Vargas Llosa's insistence on reading and privileging Arguedas as the primary locus from which to critique indigenismo in toto. I wish also to draw from the implications of his universalistic assumptions regarding "truth" and fiction, the individual and society, and subjectivity and reality, all of which he conceives as formal aspects of Arguedas's literary production. His reliance on these rather uncomplicated categories, as we shall see deployed in his reading of *Los ríos profundos*, will allow us to interrogate conventional understandings of orality and literacy and their representation in indigenista narrative.

I begin by asking questions of Arguedas's radically fictitious fiction, as assessed by Vargas Llosa, and the representations of orality as constitutive of it. Does the orality of indigenista narrative constitute a problem or a literary contribution to Vargas Llosa's new Peru? Do the representations of orality constitute the "creationary" aspects in Arguedas's work? In what ways? Are these instances of orality significant because they are productive of radical signification or because they are radically unintelligible? We will return to these questions later in my reading of *Los ríos profundos*, but it is first necessary to contextualize Cornejo Polar's understanding of the indigenista novel because of its pivotal contribution to the present discussion.

The Peruvian critic Antonio Cornejo Polar (1936–97) has written extensively on the indigenista literary tradition, including not only criticism and commentary but on the more formal and theoretical aspects of indigenista narrative. It is important to note that both Vargas Llosa and Cornejo Polar began writing on indigenismo at about the same time; as Vargas Llosa was making his initial critiques against indigenismo and establishing a critical relation to the work of Arguedas, Cornejo Polar (1967) was likewise making the first of many theoretical entrances into the work of a fellow indigenista novelist, Ciro Alegría. What we see is a coincident attraction to indigenista narrative, a simultaneously expressed need to return to this literary tradition that reveals a critical urgency to establish indigenismo's political and cultural status once and for all. Though each critic assessed indigenismo's political and cultural legacy separately and, as we shall see, along distinct paths and objectives, a mutually informed reading of their critical work on indigenismo gives rise to a concerted textual dynamic that, between them, allows for a remapping of the stakes of orality and indigeneity as critical concepts in contemporary Peru and Latin America.

Published prior to his death in 1997, and only two years before Vargas Llosa's *La utopía arcaica*, Cornejo Polar's *Escribir en el aire* (1994) focuses on the literary manifestations of Peru's constitutive tensions and its irresolvable cultural and social heterogeneity, understood geographically (sierra-coast), historically (tradition-modernity), linguistically (Quechua-Spanish), and cognitively (orality-literacy). Through an analysis of the legend of Atahualpa's death, the Incan historian Garcilaso de la Vega, and modern indigenista narrative, Cornejo Polar asserts the essentially conflicted and heteroclite nature of Peruvian literary production as symptomatic of Peruvian society. *Escribir en el aire* addresses "the heterogeneous plurality that defines our society and culture, isolating regions and strata and placing emphasis on the abysmal differences that divide and oppose, often to the point of violence, the various socio-cultural universes, and in the many historical rhythms that coexist and overlap even within national spaces. It was—is— the moment of the revaluation of ethnic and other marginal literatures and of the refinement of critical categories that attempt to give meaning to this confused corpus" (6–7). As such, far from constituting an unadulterated space of Western linguistic and literary conventions, from which non-Western forms of cultural expression are excluded, Cornejo Polar claims that Peruvian literature, despite itself, is an unstable and internally contradictory hybrid of literate and oral expressional modalities. Peruvian literature's internal tensions are ultimately a symptom of the sociocultural heterogeneity it cannot but represent, even if inadequately. Further, the heteroclite (literally, irregularly grammared signification) constitution of the Peruvian literary canon speaks not so much to its lack of literary sophistication ("primitiveness" in Vargas Llosa) as to the inadequacy of Western literacy to accommodate non-Western expressional forms.

Given this claim, Cornejo Polar (1994: 200) aims to reconceptualize the Peruvian canon, not from some principle of homogeneity and consistency as Vargas Llosa proposes, but rather, and perhaps more representatively, on its irreducible heterogeneity and plurality:

> Therefore, it is not about founding a "linguistic model" that while "overcoming the contradictions between two communities and two cultures" projects itself towards the constitution of a new and presumably homogeneous society, but rather to recognize the impossibility and perhaps even illegitimacy of such a model that unifies what is different, diverse, and discovered. This confused material, now at a boiling point, appears to demand the negation of monological discourse and of the autonomous subject that settles it, and to give way to a radical heterogenization of them both and of the entirety of the linguistic system (including the representationality it implies) that it emits to men when they comprehend that their own identity comes from many, varied, and powerful sources.

It is here that Vargas Llosa's and Cornejo Polar's analyses diverge. Whereas for Vargas Llosa the Peruvian literary canon needs to purge indigenista narrative and the work of Arguedas because of its incommensurability (or ambivalence) with the new Peru, for Cornejo Polar, indigenismo represents a critical manifestation of Peru's inextricable sociocultural heterogeneity and is the very reason why Peru (and its canon) is not and cannot be conceived as a homogeneous entity in the first place. Far from rejecting indigenista narrative for its inconsistency and antagonism with the rest of Peruvian literature, Cornejo Polar argues that the former is precisely the reason why the latter can exist only in contradiction with itself. Thus between Vargas Llosa and Cornejo Polar, indigenista narrative becomes a pivotal stake in Peruvian cultural and literary history, even if only through its ambivalent and polarizing relationship to them.

While he previously published essays of criticism on indigenista authors such as Clorinda Matto de Turner (1852–1909), Ciro Alegría (1909–67), and Arguedas himself, in "Para una interpretación de la novela indigenista" (1977b) Cornejo Polar advances his first theoretical approximation to indigenista narrative.[7] Departing from his earlier work on indigenista authors, Cornejo Polar turns to a critical elaboration of the indigenista novel's formal structures, conceptualizing it as a peculiar narrative form emerging from a specific set of cultural and historical circumstances in Peru and in the Andean regions of Latin America.[8] In particular three historical factors ground his analysis of indigenista narrative: (1) the heretofore unresolved cultural and linguistic binary of Quechua-Spanish, specific to Peru and the Andes (which simultaneously inaugurates and troubles the assumption of Peruvian cultural production as a homogeneous literary entity); (2) the inevitably limited framing of the indigenista movement in Peru as a socialist project (when indigenous populations continue to live within an agrarian, feudalist economic system); and (3) the production of indigenista narrative not by the indigenous communities themselves but by the urban, assimilated sectors of Peruvian society (i.e., the same sectors of society advocating a socialist response to the "Indian problem," thereby disallowing it as an indigenous project and foreclosing the possibility of presenting indigeneity in any "authentic" fashion). These historical premises provide Cornejo Polar with the cultural terms for engaging in a critical analysis of indigenista narrative's formal aspects; these historical factors, he argues, provide both the condition of possibility for the indigenista novel and its irretrievably dysfunctional manifestation as literary production.

Among the more formal attributes of indigenista narrative, Cornejo Polar (1980a: 22–24) distinguishes between the "two universes" that constitute Peruvian society and condition its internal dynamic: the criollo, literate, hispanophile of the capitalist metropolitan coast (Lima) and the indigenous, Quechua-speaking, traditional communities of the precapitalist Andean highlands, "la sierra." While these universes are grounded in different cultural, economic, and cosmographic processes, indigenismo remained an urban, mestizo project conceptualizing itself through the social problems of the metropolitan center. Though indigenista narrative predominantly narrates events that take place in the Andean highlands of Peru, paradoxically it is configured to do so only through the language, logic, and lens of criollo coast, in other words, through the Spanish language, the novel, and capitalism.[9] According to Cornejo Polar (1979: 67), these are seemingly contradictory apparatuses to address the cultural, social, and political question of indigeneity in Peru: "It is not accidental that indigenous cultures never produced, nor produces, novels and that indigenismo, in apparent contradiction, prefers the novel as a genre specific to its needs." In other words, he argues, to the extent that the majority of indigenista authors reside in the coastal, metropolitan center of Lima and not in the settings where their novels take place—the Andean highlands, "la sierra"— and to the extent that their use of the novel, a cultural form entirely foreign to the cultures depicted therein, requires a certain understanding of Western temporality, the Spanish language, and literacy to appreciate, indigenista narrative is neither designed nor intended for the indigenous groups that are taken as indigenismo's thematic reference (1978b: 54).

In contrast to Vargas Llosa, who reads indigenista narrative as only one literary tradition among others, of greater or poorer literary merit and of greater or lesser historical value for Peru, Cornejo Polar sees it as an inextricably Peruvian literary form with its own culturally specific mode of production. He attributes to the indigenista literary tradition the virtue of unconcealing the violent and conflicted relations in Peru between Western and indigenous societies, urban and feudal economic systems, and oral and literate expressional forms, all within the representational structural of the novel. This, according to Cornejo Polar, is indigenista narrative's greatest contribution: it breaches the novel's expressional and representational capacities and exposes its limits as to the cultural heterogeneity that it cannot integrate. That is, the novel proves incapable of representing Peruvian sociocultural reality: the novel simply breaks in the process. These failures of the novelistic form are precisely the lesson; indigenismo's legacy is to be found in the literary problems it cannot overcome in its representation of Peru's sociocultural heterogeneity. Far from representing an inferior, incongruous, and radically fictitious literary tradition, the indigenista novel is an exceptional literary tradition in that it is congenitally plagued with formalistic failures and irrevocably contradictory, but precisely one that is most symptomatic, hence truly representative, of twentieth-century Peruvian society and culture.[10] These failures, as it were, are not signs of this literary tradition's inability to adequately represent Peruvian social reality, but are instead critical confirmations of just such an achievement.

This disruptive heterogeneity manifests itself structurally in three forms: temporally, perspectivally, and linguistically. Indigenista narrative operationalizes certain authenticating features of realist narration in order to condition a particular narrative effect. For instance, the novel's temporal setting is employed in indigenista narrative as a way to accomplish two narrative goals: (1) to initially establish its setting in a time register other than historical (call it mythic, traditional, or cyclical), usually of an indigenous community living in spatial and temporal harmony untouched by civilization; and (2) to immediately disrupt such pristine temporal order by depicting the dramatic and irreversible incursion of capitalist processes into the

area, that is, to create the conditions that inaugurate world-historical temporality and thus novelistic narrative possibility. As Cornejo Polar (1977b:
43–44) explains:

> One constant of the indigenista novel is the representation of
> indigenous society in a state of relative perfection, where a human
> group manifests, without much difficulty, unquestionable values, and
> simultaneously enjoys, a certain stability and economic plenitude; this
> state, however, is immediately destroyed through external forces: the
> interference by centralist powers, the expansion of feudalist structures,
> and the emergence of exploitative mining projects, to name only the
> most frequent cases. The social scheme of this strategy is obvious,
> as is obvious its representative fidelity, but, underneath all this, lies
> the necessity to novelistically narrate the indigenous world in its
> originary condition, defined to a certain degree by isolation, if not in
> its relation with a distinct and aggressive environment. From this initial
> premise, we see the internal contradiction of the indigenista novel:
> the indigenous world is not revealed in its autonomy, not from within
> the isolated state that, according to the indigenista perspective, should
> clarify its values, but rather, from the external pressures that disfigure
> them. . . . The indigenous world lacks the virtualities that would allow
> for novelistic development. Uniformly virtuous, harmonious and
> prosperous, the indigenous world cannot support the tensions necessary
> for a properly novelistic treatment.

Here Cornejo Polar suggests that the autonomous indigenous universe as
it is imagined is simply not novelistic phenomena without external forces
acting upon it from without, in this case, forces emanating from the time
horizon of capital into previously untouched indigenous space. In short,
indigenista mythic and cyclical temporal frames need to be ruptured to
initiate a historical temporality commensurate with the novelistic narrative form. The result, however, is never a complete historicization of
mythological time but rather a heterogeneous temporalization of narrative and narration, where both cultural universes continue to inhabit the
same narratological space, textually converged between traditional and
historic time: "In the indigenista novel both temporal orders converge,
the historical and the mythic, and their conflict takes place at the level of
narrative representation" (1979: 65).

Second, as it relates to the novel's capacity to authentically depict realist narration from nonomniscient, indigenous sources (first and third person, in particular), we encounter yet another unrealizable objective in the indigenista novel. According to Cornejo Polar, indigenista narrative's essentially translational nature, in which a certain distinct sociocultural universe is revealed by and from the terms of another, implies an inevitably exterior narrative perspective, which is to say, try as the novel might to stylistically produce a realistic depiction of an "insider" account of indigenous culture and cosmography, even a fictional one, this will always prove an impossible goal.[11] In other words, because the novel form cannot incorporate elements that are not commensurate with historical temporality and its Western epistemological conventions, such as indigenous cosmographies and nonindividual, collective subjectivity, as would be assumed in "indigenous narration," the indigenista narrative exhibits, despite itself, a conflicted and contradictory narrative perspective.[12] And again, these narratological failures are precisely the lesson of indigenista narrative, Cornejo Polar (1977b: 45) adds: "It is from the self-image of the indigenista novel, which likes to think of itself as an interiorized expression of the indigenous world, like an 'insider's' vision of that universe, that it cannot accept itself as anything more than a wishful exposition of an unrealizable project: converting the indigenista novel to the indigenous novel." The novel's own epistemological limits are laid bare in the indigenista novel's failed project to become the "indigenous" novel. In this way, Cornejo Polar argues, the indigenista novel is the manifestation of the modern novel taken to its cultural and formal limits, short-circuiting it in the process.

But the temporal and perspectival modalities of the novel form are not the only structural components Cornejo Polar sees at work here. The depiction of indigenous oral expressional forms becomes a crucial obstacle for indigenista authors seeking to produce authentic indigenous representations. The question is precisely how to represent orality in a Western literary device such as in the novel.[13] Moreover, in a genre form where dialogue (both intersubjective and internal) is critical, so too is the conversion of indigenous language into a monolinguistic format (Spanish), which is to say, the assumption that narration and dialogue transpire within a single linguistic field and that all information contained therein is communicable within that field. It is not simply a matter of depicting evidence of a foreign language within the course of the narrative, even of oral forms, but, more important, that this foreign language needs to be represented as intercommunicable with the language of the novel, that is, the language of narration and dialogue. For instance, even for a novel that presents an indigenous, first-person narrator, though the assumption will be that the narrative is expressed in the narrator's language, to the novel's reader the language will nevertheless be presented in Spanish. For the indigenista novel the assumption of commensurability and transparency between indigenous and hispanophile characters and readers is key to linguistic authenticity. To this extent, the artifice of oral expression in indigenista narrative is less about accurately representing "actually existing" oral speech patterns than about structuring orality's very relation to literacy itself.

According to Cornejo Polar, the more mimetic representational strategies deployed by previous indigenista authors to depict indigenous language proved, paradoxically, less authentic and realistic than more stylized approaches. As a result, what we've come to see is the development of a new language, an artificially indigenized language, which resolves the issue of authentic representation altogether. He notes:

> More than the crude and massive incorporation of Quechua words, which was the commonly used strategy by previous indigenista novels, the creation of this new, non-mimetic language reached astonishing levels of authenticity; for on the one hand it reveals the nature of the world to which it refers, on the other it also reveals, illuminatingly, the root of a larger conflict, the dismembered constitution of a culture and society that still, after centuries of coexistence within the same national space, cannot tell their history without the attributes of a contentious dialogue. (1977b: 45–46)

Cornejo Polar does not seem surprised that the more mimetic representations of oral forms provided less assurance of narrative authenticity; in fact he finds it consistent with the social dynamic that indigenista narrative can only represent heteroclitially and catachrestically. As such, he argues, more than presenting itself as an accurate depiction of oral expression, what this "new" language ultimately presents is the incommensurability between the Western literary form and the semiological margins that it cannot accommodate. This new language figures as the semiological register of otherness that indexes the indigenous language forms it cannot but incorporate, even nonmimetically.

Nevertheless Cornejo Polar (1978b: 55) acknowledges that this new language's most immediate value has less to do with the formal and stylistic conventions of the literary device than with cultural assumptions relating to intercultural knowledge and communication:

> It seems indisputable, at least now, that indigenismo's "artificiality" is a derivation of its heterogeneous foundation; in effect, the representation of a foreign referent through a literary system that linguistically constitutes it, cannot be accomplished without the use of formal methods and recourses that illustrate the movement between two distinct universes. This movement is what marks indigenismo's specific "artificiality" in that it does not correspond to the artifice implicit in all artistry (like the use of aesthetic conventions), but rather, acquires the feel specific to intercultural and intersocial knowledge and communication.

The issue here is with representation itself, in particular the issue of the representation of orality and oral speaking beings in indigenista narrative. Far from orality's use in the establishment of novelistic authenticity, as we saw with narrative temporality and perspective, the epistemological value of the representability of orality is what proves most critical in this discussion. What implications inhere in the attempt, successful or not, of "literalizing" oral expressional forms? Is there more at stake in this literary process than simply the exoticization of the narrative through its incorporation of indigenous language? In effect, the literary rendering of indigenous language has less to do with introducing the global reader to reproductions of indigenous expressional forms (1977b: 45) than with reproducing literacy's very capacity to capture and record differential semiotic forms such as orality, to translate it, transcribe it, make it grammatical, and encode it with meaning, even incorrectly or artificially.

It is from this vantage point that Cornejo Polar's own analysis reveals a critical limitation: while his analysis attempts to go beyond orality's and literacy's ontological assumptions, it is nevertheless framed and bound by it. His distinction between "artificial" and "authenticating" representations of oral discourse, far from confirming a heterogeneous cultural foundation, ultimately relies on orality and literacy as alibis that guarantee the distinction. One simply cannot insist, as he does, on the culturally heterogeneous nature of Peru and at the same time appeal to the categorical stability of (authentic and artificial) orality and literacy in order to substantiate it. By positing the distinction between authentic and artificially produced indigenous language in indigenista narrative, Cornejo Polar is caught between the need to go beyond orality-literacy and the critical implications of their dissolution in the production of cultural meaning.

In other words, Cornejo Polar's distinction between authentic and artificial orality results in a crucial admission: that just as much is known about oral indigenous speech as about the formal structures of Western writing. That is, Cornejo Polar concedes, the binary of orality and literacy in Peru is not one opposing an unintelligible realm of cultural expression unknown to Western logics of grammar and deductive reason; rather orality and literacy exist only as an internally constituted tension within the realm of literacy itself. The implication is not that there is not enough knowledge relating to indigenous oral discourse, that orality represents some unquantifiable, unqualifiable entity, but rather that oral speech forms are sufficiently ontologized so as to render the entire question of authenticity and artificiality into one of simple representational accuracy and verification. That is, the cultural problematic of orality and literacy is actually one between two already institutionalized formalizations of cultural expression in Peru. For Cornejo Polar, orality and literacy may be inadequate categories, but they remain indispensible for him as he simply cannot dispense with either category without also jeopardizing Quechua's very institutionalization as an officially recognized language.[14]

For Vargas Llosa (1996: 335), in contradistinction, the binary of orality and literacy fails to elicit any meaning except as radical fiction, as this dynamic, a remnant of Peru's troubled historical past, has withered away along with Arguedas's vision of Peru while making way for the "new" Peru: "What is indisputable is that Andean society—traditional, communitarian, magico-religious, Quechua-speaking, conservationist of collective values and atavistic customs—which fueled indigenista ideology and literary production, no longer exists, and will never return." In Vargas Llosa's vision of a postindigenista Peru, orality and literacy have been supplanted by a presumably far less complicated tension: literacy and nonliteracy (quite simply, between those who can read and those who can't). Orality and oral expression are subjects of no interest to the new Peru, except as notable artifacts in Peru's literary archive.

So which one is it? Must we choose between them? I advance that we read indigenista narrative *against both* Vargas Llosa's and Cornejo Polar's theoretical claims. Faced with the obligation to choose between Vargas Llosa's or Cornejo Polar's propositions, I am instead drawn to the theoretical space that is revealed between them, the space unoccupied by either, the space that acts as a repository for indigenismo's most ambiguous, unreadable, and unmanageable qualities. In other words, I am drawn to moments in indigenista narrative that escape the conceptual distinctions stressed by Vargas Llosa *and* Cornejo Polar, which might in turn problematize, if not threaten to collapse, the very theoretical elaborations designed to explain them. Is it possible, in effect, to trace in indigenista narrative, and against the latter two critics, forms of expression that cannot be accounted for as either oral or literate—the illegibly nonoral and nonliterate—that both hides and reveals the tenuous and ultimately unstable character of the orality-literacy relation in Latin America? And is it possible, after coming all this way, that Arguedas's own narrative work will serve to unconceal and unleash the illiterate space between them?

Written in 1958, *Los ríos profundos* represents Arguedas's most widely acclaimed novel, winning literature awards both in Peru and abroad. The novel tells the story of a criollo boy, Ernesto, son of a traveling lawyer who, though raised most of his life in an indigenous community, is once again introduced into an urban environment with his placement and enrollment in a Catholic school in Abancay, Peru. Due to the culturally bifurcated nature of his upbringing, Ernesto inhabits both Andean and criollo worlds but must now navigate by himself the socially heterogeneous and unpredictable world of Abancay, a social space in which neither of these cultural groundings provides sufficient coherence or meaning. Through the depiction of a series of politically crucial events while Ernesto is in the city, the novel proceeds to narrate the adolescent's experiences as they confront his assumptions, his disenchantments, his attempts to comprehend, and ultimately his failure to resolve internally the sociocultural contradictions he faces while in Abancay. Though many readings of *Los ríos profundos* have been proposed in recent years, those issued specifically by Vargas Llosa and Cornejo Polar have together come to reveal, as outlined in the previous pages, a particularly salient and heretofore concealed discursive tension traceable within Arguedas's novel itself.

In "Ensoñación y magia en José María Arguedas," Vargas Llosa (1996: 176) summarizes *Los ríos profundos* as a narrative pitting a gamut of social actors and incidents in the Andean sierra against the psychological fragility of a young modern subject, Ernesto, who wishes only to exist in the peace and idealized harmony of his past: "Through the narrative are paraded contrasting Andean social groups—indentured Indians and estate holders, mestizo artisans and poor to middle-class proprietors, soldiers and local bar owners, priests and civil authorities, merchants, musicians and sanctuary caretakers. But its nucleus is the cruel and innocent ceremonies of puberty and apprenticeship that a youth makes of the adult world, a social structure replete with strict hierarchies, and pregnant with violence and racism." Vargas Llosa proposes to read *Los ríos profundos* as a form of Bildungsroman, a narrative in autobiographical structure depicting a protagonist's coming of age. In this case we are to see in Ernesto's character development the eventual and indisputable recognition and understanding of the "real" world. Cornejo Polar's (1973: 100) "*Los ríos profundos:* Un universo compacto y quebrado," on the other hand, contends that the novel's essential conflict is not between the individual and the world, but between two cosmographic understandings of the sierra and their cultural and historical incommensurability: "But this conflict is an individualist struggle only in appearance; in reality it involves the fate of its universe in its entirety. This is because *Los ríos profundos* conceives of the universe as a coherent totality, compact, and completely integrated. The contrast between this conception and the reality of a disintegrated and conflictive world is the nucleus of the novel." In these passages one can feel the analytic tensions between these readings, as Vargas Llosa reads *Los ríos profundos* as objective reality's forceful and merciless imposition onto a hopelessly naïve and impressionable young individual, while for Cornejo Polar, the narrative is a conflict between two cultural visions of the Andean sierra as they are constituted in Ernesto's fragmented and heterogeneous subjectivity. These two distinct framings of *Los ríos profundos* result in a very illuminating juxtaposition: whereas for Vargas Llosa, Ernesto's relationship to the world is conceived as an individual effected by an objective reality, for Cornejo Polar, Ernesto represents a hybrid and fragmented subject caught between two conflicting and mutually exclusive discursive formations: Andean and Occidental cosmographies of Peru. While for Vargas Llosa, Ernesto's persistent attempts to free himself from the bounds of reality induces a tactical psychosis in the form of a retreat to an indigenized relationship to his environment, for Cornejo Polar, the elements that constitute Ernesto's retreats from reality are not incoherent, irrational flights of fancy with no bearing on the immediacy of his environment but rather represent ethnographically verifiable rehearsals of the Andean cultural practice. Both Vargas Llosa and Cornejo Polar, however, acknowledge that the contradictions of Abancay prove overwhelming to Ernesto, and as we shall see, the rest of the narrative amounts to an ultimately impossible search to validate any principle, any formal logic, any logos (indigenous or Western) that accounts for the critical realities of Abancay. We shall see that neither of Ernesto's cultural competencies proves adequate to both express and reconcile the incommensurate nature of modern Peru for which Abancay is a metonym.

Ernesto's immediate relationship to Abancay begins at the moment when his father, finding work, departs Abancay for Chalhuanca, leaving Ernesto in the care of the Catholic school where he had just enrolled. Ernesto's thoughts about his departing father anticipate what he expects to find in Abancay: "And while he would miss me, as he talked with friends of Chalhuanca, playing the role of the newly arrived stranger, I would explore the great valley and town inch by inch; and I would feel the force of the sad and powerful current that buffets children who must face, all alone, a world fraught with monsters and fire and great rivers that sing the most beautiful of all music as they break upon the stones and the islands" (Arguedas 1978: 38; 1958: 43).[15] What Ernesto alludes to in this passage is an awareness, developed from previous travels with his father, of the existence of a hostile world in which he finds "people everywhere suffered [encontré que en todas partes la gente sufría]" and of his fear of the city, the urban centers of Peruvian life, as people there suffer the most: "Nowhere else must human beings suffer as much as here [en ningún sitio debía sufrir más la criatura humana]" (1978: 15, 20; 1958: 19, 24). For reasons he can already foresee, he knows to fear Abancay, calling it the "world of monsters and fire," and he must now face the perils of its contradictions by himself.

However, within this same passage Ernesto reveals his understanding of a bifurcation within the Peruvian landscape, one side of which might offer respite from the monsters and the fire of the city: the river Pachachaca or the "bridge over the world [puente sobre el mundo]." We first see Ernesto's reliance on an indigenous cosmographic understanding earlier in the narrative, when he and his father visit Cuzco and stop to see the Incan stone ruin of Inca Roca. Upon approaching the stone mural, Ernesto is reminded of Quechua songs invoking the wall's animistic qualities, immediately afterward telling his father that its individual stones were speaking to him: "Papa, every stone is talking [Papá—le dije—. Cada piedra habla]" (1978: 8; 1958: 12). In his invocation of the great river in the previous passage, we sense Ernesto's anticipation that the river Pachachaca will communicate to him within a similar semiotic register as the Incan wall and will provide him with the coherence, comfort, and reassurance of Andean culture. As we saw earlier with the balseros of the Marañon River in *The Golden Serpent*, the Pachachaca serves Ernesto as cultural grounding, while its musical incantations will protect him from the monsters and fire in Abancay.

But who or what constitutes the monsters of Abancay? A look at the student body of Ernesto's school provides a clear illustration of the monsters of Abancay, as they can be read as a microcosm of Peru's modern social body. Constituting the diverse base of the region's populace, the students are whites (Añuco, Antero, Rondinel), mestizos (Romero, Wig, Ismodes, Valle), cholos (Palacios), and a ward of the school (Lleras). Of course, the monstrosity lies not in the immediacy of their placement in the school but in the social roles they reproduce while there. Arguedas provides the space of the schoolyard as the primary setting for several racially and culturally related fistfights among the students, most often instigated by Añuco and Lleras, as well as the setting for several disturbing scenes of the gang rape by some of the students of a homeless, demented woman ("La demente") who frequents the school. While we are made aware of the psychological toll these activities, among others, have on all of them while at the school, we are also presented a specific portrait of Ernesto, who is continuously made both a victim and a helpless observer of the increasingly violent, torturous, and humiliating rituals of a classed, raced, and culturally politicized student body.

But perhaps what most significantly affects Ernesto's state of mind are those elements in Abancay that cannot be reproduced in the schoolyard, those social elements by which he had first felt encouraged when invoking the cultural comforts of Andean society, the presence of the great river to counter the monsters and fire: his knowledge that along the borders of Abancay, in quarters along the hacienda territory, live indentured indigenous folk, *colonos*, with whom he hopes to find respite. We find Ernesto making his way to the colono quarters and appealing to their cultural fluency. In an almost tragic scene, he is immediately rejected by them. I quote at length:

> The Indians and their women didn't speak to strangers.
>
> "*Jampuyki mamaya.* (I am coming to see you, little mother)," I would call from the doorways of the houses.
>
> "*Mánan! Ama rimaychu!* (No, I don't want you to! Don't speak to me!)," they would answer.
>
> They looked like the Old Man's *pongo*; black sweat ran down their heads onto their necks. But they were even dirtier than he and were barely able to remain standing on the dusty ground of the quarters and the factory amid the clouds of mosquitoes and wasps that swarmed over the cane trash. All of them wore hats made of wool, stiffened with grease from long usage.
>
> "*Señoray, rimakusk' ayki!* (Let me talk to you, *señora*)," I often insisted, in my attempts to enter a house. But the women would look at me fearfully and suspiciously. They would no longer even listen to the language of the *ayllus*; they must have been compelled to forget it, because when I spoke to them using those words and tones of voice they paid no attention to me. (1978: 41; 1958: 46)

The implications stemming from this scene are severe. At the moment when Ernesto seeks solace from the monsters and fire in the schoolyard his desire to seek out, communicate, and participate with the indigenous community is thwarted by the very people from whom he sought reassurance. At this moment he is reminded of the indentured house servant from his earlier visit to Cuzco, the Old Man's "pongo" who helped carry his and his father's luggage to their room. At the pongo's seemingly inhuman silence following Ernesto's friendly inquiry, he asks his father, "Doesn't he know how to talk? [¿No sabe hablar?]" (1978: 14; 1958: 17). Afterward Ernesto thinks, "I had never seen such a humiliated being as the Old Man's pongo [a nadie había visto más humillado que a ese pongo del Viejo]" (1978: 15; 1958: 19). Here, and for the second time, Ernesto is rebuffed and immediately interprets the colonos' silence as *their* inability to communicate with *him*: "They would no longer even listen to the language of the ayllus [traditional indigenous community] . . . because when I spoke to them using those words and tones of voice they paid no attention to me." In other words, Ernesto concludes, it must be they who have lost the ability to speak, because he is confident he spoke to them accurately and presumes no other reason why they would not understand him.

Slowly, between the school and the haciendas, he finds himself rejected by every community in Abancay: the criollos, as evidenced by Añuco and Rondinel's racism toward Indians; the mestizos, as seen through Valle's cosmopolitanism and rejection of Andean culture and language. Furthermore those who were initially considered an antidote to the monsters and fire of Abancay, the colonos, have also become monsters, as they have failed to respond adequately to Ernesto's entreaties. We see that Ernesto's confidence in his cultural fluency determines his use of categorical distinctions for the people he encounters in Abancay. His unilateral strategy, to ask "Can *they* understand *me*?," establishes a dichotomous social map among Abancay's parts, that is, between those who can understand him and those who cannot. However, the posing of the converse question, "Can *he* understand *them*?," has yet to reveal itself as a dialogic possibility or as the conceptual limit we will see it become later.

Confronted by these most frightful aspects of Peruvian society, his subjection to the effects of social conflict and his inability to find assignment within any particular ethnic community in Abancay, including the colonos, Ernesto seeks refuge elsewhere, in a domain external to human society. He turns to the river Pachachaca for the coherence and reassurance remembered from his younger days, where "all of the mournful images, doubts, and evil memories were erased from my mind" (1978: 63; 1958: 69). According to Vargas Llosa (1996: 179–80), Ernesto's strategy for surviving Abancay involves the psychological, subject-preserving mechanisms of the modern subject, in this case dreams and magic: "The world of men is for Ernesto an impossible contradiction. . . . One needs to live, however, and Ernesto, who cannot escape his condition, must search for a way to tolerate it. For this, he has two weapons: the first is refuge into subjective interiority, dreaming. The second, a desperate need to communicate with what is left of the world, after the exclusion of humans: Nature." Dreams and magic enable Ernesto to leave the present condition in Abancay and return to those moments spent in cultural coherence and purity. He seeks out that natural space that reminds him of those moments: the river Pachachaca. There, seeking strength, he engages in an animistic, "magical" engagement with the river, attributing to it qualities and powers that he himself wishes to possess: "Yes! I must be like that clear, imperturbable river, like its conquering waters.

Like you, Pachachaca! Handsome, glossy-maned steed, who runs undetainably and unceasingly along the deepest of earthly roads!" (Arguedas 1978: 63; 1958: 70). What this psychological compensation amounts to, argues Vargas Llosa, is Ernesto's substitution of one ideological order of reality for another, that is, nostalgia, nature, and musicality for the monsters and fire of Abancay.[16]

However, neither Vargas Llosa nor Cornejo Polar treats these scenes with any presumption of veracity. In other words, neither of them takes seriously Ernesto's assertion of being capable of wielding nature in this way; *Los ríos profundos* does not accede to this possibility either. But what these critics do take seriously and want to account for is Ernesto's assumption that such an magico-religious semiotic system exists in nature, that communication within that system is both possible and desirable, and that his desire to communicate within this register exceeds his desire to communicate with Abancay society. For Vargas Llosa (1996: 183), this results in the claim that nature becomes the dominant character in the novel, as it will be the only element that manifests his innocence and idealism. However, Vargas Llosa's reading is soon drawn into an irreconcilable position when Ernesto's innocent and idealistic relationship to nature is corrupted by his rehearsal of certain indigenous traditions and rituals:

> His sensibility, exacerbated to the point of becoming one with nature,
> leads Ernesto to the pagan idealization of plants, objects, and animals,
> and to their attribution of not only human properties, but divine
> ones as well: a consecration of them. Many of Ernesto's superstitions
> come from his infancy, like a legacy of a spiritually Indian half, and
> the child stubbornly clings to them as a subconscious manifestation
> of his solidarity with that culture: moreover, his personal situation
> favors that inclination to reject reason as a link to reality and to prefer
> magical intuitions and devotions. This results in his irrational fatalism,
> his animism and fetishism, all of which lead him to venerate the most
> diverse set of objects with religious unction. (185)

Though centered on Ernesto's accession to nature, what is made clear in this passage is how Vargas Llosa's reference to a certain anthropological discourse actually determines his approach to *Los ríos profundos* and modern Peru's relationship to it; terms such as *pagan, superstition, fatalism, animism,* and *fetishism* accomplish much of his critique of Andean society by rendering its system of beliefs and cultural practices obsolete and incompatible with modernity. To be clear, the critique here is not that the narrative itself depicts Ernesto actually wielding any kind of real psychic connection with the natural environment. Vargas Llosa's contention with *Los ríos profundos* is not that its narrative framing is not secular or world-historical enough; the problem is that Arguedas depicts Ernesto as believing that he does have such power. In Vargas Llosa one senses discomfort in his tone as he elaborates on the extent to which Ernesto goes to establish a coherent, reassuring order of reality for himself, however irrational. Seen in this way, Ernesto's sincere or "earnest" appropriation of indigenous customs provides Vargas Llosa with a perfect exemplification of the claims subtending postindigenista discourse: that Andean indigenous practices, like the one Ernesto is shown reproducing, are remnants of a culture that no longer predominates, are based on erroneous beliefs anyway, and are therefore of no use to modern Peru. What was initially conceived as imaginative child's play results, for Vargas Llosa, as Ernesto's betrayal and abandonment of Western reason through his counterfeit, though still troubling, indulgence in Andean culture's magico-religious traditions and rituals. While Vargas Llosa rejects the legitimacy, let alone the continuing primacy attributed to Andean indigenous customs, he still senses a menace in Ernesto's sincere rehearsal of them. In other words, for a cultural tradition of no further significance, as he argues, why is he so resistant to Ernesto's role-play, particularly when even *he* doesn't find it narratologically earnest anyway? Why this ambivalence toward Ernesto's poor and childish imitation of already "obsolete" Andean customs? Where does this threat emerge from, or rather what is ultimately at stake here in this reading of *Los ríos profundos*?

Unfortunately Vargas Llosa's analysis is limited to this examination of Ernesto's "primitive" appropriation of the natural world through indigenous rituals and traditions and makes no further effort to use this in refining his understanding of Ernesto's sociocultural positionality in Abancay. As we see in "Ensoñación y magia," by simply illustrating how the monsters of Abancay determined his relationship to nature and by focusing solely on the therapeutic and radically fictitious nature of Ernesto's imagination, Vargas Llosa ultimately flattens Ernesto's exceedingly complex relationship to Abancay. Past this point, Vargas Llosa provides no further insight into how Ernesto's relationship with nature structures his relationship with Abancay society. Not surprisingly, we see a similar dilemma invade Cornejo Polar's analysis.

Cornejo Polar (1973: 109) too makes a crucial concession in characterizing Ernesto's play, remarking that his fluency in Andean nature and folklore is self-attributed and not a narrative fact: "Ernesto presents himself as in possession of an unusual capability: that of revealing the hidden meaning of these [natural] signs, and of the ability to communicate intensely with [nature], all within a social context that either ignores or mocks it." A subject who thinks he can read and talk to nature is a version of Ernesto not too dissimilar to the one Vargas Llosa has been proposing; both Vargas Llosa and Cornejo Polar seem to suggest that Ernesto's relation to nature is a fanciful one and therefore not an "authentic" rendering of indigenous religious assumptions. Cornejo Polar's assertion that Ernesto's special trait, the ability to communicate with nature, is "unusual" implies its being unusual even to Andean cultures themselves, thereby suggesting that Ernesto is taking liberties with his knowledge of indigenous customs. However, if this were the case, then one would need to already know definitively whether or not Ernesto's play exceeded the boundaries of indigenous practices. Once again, this assessment could emerge only from a totality of knowledge of the indigenous world that might or might not reproduce the same assumptions as those already inscribed in the Western archive of oral representation. Therefore we must ask: Is Ernesto misguided by his invention of customs and rituals that prove unusual to the indigenous orders of reality that he appeals to, or is our investment in indigenous knowledge misguided to the extent that it thinks it can prove conclusively whether or not Ernesto's behavior is unusual by indigenous cultural standards? In other words, is Ernesto out of his mind, or are we for thinking we can tell the difference?

As such both Vargas Llosa and Cornejo Polar are each caught in an analytic dilemma. They each juxtapose Ernesto's behavior and attitude to a discursive formation that provides them with differential significance. While Vargas Llosa opposes Ernesto's anthropological play to the extinct indigenista cultural vision for Peru, Cornejo Polar opposes Ernesto's "unusual" ritual traits to still living Andean cultural traditions. In each case, in attempting to account for Ernesto's relationship to nature, because they both agree Ernesto never really communicates with nature, Vargas Llosa and Cornejo Polar both reinforce the ontological status of the opposing category. Ultimately, what is conceded here is the indeterminacy of indigenous knowledge, lying somewhere between its primitive anthropological formalization (superstition, fetishism) and its insertion into the logic, grammar, and literacy of Western knowledge (authentic cultural practice).

It would be misleading to imply, as Vargas Llosa's analysis does, that Ernesto spent the entire narrative inhabiting this alternative order of experience and failed to establish any communicational links with anyone. In a very significant segment of the novel, he finds a community in the patrons, merchants, and musicians of the local *chichería* bars, where he spends much time listening to Andean music and conversing with the mestizo and cholo sectors of Abancay. It will be his familiarity with the owners and waitresses of the chichería bars that enable his active participation in the chola insurrection, an episode of social upheaval in Abancay in which working-class women revolt against skyrocketing salt prices by sacking the salt warehouse and redistributing the salt among themselves and among the colonos of the haciendas. Ernesto participates in the procession of cholas from the warehouse to the *comunero* quarters, while they applaud him for his engagement: "That's the way! Brave boy! Onward, onward!" (1978: 93; 1958: 101). Oddly enough, the chola insurrection provides Ernesto with some feeling of community, if only briefly and if only from overwhelming circumstances, but not without the racial tensions he has experienced elsewhere. And of course, it still isn't the community he is hoping to be accepted by, as one of the very reasons for going to the chichería bars was to look for the presence of more colonos: "I never lost the hope that I would be able to talk to them" (1978: 46; 1958: 52).

In addition to the cholos and mestizos at the chichería bars, Ernesto acquires a very special friendship at school. Antero "Markask'a" proves a very ambiguous figure in relation to the rest of the student body, who, to a greater or lesser extent, have been flatly characterized by their racial and class affiliation. We know that Antero is blond and from a small, landowning family, yet ironically he appeals to Ernesto's indigenous sensibilities as no other student does. Antero is the student who presents him with "el zumbayllu," the spinning top that fascinates Ernesto because of the musical sounds it produces when in motion. It is a musicality that appeals to his cultural Andeanism: "The song of the top penetrated deep into my ear, reviving memories of rivers, and of the black trees that overhang the walls of the abysses" (1978: 68; 1958: 76). Ernesto's relationship with Antero, both as a friendship and as confirmation of their cultural and ethnic commonality, is established very early in the narrative. In a very critical way, Ernesto's relationship to the criollo Antero proves a catalyst, providing the literate grounds for the formalized expression of his previously internalized desire for oral communication. Antero serves in this capacity not as a foil, nor in relief to Ernesto's desires, but rather as a mentor.

Antero manages to inspire Ernesto through his knowledge of Quechua, indigenous customs, and folklore. On one occasion, he tells Ernesto a story of his swimming across the Pachachaca River and how the Indians of his family's hacienda believed he was bewitched. To this story Ernesto responds in awe, "Markask'a was better than I; he had explored a river, an awesome river, and not just as a traveler explores it. Pachachaca! . . . Markask'a's voice was like that of an angry Pachachaca" (1978: 107; 1958: 116). Ernesto seems to relate well to Antero, if only because of their shared fascination with indigenous culture; this feeling proves mutual, as Antero confesses to Ernesto, "You've made me talk. . . . All the things I think of when I'm alone, I've sung to you. I don't know why, when I'm with you I open my thoughts, my tongue is unloosened" (1978: 107; 1958: 116). This conversation between Antero and Ernesto accomplishes much to establish Ernesto's sociocultural positioning in relation to the rest of the student body and in his fraught relationship with the colonos. As Antero reveals that being with Ernesto makes him more willing to talk, we are also reminded of Ernesto's inability to evoke the same feeling among the colonos as well as in the Old Man's pongo. Despite Ernesto's assumptions about himself, he has more in common with the criollo, landowning class and with the cholo working class than with the indigenous community to which he wishes to belong.

Yet another characteristic that Antero brings to light in Ernesto, something that further defines his distance from the other ethnic communities, is his coextensive attraction to the written word, that is, to his literacy. In distinction to Ernesto's ability to hear the animistic appeals of nature, like the stones of the Inca Roca and the river Pachachaca, he too is a confident, literate subject. After some initial difficulty at school, Ernesto tells us he has become one of the better readers in the class: "I was among the most preferred readers by all the priests and brother Miguel" (1978: 75; 1958: 83). Moreover the chapter establishing Ernesto and Antero's friendship through the gifting of the zumbayllu begins with an etymological discussion of the relationship between the Quechua suffixes -*yllu* and -*illa*:

The Quechua ending *yllu* is onomatopoeic. *Yllu*, in one form, means
the music of tiny wings in flight, music created by the movement of
light objects. This term is similar to another broader one—*illa*. *Illa* is
the name used for a certain kind of light, also for monsters with birth
defects caused by moonbeams. *Illa* is a two-headed child or a headless
calf, or a giant pinnacle, all black and shining, with a surface crossed by
a wide streak of white rock, of opaque light. An ear of corn with rows
of kernels that cross or form whorls is also *illa*; *illas* are the mythical
bulls that live at the bottom of solitary lakes, of highland ponds ringed
with cattail reeds, where black ducks dwell. To touch an *illa*, and to
either die or be resurrected, is possible. The term *illa* has a phonetic
relationship and, to a certain extent, shares a common meaning with
the suffix *yllu*. (1978: 64; 1958: 70)

Though this passage inaugurates the chapter, it is not an object of narration;
rather this section proceeds as a piece of expository writing describing
the etymological relationship between these suffixes. The intent of this
section, as we shall see, is to establish a semiotic connection between
the word *zumbayllu* and Ernesto's zealous attraction to the spinning top.
Whether it is Ernesto who is providing this etymological survey is doubtful,
the significance of which nevertheless pales in comparison to the larger
implication that in order to best understand and appreciate indigenous
traditions and oral expressional forms such as these, one must approach
them philologically. That is, as writing.

Striking, however, is Cornejo Polar's (1973: 123) assertion that the
etymological information presented in the novel is a fabrication. This
assertion now weaves a literate, grammared logic into Ernesto's fascination
with the zumbayllu. When Antero first arrives with the zumbayllu, some of
the other kids, including the cholo Palacios, already know what a zambayllu
is, while Ernesto does not. He is, however, familiar with the suffix *-ayllu*. As
the rest of the students run off to the schoolyard to play with the top, Ernesto
is left standing, wondering, "What could a *zumbayllu* be? What did this
word, whose last syllables reminded me of beautiful and mysterious objects,
mean?" (1978: 67; 1958: 74). In this instance Ernesto's referential cultural
horizon proves limited and is enabled only by a linguistic approach to the
word *zumbayllu*. It proves critical that the philologically based understanding
Ernesto derives from hearing the word will actually determine the form,

function, and beauty that the top holds for him; ultimately his literary approach to the word determines his spiritual relationship to this object, even if the meaning derived is etymologically indeterminate or epistemologically suspect. His analytic approach to a word in which he has no referent—to separate and identify prefix, suffix, and root—gives him the grammatical terms to derive meaning from the zumbayllu and to establish a particularly intense and significant relationship to it, a level of zeal no other child manifests. However, we must remember that this zeal is derived primarily from his philological approach to a signifier for which he has no referent; in this instance, the object signifies less than the meaning derived from the word, as Ernesto proves more attached to the signifier than to its referent. In the episode of the zumbayllu, which happens to be the most significant object in *Los ríos profundos*, we see an instance wherein an indigenous, oral expressional form, to the extent to which the suffix *-ayllu* provides Ernesto the philological means to understand the word *zumbayllu*, is understood as already systematized into a literate, etymologized, and grammared system. That is, we see Quechua presented as having some preestablished system of writing, where, like Western languages, Quechua too can be broken down into grammatical and etymological units and it too can provide meaning from these codified units, even artificially or inaccurately.

Another critical demonstration of Ernesto's literacy occurs when Antero asks him to write a love letter to a girl he is courting. The scene depicts Ernesto beginning the love letter, being interrupted by an internal tension, and commencing the letter anew, but this time writing the letter not in Spanish but in Quechua, and addressing it not to Antero's love interest but to his own imagined love interests, figures presumably drawn from his memory, from his time in the indigenous community. I quote at length from the moment of interruption:

> But a sudden discontent, an intense feeling of shame, made me
> interrupt the writing of the letter. I laid my arms and head down on
> the desk; with my face hidden, I paused to listen to those new feelings.
> "Where are you going, where are you going? Why don't you continue?
> What has frightened you; who has cut short your flight?" After asking
> these questions I went back to listening to myself eagerly.
> "And what if they knew how to read? What if I could write to
> them?"

And they were Justina, or Jacinta, Malicacha, or Felisa, who had
neither long hair nor bangs, nor wore tulle over their eyes. Only black
braids, and wildflowers in the bands of their hats. . . . "If I could write
to them my love would flow like a clear river; my letter could be like
a song that goes through the sky to reach its destination." Writing!
Writing for them was useless, futile. "Go; wait for them on the roads
and sing! But what if it were possible, if it could be started?" And I
wrote:

"*Uyariy chay k'atik'niki siwar k'entita.*" . . .

"Listen to the emerald hummingbird who follows you; he shall speak
to you of me; do not be cruel, hear him. His little wings are tired, he
can fly no farther; pause for a moment. The white stone where the
travelers rest is nearby; wait there and listen to him; hear his sobs; he
is only the messenger of my young heart; he shall speak to you of me.
Listen, my lovely one, your eyes are like large stars; beautiful flower, do
not flee any more, halt! An order from the heavens I bring to you; they
command you to be my tender lover. . . !" (1978: 74–75; 1958: 82–83)

Like the previous scene with the zumbayllu, Ernesto is depicted as having
command of the Quechua language, but this time he is shown with
a command of a written, literary, form of Quechua. At the moment of
interruption he asks himself two very critical questions: "What if they knew
how to read? What if I could write to them?" The second question proves
an already established point, as the passage concludes not only with a short
depiction of his letter written in Quechua but also with a more extended
translation of this letter into Spanish for the reader. In this instance, the
answer to his question is not only affirmative (Yes, he can write to them)
but also implies his letter's already formalized integration into a network
of literate signification that exceeds the capabilities of the addressees
themselves, and that distinguishes him categorically from them: Yes, he
can write. However, the first question, "What if they knew how to read?,"
now takes on a fuller, critically refined meaning, in that Ernesto's literacy
finally presents itself as an obstacle to communication.

While Ernesto conceives of the letter he writes in Quechua as a song,
orally emitted and reverberating toward its destination—"my letter could
be like a song that goes through the sky to reach its destination"—he is
simultaneously confronted by the circularity of his metaphor: "Writing!

Writing for them was useless, futile." The irony here is that at the moment of his most elaborate approximation to indigenous culture, the very act of writing, his literacy, irrevocably distances him from it. His distantiation is not bound by the simple gesture of putting pen to paper for, as we saw with the zumbayllu, the form of orality Ernesto exhibits is processed cognitively through a philologically systematized, grammared form of written Quechua that he has now internalized. The act of writing in Quechua is merely a symptom of Ernesto's already pronounced cognitive shift along the axes of both conceptual fields: both Spanish and Quechua, and orality and literacy. Is it therefore possible that his literacy is the fundamental distinction preventing him from communicating with the colonos?

The question before him now is not "Can I write?" but, more problematically, "Can they read?" We can see now that this very question has plagued him since the beginning, first with the Old Man's pongo in Cuzco ("¿No sabe hablar?") and later with the colonos in Abancay ("Ya no escuchaban ni el lenguaje de los ayllus"), where, though their refusal to communicate may have seemed to imply an unwillingness to communicate, to Ernesto it registers as an inability to communicate. In both instances, we hear him ask, "Do *they* not understand *me*?" This question, however, has yet to be answered narratologically; the very issue of its undecidability is precisely the point; Ernesto is never fully confident in whether or not any of *them* understand *him*. More than simply a rhetorical question, "Can *they* understand *me*?" signals a critical short-circuiting of meaning occurring at the threshold of two orders of signification within Ernesto: his desire to be understood orally but to understand literately. Ultimately, when Ernesto asks himself "Do *they* not understand *me*?," what he actually means is "Can *they* not read?" This semiological breakdown will later be taken to its most radical point by the colonos themselves, when it is finally asked of Ernesto, "Can *he* understand *them*?" It is to Ernesto's cognitive collapse resulting from this fundamentally indeterminate and uncategorizable enunciation that I now wish to draw attention.

It is during the last episodes of the novel that Ernesto and Antero's relationship begins to wane. As we saw, the criollo Antero provides Ernesto with the impulse to indulge and experiment with oral and literate forms of expression in Quechua, both with the philological play of the zumbayllu and through the letter he wrote. Now, however, we see Ernesto's rather paradoxical access to linguistic hybridity close off when Antero finds new friends (1978: 195; 1958: 207). Ernesto reacts to this rejection by resolving to immediately return the zumbayllu to Antero in protest. When Antero refuses to take back the zumbayllu, Ernesto proceeds ceremoniously to bury it in the schoolyard: "'It must surely be his destiny, the destiny of his blood!' I said, thinking of Antero, as I walked slowly toward the playground. At the end of the dark courtyard I dug a hole with my fingers, using a sharp piece of glass to help deepen it. And there I buried the *zumbayllu*. I laid it to rest in the bottom of the hole, patted it, and buried it. Trampling the dirt down firmly, I felt relieved" (1978: 202; 1958: 214). As he buries the zumbayllu, we hear for the first time Ernesto remark on Antero's racial identity, as if he has realized that his friendship with Antero has compromised his assumptions about his own cultural purity, rendering ambiguous a cultural identity Ernesto believed was concrete, stable, and coherent. This newly perceived ambivalence of self, brought on from Antero's rebuff, is then transferred to the zumbayllu, as it begins to symbolize, to Ernesto's horror, the now contradictory nature of his relationship to the criollo Antero. Though he still believes the zumbayllu possesses spiritual powers, he now seems troubled by its inability to protect him from such cultural contradictions: "'*Zumbayllu, zumbayllu*! Adiós! I feel sorry for you,' I said to the top. 'You're going to fall into dirty hands and pockets. The boy who made you is now a godchild of the devil'" (1978: 198; 1958: 210). It is at this moment of Antero's break with Ernesto, at the moment when the now incoherent nature of the zumbayllu is buried and divested of all semiotic value, that we begin to see a critical breakdown of meaning in Abancay.

Specifically, we witness confusion emerging from rumors of an outbreak of typhus among the colonos, causing fear that it might spread from the haciendas on the outer reaches of Abancay to the city itself. Panic among the students begins to swell as more and more rumors are told about the outbreak: from stories that seem to confirm the outbreak, such as that the military police have set up a command post along the only bridge that connects Abancay to the haciendas, to more gruesome depictions of colonos practicing *usa waykuy*, biting the heads off the lice found on the dead as an attempt to contain the plague (1978: 206; 1958: 219). Many students begin making plans to leave the school and Abancay as soon as possible.

These stories affect Ernesto in a profound and unpredictable way. He reflects on the manner of the colonos' inevitably gruesome fate on the other side of the bridge. To Ernesto, this hypothetical scene is so disturbing not because countless colonos would be dying from the plague but because they, he determines, no longer "know" how to die, as they have forgotten the cultural traditions that provide death with dignity and meaning. As a result, he forecasts, they will perish "insignificantly":

"The *colonos* will come down like a landslide from the other side of the river," I thought to myself, "or else they'll just die peacefully in their thatched huts! They have no fear of death. They receive it with mournful hymns, even though no one else pays any attention to an Indian's death. In the Indian communities they wear mourning, but the colonos don't even know about that any more; they teem in the alien earth like worms; they weep like little children; like Christians they take orders from the overseer who represents God, who is the master, the son of God, as unattainable as He is. If one of those masters were to say 'Feed your tongue to my dog,' the colono would open his mouth and offer his tongue to the dog. They will die, trembling, like the idiot Marcelina, and go to heaven to sing eternally! They won't go down to the bridge," I said. "They won't dare! And if one of them does go down and sees the guardias armed with their rifles, and with those wide-brimmed hats and leather leggings and spurs, he will fear them worse than death." (1978: 213; 1958: 224)

The rather unambivalent feelings expressed in this passage confirm that the typhus outbreak has effected a profound change in Ernesto's attitude toward the colonos. What was originally an earnest desire to seek them out has now been transformed into abhorrence, contempt, and ultimately a mortal fear of them. It is a fear, however, not limited to the circumstances of the outbreak but rather a fear expressing the monstrosity they have become from their abandonment of the Quechua culture and language.

In this image of the typhus-stricken colono we are presented with what, for Ernesto, results from the loss of one's cultural identity and mother tongue: bare life, life that can be killed but is not worthy for sacrifice. While at the beginning of the novel the colonos are considered indigenous folk, a safe haven from the monsters and fire at Abancay, they are now reduced to a frightful comparison of what they once were: "In the Indian communities they wear mourning, but the colonos don't even know about that any more." According to Ernesto, the colonos are incapable of even the basest impulse for survival; if they no longer even speak like indigenous people, how can they be expected to die like them? His reference to the useless and literally insignificant colono tongue makes their death all the more meaningless: "If one of those masters were to say 'Feed your tongue to my dog,' the colono would open his mouth and offer his tongue to the dog." Through Ernesto's image of colonos offering their tongue to the master's dog the reader is given the foundational figuration of their lack of position within the police order as the "part of no part," as "beings without a name, deprived of logos" (Rancière 1999: 22). For Ernesto, this does not absolve the colonos of condemnation; rather it further serves to justify his insistence that it is *they* who cannot understand *him*. *They* are literally *insignificant*; though they could never read, they can now no longer even speak. As we saw earlier, *their* inability to understand *him* positioned them in a space beyond Ernesto's understanding, beyond comprehension, beyond meaningful signification. Now we see that *his* inability to understand *them* threatens his entire cosmographic horizon; the trace of radical colono illiteracy reveals the breakdown of the coherency provided by the orality-literacy relation. Ernesto needs to bury the zumbayllu because it begins to signify the impure heterogeneity of his orality and literacy, which he maintains as distinct, stable categories; here the colonos reveal the abyss separating his (oral and literate) fluency from a domain of illiterate signification enunciated by the colonos themselves.

In his reading of *Los ríos profundos*, Cornejo Polar (1973: 130) provides a crucial note on the significance of the colonos to the narrative: "Ernesto informs us that these people, at the brink of annihilation (keep in mind that they have lost their memory, one of the most valued qualities in the novel's axiological constellation), are, however, similar to those who, years ago, taught him to love the indigenous world." In this passage Cornejo Polar informs us that though Ernesto still believes that the colonos are related, somewhat, to the indigenous tribes who inculcated in him the values of the indigenous world, the fact of the loss of their cultural memory distinguishes them categorically from the "authentic" indigenous folk of his youth. But if we note Ernesto's exact phrasing of his first encounter with the colonos—"They would no longer even listen to the language of the *ayllus*; they must have been compelled to forget it, because when I spoke to them using those words and tones of voice they paid no attention to me [Ya no escuchaban ni el lenguaje de los ayllus; les habían hecho perder la memoria; porque yo les hablé con las palabras y el tono de los comuneros, y me desconocieron]"—we can see that the assumption of the colonos' loss of cultural memory is only Ernesto's contention and is never established as narrative fact. Ernesto cannot inform us of this fact, because it is not a fact but ideologically based speculation. It would ultimately be impossible for him to ascertain with any certainty whether the colonos have retained or lost their cultural memory, regardless of *their* inability or unwillingness to understand *him*. In effect, Ernesto comes to believe as fact what is essentially a supposition that he himself fashions as a means to reconcile their sad, miserable, existence. Unfortunately Cornejo Polar, in not questioning Ernesto's assumption, falls for the same trap. He too accedes to the idea that the colonos are no longer the same people from Ernesto's youth; he too concurs in the assumption that it is *they* who have lost the ability to speak to *him*. Ultimately Cornejo Polar imposes onto the colonos the same unilateral logic used by Ernesto to account for *their* cultural incommensurability; he too insists that it is *they* who should be understanding *him*. In this regard Cornejo Polar's analysis proves no more capable of recognizing the limits of the hegemonic relation than Ernesto himself. Cornejo Polar is content simply to reproduce the logic and limits of Self and Other as they are expressed in Ernesto's relation with colonos. What Cornejo Polar fails to see, and what *Los ríos profundos* is at pains to demonstrate, is that Ernesto is himself that hegemonic relation.

Meanwhile, as evidence of the validity of the rumors of the typhus outbreak among the colonos begins to emerge, Ernesto hears from a family fleeing the city that the colonos, despite the containment barricades, are nevertheless beginning to cross the river en masse: "They've come across from the other side of the river on a rope bridge, hanging baskets. They're arriving now" (1978: 225; 1958: 238). Furthermore he is told that the colonos are demanding a church service: "They say the colonos are crying, 'Church, church; mass Padrecito!' There's no escaping the plague, now; they want a high mass, they say, from the great father of Abancay. Then they'll sit down and be still; shivering, they'll die and be still" (1978: 226; 1958: 239).

To this news Ernesto remains incredulous: "That's a lie! They couldn't do it. They couldn't. Didn't they get scared when they saw the guardias?" (1978: 225; 1958: 239). To Ernesto, this signifies more than the spread of the disease: the colonos, as they breach the barrier of the Pachachaca River, are simultaneously breaching the limits of orality and literacy, breaching the barriers that both bind and separate his cultural horizons. Ernesto insists against the breach of either threshold, as both represent key elements in his cosmographic understanding of the Andean universe. More than the typhus itself, a loss of cultural grounding is what Ernesto seems to fear, and in one instant the colonos have overwhelmed his ability to sustain a coherent cultural order. In his frantic securing of his conceptual borders we are seeing the failure of dreams and magic to counter the monsters and fire.

Still disputing claims that the colonos have breached the river and are now overrunning the city of Abancay in search of absolution, Ernesto proceeds to the barricaded bridge to see for himself. There he receives visual confirmation of what, until then, were only rumors and speculation: "The colonos were really coming up the hill like a herd of sheep, like thousands of sheep. They had spilled out over the edges of the road and were climbing up through the brush, between the bushes, clambering over the stone or adobe walls that enclosed the sugar-cane fields" (1978: 228; 1958: 241). Ernesto finally sees for himself the uncontainability of the colonos's desperation, of their radical signification, and of the Pachachaca River's inability to retain the coherent distinction between Western and Andean cultural realms. It is during this moment of confirmation that Ernesto proclaims the colonos' inferiority to the Indians of his youth: "I was brought up by the Indians, by other men, better than these, better than the colonos" (1978: 229; 1958: 242). No more apt illustration of the critical breakdown in Ernesto's dichotomous conceptual horizon, the one he relies on to maintain strict semiotic and cultural coherence in his life, than the image of typhus-stricken colonos sprawling over the sides of the Pachachaca River. Representing the only active marker within the time horizon of capital, the colonos disrupt Ernesto's culturally ahistorical fluencies; they disrupt not only his assumptions of a pure, uncontaminated, Quechua-speaking identity, existing in externality from the logic of Western literacy, but also his even more foundational conception that only two—mutually exclusive—registers of signification exist: orality and literacy.

Ernesto nevertheless survives the colono onslaught of Abancay. That night they arrive in Abancay and proceed to the church in utter silence; later that same evening they return to the other side of the river, singing funeral songs. However, Ernesto will never recover from the destabilizing effects colono illiteracy had on him (1978: 232; 1958: 245). The remaining part of the narrative makes amply clear his resolution to avoid any further interaction with colonos; he leaves Abancay forever, abandoning this threshold of illiteracy in search of more stable, even if fictitious grounds where literacy and orality can continue to provide him with cultural stability and coherence he seeks.

The colonos of Abancay reveal the trace of illiteracy at play in indigenista cultural politics. In *Los ríos profundos*, they present the fissure between literacy and orality that subsequently breaches the latter's conceptual field of intelligibility, revealing forms of signification that cannot be captured by Ernesto's, nor our, assumptions of orality and literacy. What began as a question of whether Ernesto's subjective retreat from the monsters and fire constituted a radical fiction or an "authentic" attempt to counter reality with Andean cultural practices has resulted in the textual divulging of his cognitive dependence on Western literacy to integrate himself into oral, Andean culture ("Can *they* understand *him*?"). And as we saw, the fundamental inadequacy of Ernesto's strategy is revealed by the typhus-stricken colonos of the haciendas, whose attitude, behavior, and expressional form prove utterly overwhelming to his understanding of Andean culture ("Can *he* understand *them*?"). Neither Ernesto nor the reader will ever be able to determine if the colonos indeed understand him. But what we can determine is that their failure to respond to his inquiry is insufficient proof of their incommensurability; Ernesto falls victim to this logical fallacy, as did Cornejo Polar. However, it is at the threshold of the hegemonic articulation of signification, between two linguistic codes (Spanish and Quechua) and two indeterminable cognitive positions (orality and literacy), where, in the failure of the colonos to be hailed, the trace of illiteracy presents itself. The threshold separating the colonos from Ernesto neither is accounted for by orality nor exists beyond literacy; rather it is unconcealed between them. What indigenista narrative provides the conceptual grounds for, and what *Los ríos profundos* narratologically confirms, is the vacuous semiological core inhering in the binary of orality and literacy and, in this case, its unreconcealment as illiterate, colono signification.

My reading of *Los ríos profundos* explores the limits of orality and literacy from the theoretical residue left behind from Vargas Llosa's and Cornejo Polar's confrontations over Arguedas; instead of taking seriously the destabilizing effects that radical colono signification enacts on the cultural binary of orality-literacy, they both use the latter to catachrestically encode the former. And like Ernesto himself, both Vargas Llosa's and Cornejo Polar's notions of orality fall victim to the truly irruptive grounds of colono illiteracy. It is not surprising then that their conceptualizations of indigenismo prove symptomatically consistent with Ernesto's instinctual decision to avoid contact with any more colonos. They too wish no further contact with abject signification in indigenismo; for both Vargas Llosa and Cornejo Polar, there is no place for colonos in literary indigenismo nor in modern Peru. Ultimately, suspended somewhere between an extinct primitivism ("dreams and magic") on the one hand and authentic, legitimate, and formalized cultural practice ("el zumbayllu") on the other, neither Vargas Llosa's nor Cornejo Polar's simultaneously catachrestic notions of orality prove able to account for and contain the undesirable impact of colono affectivity in *Los ríos profundos*. More significantly, however, together they unconceal the discourse of orality and literacy to be constitutive of precisely that *other* Peru from which emerged colono illiteracy in the first place, thereby revealing the sheer contingency of any semiotic order and the complicity of counterhegemonic ideological practice that only seeks to invert it.

Secrets Even to Herself: *Testimonio*, Illiteracy, and the Grammar of Restitution

In 1996 a collection of essays appeared under the title *The Real Thing: Testimonial Discourse and Latin America* (Gugelberger 1996). Proposed as an anthology of critical *testimonio* discourse, containing essays from the early stages of the testimonio debate in the late 1980s and early 1990s, it would also include many recent reformulations of the stakes of testimonio discourse since its initial elaborations.[1] In one such essay, "The Real Thing," John Beverley (1996: 280–81), who had years earlier announced the emergence of a new world-historical narrative form in testimonio, now pronounces its death:

> This is perhaps the best way to confront the circumstances that frame
> this collection: the moment of testimonio is over. Not, so that I am
> not misunderstood on this point, testimonio as such: that will go on,
> just as testimonial forms have been present at the margins of Western
> literature since its constitution as a modern episteme in the sixteenth

century. But testimonio's moment, the originality and urgency or—
to recall Lacan's phrase—the "state of emergency" that drove our
fascination and critical engagement with it, has undoubtedly passed, if
only by the logic of its aesthetic familiarization.[2]

Though acknowledging that the production of testimonio narratives will
continue in one form or another, Beverley asserts that its critical value
for Latin American studies has nevertheless been exhausted. While we
can be sure this statement was not made in haste and not without much
deliberation, it is still a quite curious statement since he was among the
first in the North American academy to make the case for testimonio as a
critical object of study in Latin American literature and politics.[3] In light
of this pronouncement one might ask: Why this shift in position? What
caused this change? And what is ultimately left of testimonio as a result of
its abandonment by North American Latinamericanists?

It is important to remind ourselves that Beverley is by no means a late
arrival on the subject of testimonio. As early as "Anatomía del testimonio"
(1987), Beverley proposed that, like the short story and the novel, both of
which emerged from a particular set of historical circumstances and transitional periods in Europe, so too might testimonio be signaling the emergence of a new global, proletariat order. However, it would not be until
"The Margin at the Center" (1989: 12) that we see Beverley's articulation of
testimonio as a fully conceptualized narrative form: "We should expect an
age such as our own—also one of transition or the potential for transition
from one mode of production to another—to experience the emergence
of new forms of cultural and literary expression that embody, in more or
less thematically explicit and formally articulated ways, the social forces
contending for power in the world today. . . . One of these new forms in
embryo is the kind of narrative text that in Latin American Spanish has
come to be called testimonio." Here Beverley conceives of testimonio as an
emerging narrative form inextricably linked to the rise of national liberation movements and the sociocultural radicalism of the midcentury across
the globe, particularly in Latin America. Moreover, his asserting that testimonio represents a "popular-democratic" and "fundamentally egalitarian"
narrative form (16) further emphasizes the distinctness of testimonio's discursive genealogy, as it is ascribed in direct opposition to the formal and
historical principles of the novelistic form which has dominated political

modes of narration from the eighteenth century onward. Further grounding this distinction, Beverley argues that, unlike the novel, testimonio is
not fiction (or rather its reality effect is born from its reality) and, further,
that it is geared less toward an individualist, novelistic narrative experience
than a narrative representation of or for a particular social group in its col-
lectivity (15).

What Beverley (1989: 26) saw in testimonio was a narrative form signaling the rise of a new historical and narratological culture, or rather a new
narratology for a new historical subject: "If the novel has had a special relationship with humanism and the rise of European bourgeoisie and with
colonialism and imperialism (and thus with the founding of the conditions
of social oppression and inequality that testimonio represents), testimonio
is by contrast a new form of literary narrative in which we can at the same
time witness and be a part of the emerging culture of an international prole-
tarian/popular-democratic subject in its period of ascendancy and struggle
for hegemony." Ultimately, Beverley conceived of testimonio, like the novel
before it, as a revolutionary literary form signaling a shift to another mode
of production and subjectivity. Testimonio, as the passage itself indicates,
is very similar to the novel in its implied deployment in the consolidation
of "imagined communities" (national, proletariat, or otherwise) and as a
means toward gaining hegemony.[4] However, Beverley ultimately insists on
the categorical difference between the novel and testimonio as they emerge
from different socioeconomic and ideological conditions. This assertion
will prove a major point of contention for critics like Elzbieta Sklodowska
(1992: 91–97), who contend that testimonio does not constitute a rupture
of the novel form but rather the latest manifestation of the novel's adap-
tive capacity to absorb, incorporate, and reproduce nonliterary discourse
such as those found in testimonio. We will come back to Sklodowska a bit
later in this discussion, but suffice it to say that though Beverley establishes
these formal distinctions only in passing and without much elaboration, the
very need to provide a foundational distinction between testimonio and the
novel, as well the terms he uses to oppose them, will prove crucial to the
theoretical course of testimonial discourse. Whether or not this distinction
between testimonio and the novel is able to secure itself in the way that Beverley needs it to do remains the pivotal question.

The distinction is a precarious one. Beverley's problem is that the significance he attributes to testimonio as a marker of an emergent historical,

narratological, and subjective shift is so deeply tied to the novel that its own identity ultimately hinges on it. This is a problem because, first, it posits testimonio as meaningful only to the extent that it is *not* the novel, and second, since this categorical distinction obtains as its very condition of possibility it becomes vulnerable to any intellectual labor that seeks to trouble it. Even without Sklodowska's assertion of the novel's ability for appropriation and adaptation, one can see a certain conceptual slippage within Beverley's notion of testimonio. For, while he insists on this literary distinction to further testimonio's political claim, he at the same time attributes to testimonio other novelistically characteristic features. That is, to the extent that for Beverley testimonio is reproductive of the same discursive effects as the novel—facilitating the historical consolidation of the modern nation-state and the national community—such congruency might itself begin to problematize the integrity of the opposition to begin with, even if testimonio is conceived as a nonliterary or even antiliterary mode of textual production. This ideological congruency between the two might trump their otherwise differential literary qualities (which are arbitrary), for in either case literacy's ability to interpellate is still functional and operative. Thus, while Beverley needs testimonio to be placed in opposition to the novel, he also, paradoxically, needs it to behave in the exact same way as the novel. What is therefore ultimately at stake for Beverley is that the degree of testimonio's distinctness from the novel is in inverse proportion to the degree to which testimonio is deployed, like the novel, to constitute the new imagined community he sees emerging globally at its moment. Is this what Beverley meant by "the logic of aesthetic familiarization"? Might this internal contradiction, inscribed at the core of "The Margin at the Center," have something to do with his charge that testimonio's "moment is over"? Might his subsequent abandonment of testimonio in "The Real Thing" have already been announced in his earliest conceptualization of testimonio in "The Margin at the Center"?[5]

Beverley provides a number of clues in the concluding pages of "The Real Thing," the most significant of which is his concession that, for all of the glimpses and critical revelations of subalternity, radical alterity, and all "that resists symbolization absolutely," provided by his and others' interpretations of *Me llamo Rigoberta Menchú* (1983), for Beverley (1996: 278–79) the "Real" was ultimately the exploitation of the testimonio form by an unapologetic, political activist hoping to advance the interests of her community:

The Real that *I, Rigoberta Menchú* forces us to encounter, in other
words, is not only that of the subaltern as "represented" victim of
history but also as an agent of a transformative project that aspires to
become hegemonic in its own right. For this project, testimonio is a
means rather than an end in itself. . . . Menchú is certainly aware that
her testimonio can be an important tool in human rights and solidarity
work that might have a positive effect on the genocidal conditions the
text itself describes. But *her* interest in creating the text is not in the
first place to have it become part of the canon of Western civilization,
which in any case she distrusts deeply, so that it can become an object
for us, in a sense our means of getting the "whole truth"—"toda la
realidad"—of her experience. It is rather to act tactically in a way that
she hopes and expects will advance the interests of the community
and social groups and classes her testimonio represents: "poor"
Guatemalans.

What is most compelling here is Beverley's suggestion that, all along,
it might have been Menchú who had us more astutely read, and not
the other way around. In other words, it was Menchú who understood
the ultimate value of the testimonio form, and it had little to do with
literary history, genre studies, or narrative structure; rather it involved
drawing the maximum amount of attention, by any and all means
necessary, to the violent and brutal consequences of the civil war in
Guatemala and primarily to the indigenous victims of both the conflict
itself and the historical roots leading up to it. To put in another way, by
1996 testimonio's literary distinction and historical conceptualization,
such as proposed by Beverley in "The Margin at the Center," suddenly
appeared superfluous and utterly off the mark, even to Beverley himself.
However, he seems to have foreseen the consequences for the academic
Left when it would one day be forced to confront its attempts to
reconcile its theoretical positions on testimonio with the increasingly
unpredictable and problematic consequences Menchú's testimonio
produced. In this regard Beverley's critical insight is crucial: ultimately
the Real was not that testimonio proved too easily co-opted and defused
by the transparency of its subversive political tactics but rather that it
was too subversive, uncontrollable, and unwieldy for both the Right *and*
the Left.

As it turns out, *The Real Thing*'s critical retreat from testimonio was somewhat timely, and preemptively so, as by then *Me llamo Rigoberta Menchú* was coming under increasing scrutiny, with questions regarding the veracity of Menchú's testimonial account. In 1999 the anthropologist David Stoll published *Rigoberta Menchú and the Story of All Poor Guatemalans*, a controversial study on the historical veracity of Menchú's account as depicted in *Me llamo Rigoberta Menchú*. Drawing on sources encountered while doing field research in Guatemala in the late 1980s and early 1990s, Stoll contests the veracity of several crucial elements in Menchú's narrative account: namely, her assertion of the popular and familial roots of the guerrilla movement in her locale; the inclusion of nonfactual events, like the death of Menchú's brother, as actually witnessed by her; and her omission of the details of her education and literacy at the time of the interview.

Despite Stoll's (1999: xi) expressed wish only to enable a frank and honest discussion of the civil war in Guatemala, his book was nevertheless received as a politically motivated attack on Menchú's historical and cultural legacy as a Nobel Peace Prize–winning indigenous activist. Many of these critics claimed that Stoll's book was the American Right's attempt to curb Menchú's rising popularity and leadership by questioning the accuracy of her testimonial account and threatening not only the political figure of Menchú but also the radical legitimacy of the testimonio form itself. The book provoked responses in defense of Menchú and the testimonio form. However, in the academic Left's perceived urgency to respond to the allegations, the frame of the debate irrevocably changed the nature of testimonio's formalization.

Conceived as a response to the debate spurred by Stoll's book, *The Rigoberta Menchú Controversy* appeared soon after, in 2001. Edited by Arturo Arias, the compilation comprises domestic and international newspaper articles documenting the controversy over Menchú's authenticity, as well as numerous critical essays. However, though the precedent was set to engage Stoll's argument through the critical frame of analysis established previously in the edited volume *The Real Thing*, the empiricist thrust of Stoll's critique overrode this possibility as the compilation simply and only reproduced the same appeals to empirical truth as those initiated by Stoll. That is, we see in *The Rigoberta Menchú Controversy*, as in Stoll, an overriding concern to establish and prove historical facticity, this time in defense of the veracity of Menchú's account. What was initially conceived as *Me llamo*

Rigoberta Menchú's most compelling feature, the text's "counterdiscursivity,"[6] was conceded in defense of her empirical validation—historical, sociological, anthropological, or otherwise. This rush resulted in an interpretive agenda whose critical implications were perhaps the very thing Beverly foresaw happening to testimonio discourse in "The Real Thing."[7]

As a particularly illustrative example of the type of critique spurred by Stoll's charges, Claudia Ferman narrates her visit with Elizabeth Burgos-Debray in Paris, where she was shown the material evidence of *Me llamo Rigoberta Menchú*'s production including cassette tapes, handwritten notes, original transcripts, and manuscripts. It is at this moment of visible confirmation, Ferman tells us, that she realizes the project was never Menchú's to begin with, that she didn't write it, and is therefore not responsible for its claims:

> Looking through the manuscript, I was able to corroborate the undeniable literary nature of the text—its emergence and materialization as a written artifact. The literary discursiveness of *Me llamo Rigoberta Menchú y así me nació la conciencia* was not achieved by undermining the oral tradition of which Menchú is heir and also model. Undoubtedly it is Burgos who, by defoliating, ordering, and harmonizing the rhetorical expression of the spoken word, inscribes and incorporates a story and a world vision within the tradition of the book. The *mestizaje* of the mediums and languages reaches a point where the double voice becomes one: the voice of Menchú, who speaks out against the disasters of war in Guatemala and demands her people's right to their tradition and their culture. (Arias 2001: 166)

"Undoubtedly," Ferman argues, it was Burgos who is responsible for the "personage" that Menchú became. Further evidence that the book is Burgos's and not Menchú's is the "undeniably literary character of the text," which, to Ferman, is the most compelling argument to make against Stoll: the figure of Menchú is a fictional product of the "eloquence inherent to [Burgos's] literary expression"; she is not the author, and therefore not subject to Stoll's critique (167).

As a result of this strategy to defend this testimonio, Menchú's "authority" was not the only thing inadvertently put into question; her speech was as well. As Ferman unwittingly suggests, without "undermining the oral tradition of which Menchú is heir and model," her enunciations have nevertheless been "defoliated," "ordered," and "harmonized," "inscribed," and "incorporated" into the materiality of the book by Burgos herself. That is,

Menchú's speech is ultimately not her own, but someone else's. But that is not all, for Ferman goes even further to advocate for, at Menchú's expense, all of our roles in authoring this text: "Thus, Menchú, is assumed to be the 'author' of (authorizes) the textuality that surfaced in those few days in Paris. But that text also has us, the multiple interpretative communities, as its authors" (Arias 2001: 167). What Ferman means here is that we are all responsible for the creation of Rigoberta, and that, like the comrades of Spartacus, anyone with an interest in her can proclaim, in defense and with all sincerity, "I am Rigoberta!"

As illustrated in Ferman's strategy to defend Menchú's narrative from attacks like Stoll's, the impulse was to de-authorize her, to displace her amid the materiality of the text's production, to disembody her from the empirical realm of analysis by containing her within the eloquence of Burgos's literary expression and disseminating her authorship among the various "interpretive communities" that constitute her. In light of Stoll's critique, for Ferman the best defense of Menchú is to erase her voice from testimonio's literalness and reinscribe her in its literariness. What this form of recuperation produced was a reading of Menchú in which she is no longer presented as the source of a "reality effect" but rather, in the post-Stoll era, as the "reality effect" itself.

However, despite the impact of Stoll's critique and the impulse to defend Menchú from it, which, one can argue, more precisely marks the passing of testimonio's moment in the North American academy, it is important to recognize that the dynamic between the literal and literary registers of signification that we see here has been inscribed at the core of testimonio discourse since its inception. Elements of the initial discussion, which centered around the distinction between testimonio and novel, one literal and the other literary, and which has now, in the post-Stoll era, shifted to a discussion of Menchú's literal or literary accuracy, are inscribed within the very definition of testimonio proposed in 1970 by Cuba's Casa de las Americas, a definition designed to formalize the genre for its yearly, international prize: "Testimonios must document some aspect of Latin American or Caribbean reality from a direct source. A direct source is understood as knowledge of the facts by the author or his or her compilation of narratives or evidence obtained from the individuals involved or qualified witnesses. In both cases, reliable documentation, written or graphic, is indispensable. The form is at the author's discretion, but literary quality is also indispensable" (qtd. in

Beverley 1989: 13n5, his translation). In this instance, we see that both "reliable documentation" as well as "literary quality" are equally indispensable for the Casa de las Americas prize in testimonio. However, in this rather vague definition we are not given parameters to adjudicate when one element presents a problem for the other, as in the case of *Me llamo Rigoberta Menchú*, or if, in such cases, one element should be privileged over the other. The definition also neglects to indicate whether the objective of testimonio production lies in its ability to reconcile the literal and the literary, or if, as we saw earlier in Cornejo Polar's discussion of indigenista narrative, the failures of the testimonio form are precisely the lesson and its virtue. But it does indicate something of a previous history to testimonio not alluded to in Beverley's initial attempts at formalization. Following his own definition in "The Margin at the Center," Beverley (1989: 11) argues, "However, because testimonio is by nature a protean and demotic form, not subject to critical legislation by a normative literary establishment, any attempt to specify a generic definition for it, as I do here, is at best provisional, and at worst repressive." While Beverley fails to explicitly address testimonio's previously established definition for the Casa de las Americas prize, he in effect challenges any and all attempts at testimonio's formalization by asserting its inherent irreducibility to institutional proscription. However, assuming that he was aware of the definition proposed by Casa de las Americas almost twenty years earlier (see n5), does his own conceptualization constitute a break from it? Is he attempting to establish another discursive genealogy for testimonio? If so, why? What is at stake here?

The formal and historical import of Casa de las Americas' institutionalized definition tells us two things. The first is that despite the immediacy of any cultural or historical context, testimonio is ultimately bound to an inextricable, internal contradiction (the literal and the literary), and second, that there are and have been other cultural and historical contexts for testimonio production in Latin America. As we know, testimonio enjoyed an institutional history prior to Menchú's reception and conceptualization in the North American academy, and this history is grounded in a set of circumstances entirely different from the one Beverley has presented in "The Margin at the Center." That is, testimonio was not always conceived as a contemporary narrative form specifically devoted to respond to present economic and political conditions that continue to reproduce subalternity; instead it was considered a foundational narrative form emanating from a specific historical and political vantage point which claims to have seen the end of subalternity itself: the Cuban Revolution. We thus have not one but two competing narratives of testimonio: one asserting that testimonio emanates from persistent conditions of subalternity, and the other asserting that testimonio originates from the end of subalternity as sociohistorical condition. That these narratives of origin are seemingly divergent, however, does not necessarily mean they are mutually exclusive, for, if considered carefully, they each rely on the other's narrative sequencing. One the one hand, Central American and Andean testimonios (such as Menchú's and Domitila Barrios de Chungara [Barrios de Chungara and Viezzer 1978]) are understood as following in the footsteps of the Cuban Revolution. On the other hand, however, the Cuban Revolution needs testimonio in order to justify itself; it needs to bring back the image or specter of subalternity in order to assert that subalternity no longer exists. Of course, this does not mean these narratives are therefore complementary, for historically they can't both be right about testimonio; either it originates as a literary form to account for subalternity, or it originates as a literary form to account for the end of it. It can be neither, but it can't be both. Such is the predicament of testimonio that as a "revolutionary" narrative caught between competing claims about subalternity, it nevertheless remains in need of a supplement of subalternity. Therefore, and as distinct from the terms given by Beverley, the earlier, postrevolutionary conception of testimonio emerges from an altogether different theoretical debate, which I rehearse below. It is the wager of this discussion that whatever is still at stake for the future of testimonio discourse resides at the threshold between Beverley's and Miguel Barnet's theoretical formulations.

In chapter 2 we saw how the terms of Vargas Llosa's essay "Novela primitiva y la novela de creación en América Latina" (1969a) were used against the indigenista narrative tradition, and against José María Arguedas in particular, in an attempt to temper and contain indigenismo's cultural influence in the forging of Vargas Llosa's "new" Peru and its canon. Read more amply, Vargas Llosa's piece can also be seen reacting to a more broadly perceived crisis in Latin American literature: a pervasive, vulgar understanding of "reality" and the inhibiting of literary potential by an ideological dependence to it. More specifically he emphasizes that the reliance on a materialistic conception of reality, infused as it is into much of Latin American literary production like indigenismo, thwarts any and all promise of significant literary value (29–30). What he proposes with "creationary" literary activity is a new relationship to reality, a new literary praxis in Latin America not built around a conventional dependence on its ideological authority and objectivity but premised on its outright rejection and rearticulation. He notes: "The creationary novel ceases to be 'Latin American,' it is now free from this servitude. It no longer serves reality; reality now is in the service of it. In distinction to what happened with the 'primitives,' there is no common denominator among these new novelists, neither of themes, style nor technique: their commonality is their diversity. These writers no longer struggle to express 'one' reality, but rather, multiple, personal visions and obsessions: 'their' reality" (31).[8] In this regard, Vargas Llosa's affirmation of creationary literary activity is not too dissimilar from Alejo Carpentier's prologue to *El reino de este mundo* (1949), in which he advances "lo real maravilloso" as the foundational principle of a new novelistic practice in Latin America, and from which emerged the boom authors' "new Latin American novel." Read in this way, "Novela primitiva y la novela de creación en América Latina" can be understood as a response to a larger crisis of Latin American fiction writing. To this extent, Vargas Llosa follows a long tradition of the essayistic manifesto that portends the emergence of new aesthetic programs in Latin America, including but not limited to José Martí's "Nuestra America" (1891), José Enrique Rodó's *Ariel* (1900), José Carlos Mariategui's "Literature on Trial" (1928), and Carpentier. In each case we see a perceived crisis that will be overcome through the avant-garde literary programs being proposed; Vargas Llosa's essay does not deviate from this general discursive form. However, his manifesto is not alone at the end of this long-established line; in fact the literary program he had proposed in "Novela primitiva" finds itself as an object of contention signaling the emergence of yet another revolutionary, literary form in Latin America: testimonio.

In the same year as Vargas Llosa's "Novela primitiva," the Cuban ethnographer Miguel Barnet published *La canción de Rachel* (1969), in which he included an essay entitled "La novela testimonio: Socio-literatura." Barnet's essay represents one of the earliest, if not the earliest articulations of testimonio in its current form; moreover this essay proposes testimonial narrative as an ideal practice for the literary self-fashioning of the newly established revolutionary state in Latin America. As illustrated by Elzbieta Sklodowska in her book *Testimonio Hispanoamericano* (1992), testimonio as a literary form and testimonio as a nationalist project consolidating the revolutionary state are inextricably conjoined. Sklodowska's study is significant because it is the first to treat the Cuban origins of the testimonio genre and its influence on Central American and Andean testimonio production during the 1970s and 1980s. But most important, it is because she establishes testimonio's institutional history in postrevolutionary Cuba at the moment of Barnet's articulation. While Sklodowska reads Barnet's essay alongside Carpentier's prologue as a means by which to flesh out the formal features of the testimonio genre (11–12), I instead critically juxtapose Barnet's essay with Vargas Llosa's "Novela primitiva" in order to uncover the political stakes between testimonio as a cultural and literary alternative to the boom's creationary designation. My reading of this debate reveals in Barnet a far more reactionary position vis-à-vis the position taken by Vargas Llosa in his essay, and less the literary manifesto as it is presented by Sklodowska.

Read alongside Vargas Llosa's essay, Barnet's maintains an uneasy, if not conservative position on the principles espoused by the former. Barnet (1983a: 12) begins by eschewing the alienating values of literary formalism and innovation for the "organic" and "primordial" experience man has with the world and expressing the need to return to the days when "life and art complemented each other."[9] Referring here to contemporary, western European literature, Barnet explains that the atrophying of Europe's sociopolitical vitality has resulted in a literary stasis: "for many years, Western Europe has not seen a movement of any great social significance, there have been no political explosions, and its literature reflected this state of innocuousness" (15). Though he concedes that this political stasis is an inevitable consequence of historical factors, he finds that these conditions have constituted a form of literary production devoid of any significant sociocultural value. He goes on to state, "Naturally, that form of literature is a noble one, it does not, in the least, interfere with any of man's social conflicts. . . . It is a literature entirely inoffensive. Its lies in exteriority to an organic whole, limited only to the elite, and delightful only those within its sphere" (15). However, he seems to suggest, this stasis is not limited to the course of European literature; his critique might also point toward Vargas Llosa's creationary literary activity as representative of this crisis. For while Vargas Llosa advocates a program of radical development in literary technique to overcome certain atavisms of contemporary Latin American literature (i.e., its "servitude" to

Latin America), Barnet seems to express the need to return to a more immediate, direct relationship of man and myth, "enabling an existential consciousness, an awareness of being in the world," which, he feels, is essential
to the founding of a Latin American identity (12).

The relationship between Vargas Llosa's and Barnet's proposals become
much more complex when the latter proposes that the cure will come from
the Western Hemisphere: "Parallel to this crisis runs yet another tendency,
within the tradition of the fictional novel, representing a healthy, vigorous
and rejuvenating stream, and it is coming from the Americas, from both
Latin and North American literatures" (1983a: 16). For Barnet, the crisis is
European, while the corrective will come from the Americas, and the contribution to be had is a literary formation inextricably linked to the formation of a new Latin American cultural and political praxis. He contends
that "this is essentially due to the fact that America is still in embryonic
form, a world that yearns to embody reality, which needs to create a site
for its own constitution for its social and cultural development. Europe is
exhausted, while America is thirsty for action. America struggles violently
against itself, against the image that Europe attempted to establish for it.
For this reason American and Latin American literatures are assisted by
inherent duality; it, by nature, needs to struggle, contest, and break away"
(17). Curiously, as Barnet presents the dilemma as one between Europe and
the Americas, it simultaneously implies a categorical distinction, under the
rubric of cultural identity, between European and Latin American literary production. Vargas Llosa, on the other hand, proposes quite the contrary: creationary activity as the liberating of literature from its servitude
to Latin America, that is, a de-nationalized literature encoded within the
terms of global literacy. Yet, might this creationary activity, by Barnet's
own standards, be a Latin American enterprise, emanating from what he
calls "the Latin American *I*, the Latin American *we*" (19)? For even Vargas
Llosa (1969a: 31) concedes that his notion of creationary literary activity is
ultimately rooted within a Latin American cultural horizon: "The worlds
created by these [creationary] fictions, though worthy of their own sake
and engaged at different levels of representation (psychological, fantastical,
mythical), are, nevertheless, varieties of Latin America." In other words, it
appears that Vargas Llosa's and Barnet's proposals are not as divergent as
conceived initially and in effect might represent some unanticipated common ground between them.

After all, both Vargas Llosa and Barnet articulate very similar stylistic stances on literary production. For instance, we see in Barnet an almost identical adherence to some of the same principles on which Vargas Llosa's notions of creationary literary production rest. Barnet (1983a: 29–30) asserts such adherence when discussing his role in literary aspects of testimonio production:

> I will never write a book in which I faithfully reproduce what the
> recording dictates to me. From the recording, I will only take the
> speech's anecdotal tone, the rest, the style and the colorations, shall
> always be my contribution. That literature is false, and as a product
> of transcription it is simplistic and flat, and leads nowhere. . . . The
> author of the testimonial novel should not limit himself. He
> should give free rein to his imagination when it will not injure his
> character's personality, when it will not betray his language. The
> only way in which an author can extract the maximum benefit from
> a situation is by applying the fantastical, inventing it from within an
> essence of reality.

Here Barnet does not apologize for his textual interventions in the construction of the testimonial text; in fact he considers it a stylistic necessity. What this passage implies, at least within the categories used by Vargas Llosa, is that Barnet's testimonio project is not representative of "primitive" literature after all; on the contrary, to the extent that his discourse emphasizes the stylistic, imaginative, and perhaps even fantastical conventions associated with Vargas Llosa's notion of creationary literary activity, it will be constitutive of it. On the other hand, Barnet legitimizes Vargas Llosa's literary strategy by appropriating many, though not all of its stylistic attributes in his own work on testimonio.

Up to now, I have been presenting Vargas Llosa's "Novela primitiva" as somehow preceding Barnet's "La novela-testimonio," as if only Barnet is burdened with the task of accounting for the other's claims. However, the fact is that they were published in the same year, and, as we can see, they are each accounted for within the other's text. To this extent, it would seem likely that the unanticipated and fortuitous exchange being established between these texts ultimately concerns the same perceived crisis, and up to this moment, asserting, essentially, the same things. However, is there another, more critical issue at work between them; is there something else at stake here, beyond the expressed crisis of literature? Are they both still talking about the same thing: both talking about a crisis, while not necessarily talking about a literary crisis? That is, over and above the stated crisis in literature in each of their formulations, is there another matter over which this register of literary discourse simply glosses a larger stake of importance?

Contrary to what we've seen so far, the issues prove as political as they are literary. In 1969 both Barnet and Vargas Llosa were writing in the midst of what will later be called "el caso Padilla." The National Union of Cuban Writers and Artists (UNEAC), of which Barnet is a founding member, was in the midst of a scandal brought about by its awarding of its prize in poetry to Heberto Padilla's *Fuera del juego* in 1968. Later considered too critical of the Castro regime, *Fuera del juego* was condemned as antirevolutionary, and its author was arrested for subversive activity and forced to issue a public statement renouncing his work (see Edwards 1974). For Vargas Llosa, this incident amounted to an irrevocable breach of solidarity between the newly established government and leftist Latin American intellectuals and writers associated with Cuba's cultural revolution. Ultimately "el caso Padilla" led many to distance themselves from UNEAC, the national editorial house Casa de las Americas, and the Cuban government entirely, including Vargas Llosa, who renounced all ties in 1971.[10]

The question for us here is whether this political situation might explain, or at least nuance, the critical stakes between Vargas Llosa's and Barnet's literary proposals. Does Vargas Llosa's affirmation of creationary literary activity represent an implicit critique of the Revolution? Does his insistence on freeing literary production from the "servitude" of being Latin American presage his subsequent decision to break ties with the Castro regime over the Padilla affair? And read in this way, does Barnet's proposal for testimonio consequently amount to a literary defense of the Revolution? In other words, if we take Vargas Llosa's affirmation of creationary activity as a literary response to the growing disillusionment with the Castro regime, and if we take Barnet's proposal for the testimonial novel as the response to the crisis of literature's social responsibility in Latin America, how else can testimonio be understood except as an institutionalized literary project intent on creating, for itself, the cultural grounding for the revolutionary state?

While the writers from this hemisphere continue being educated
Creoles, graduates from even provincial universities, or terrifying
geniuses, our literature will suffer from an astronomically integrated
vision of the world. While the Indian remains in his state of lethargy,
while the humble, Latin American black never produces a transcendent
work, our literature will continue limping along. Because that educated
Creole, that recent graduate, does not represent everybody but only one
side, one stratum, or most terrible of all, one class; a class inoculated
with the virus of bourgeois morals and prejudices. (Barnet 1983a: 19)

In light of Barnet's posture in this statement, is it not more than coincidental
that "el caso Padilla" led simultaneously to the loss of support from the
boom writers, many of whom are "creoles," and to the inauguration of the
testimonio as a privileged literary form in Cuban nation building? If indeed
testimonio is caught up within this ideological polemic, deployed as it is
in Barnet's literary program to consolidate the Revolution's cultural legacy
and the formation of the new national subject, how then are testimonio's
stakes brought to bear for the Revolution?

Confirmation of Barnet's larger political agenda is not difficult to
unearth. Sklodowska's reading of Barnet leaves little doubt regarding the
desired effects of testimonio's institutionalization in Cuba and its cultural
implications elsewhere. She notes, for instance, "Through Barnet's peculiar
rhetoric in his theoretical essay 'Novela-testimonio' one gets the feeling that
we are being faced with an 'official' project" (1992: 10, my translation). She
is forced to concede that with testimonio "the objective is not ethnological,
but political" (13). And she reminds us that "Barnet is writing from a position not distant from the official ideology of the Cuban Revolution that
relegates its racial conflicts into the past and conceives of its ethnic future
on the island as a harmonious syncretism" (117). For Sklodowska, Barnet's
understanding of testimonio was never meant to exceed the ideological limits of the Revolution from which it emerged.

This is made further evident in Barnet's *Biografía de un cimarrón* (1966),
where the life of Esteban Montejo, the subject of this testimonio, is framed
within a "revolutionary spirit" that will ultimately realize itself in the Cuban
Revolution. Esteban, who by 1966 was more than a hundred years old, tells
the story of his existence as a runaway slave in nineteenth-century Cuba
and as a participant in the War of Independence at the turn of the century.

However, writing just a few years after 1959, Barnet is enunciating Esteban's life from a historical juncture that already saw the Revolution come to pass. Esteban's placement on *this* side of the historical transition cannot be overestimated. That is, it is only now, *after* the Revolution, that these facets of Esteban's life come to represent the spirit of the Cuban people. As Barnet makes sure to note in the introduction to the 1966 edition, Esteban's life represents

> an admirable level of honesty and revolutionary spirit; the honesty of his life's actions which are expressed in key moments of his narrative, in the War of Independence, above all. The revolutionary spirit is exhibited not only in his narrative, but in his overall attitude. Esteban Montejo, at 105 years of age, constitutes a good example of revolutionary conduct and quality. His history of being a revolutionary, first as a runaway slave, then as liberator, and as member of the People's Socialist Party afterward, continues, in our time, through his identification with the Cuban revolution. (Montejo and Barnet 1966: 11–12)[11]

Barnet presents Esteban as a truly revolutionary subject, both in his actions to escape slavery and as a participant in the War of Independence. Moreover, at more than a hundred years of age, Esteban continues in this spirit as a supporter of the Revolution. However, the question becomes whether Esteban was himself ever this representative of Cubanicity prior to the Revolution, or whether what was considered revolutionary about Esteban after the Revolution would still be considered revolutionary before it?

Let us not assume that because Barnet conceives of testimonio as a literary form working in cultural and formal solidarity with the Revolution its institutionalization would amount to the reproduction of an ongoing, revolutionary spirit that might interfere with the successful founding of the emergent revolutionary state in Cuba. On the contrary, Barnet must presume the deployment of testimonio to arrest the moment of historical transition and provide the static terms of consolidation for the newly established socialist state and the revolutionary Cuban national subject. While for Barnet the subject is the product of history, and not the other way around, the subject of testimonio is ultimately bound within the static, arrested frame of his or her historical articulation, in this case from within the Cuban Revolution. Note, for instance, Barnet's vision of what *Biografía de un cimarrón* would provide for Cuban culture: "This book does nothing more than narrate the common experiences had by many people of the same nationality. Ethnology collects them for the experts of sociology, history and folklore. Our great satisfaction comes from reflecting them through a legitimate actor of Cuba's historical process" (Montejo and Barnet 1966: 12). In this passage Barnet asserts that the subject of testimonio, in this case, Esteban Montejo, is significant only to the extent to which he represents a given sociohistorical frame, that is, representing a certain class and enunciating particular historical moments from within another. Ernesto's life here represents Cuba's past, both in temporal terms and in at least theoretically defunct class distinctions. The moment of revolution in Cuba, Barnet assumes, realizes society's historical development into a classless society, allowing Ernesto, and others like him, to arise from subalternity into a fully integrated participant in the revolutionary Cuban nation-state. Barnet's testimonio is precisely the presencing of the emancipated subject at this historical moment of de-subalternization: the documenting of the historical subject's realization within the revolutionary state and arresting it, in all its plenitude, at the moment of its conscription. For Barnet, the question is not whether testimonio itself de-subalternizes, for the Revolution carried this out; what testimonio does is consolidate the de-subalternized, emancipated subject within a nationalist form.[12]

Thus for Barnet, testimonio is conceived within a narratological frame that presumes the eradication of all forms of subalternization culturally and politically, a testimonial narratology, which, however, though premised on the end of subalternity is not necessarily concerned with it. If through the Revolution all subaltern subjects were emancipated, and if through the establishment of the revolutionary state all former subaltern subjects have become fully integrated national subjects, and if testimonio is conceived as the narrative form that best expresses or arrests this moment of historical emancipation, then Barnet's conception of testimonio ultimately has more at stake in constituting hegemonic national culture and identity than as a subaltern (antiliterary) narratology, as we see later in Beverley. Though not yet theorized to the degree we recognize it is today, the notion of subalternity is nevertheless implied in Barnet as a remnant of Cuba's already historical past ("hombres sin historia"), in other words, as an already transcended sociopolitical condition after the Revolution. Therefore, as it relates to testimonio, any understanding of subalternity is secondary (though theoretically a priori) to the formation of a national subject in postrevolutionary Cuba.

Similar to what we saw in the Vargas Llosa–Cornejo Polar debate in chapter 2, what we have here in Barnet and Beverley are two configurations of testimonio, which, though articulated in different circumstances and with different projects in mind, equally continue to inform our notions of testimonio today. Ultimately, what I want to emphasize is that Barnet's and Beverley's conceptualizations of testimonio are not simply bound to each other by historical succession; for better or worse, both are still, simultaneously and to a coextensive degree, inextricably formative of the discourse of testimonio we presently inherit, and further, neither has, nor can, eclipse the initial contributions of the other. Wittingly or not, we continue to rely on them to further draw upon testimonio's unique value for Latin American studies. It might well be that the discursive conditions created by the conjunction of Beverley's and Barnet's conceptual principles on testimonio also inject a series of contradictory assumptions and shared critical lapses into its logic, revealing, perhaps, the same theoretical problems brought to bear in the Menchú-Stoll controversy.

In other words, while both Beverley and Barnet saw testimonio as a strikingly original narrative form, distinct from the conventions of the novel, and while both saw its emergence tied to larger world-historical shifts in relations of power as somehow representative or even constitutive of it, their similarities nevertheless end here. Whereas Beverley conceives of testimonio as an unclassifiable ("protean"), antiliterary ("demotic"), textual form of expression by and from subalternity, Barnet saw it as a pliable, stylized, and ethnographically sound narrative form serving a foundational literary role ("obra de fundación") in national consolidation. Whereas Beverley understood testimonio as a subaltern practice focused on the critique of the nation-state and national identity, and which is instead geared toward fostering international support and alliances in a trans- or postnational register, Barnet understood it in exclusively culturally nationalist terms, as a means for a newly established state to forge the cultural narrative of a new national community. Further, while the existence of subalternity constitutes testimonio's condition of possibility for Beverley, Barnet's is premised on the purported eradication of subalternity itself.

Despite the fragility of these oppositions—some of which are highly debatable in themselves—it is still an open question whether testimonio can indeed serve Beverley as a vehicle for subaltern expressivity (even inadequately), or whether the eradication of the condition of subalternity itself can lead from the substitution of one state form for another, as we see in Barnet. These questions are in all probability unanswerable; they are ultimately more ideologically grounded theses than critically grounded ones. However, to the extent that Beverley's and Barnet's claims place them in tacit opposition (either/or), any attempt at reconciling (or even privileging one of) the two runs the risk of reproducing the already extant problems facing testimonio. Ultimately, what we have here are two foundational conceptual models of testimonio that are ambiguously interrelated but whose interstitial space remains critically unexplored.[13]

On the one hand, Beverley's conceptualization of testimonio, as I understand him, does not represent much of a theoretical progression from Barnet's earlier, leftist though statist agenda. What we see in Beverley is an attempt to wrest testimonio from its perhaps inherent inclination toward statism and articulate it within a more progressive political horizon that formalizes its use by emancipatory movements that continue to seek international recognition and support. However, we see in both cases attempts to codify and institute the testimonio form. Despite his own earlier caveat ("because testimonio is by nature a protean and demotic form not yet subject to legislation by a normative literary establishment"), Beverley nevertheless proposes to contain testimonio's parameters by determining what it is not (the novel, autobiography) and what its function is. Second, and more important, simply because Beverley's conceptualization of testimonio postdates Barnet's does not mean that the former's understanding of testimonio is limited to its use after its institutionalization in Cuba; it presents itself not as postrevolutionary but as in direct continuity with it. In fact one can make the case that Beverley's mythology of the testimonio form in "The Margin at the Center" (subaltern expression, emancipatory ideological horizon) works quite well as a prequel to the state's subsequent appropriation of testimonio as an institutionalized narrative form for Cuban nationalism that we see in Barnet. Despite the historical moments marking their enunciations, it is ultimately Barnet who represents the conceptual limit to Beverley's notion of testimonio.

On the other hand, Barnet's limitations would be quite apparent to critics informed by Beverley's understanding of testimonio and subalternity, the most important of which is the issue of mediation, that is, the relationship between the subject and the interviewer. While Beverley (1989: 19) would propose a nonhierarchical relationship between the two, a relationship of solidarity between the poor, working class and a radicalized intelligencia, Barnet (1966: 10) chooses to articulate his testimonial model in the following way: "We know that to simply make an informant speak is, to a certain extent, making literature. But we are not intending to create a literary document or a novel [Sabemos que poner a hablar un informante es, en cierta medida, hacer literatura. Pero no intentamos nosotros crear un documento literario, una novela]." In this rather curious way of linking a talking informant with literary production, Barnet seems to propose an interface of such unequal power relations that it constitutes what might be testimonio's most absolute limit of possibility: a narrative structured around the encounter between a subject and the state. After all, "making an informant speak" is not a politically neutral metaphor, nor one consistent with de-subalternization; in fact it amounts to its reproduction. However, if Barnet's tacit admission that the textual manifestation of the absolute limit of unequal power relations is literary, then it seems clear why Beverley (1989: 22) would rearticulate testimonio's stakes as a challenge to the institution and ideological principles of literature itself.[14] Nevertheless these polarized, hierarchical conditions frame the logic of Barnet's testimonial form and are further reflected in the construction of Esteban's narrative.

As much as Esteban is deployed as representative of Cuban revolutionary nationalism, it also seems that *Biografía de un cimarrón* is framed by another essential state practice: counterinsurgency. The impulse for fact and intelligence gathering, even during a discussion of periods and circumstances far removed from the present, is not lost in the production of Esteban's testimonio. Barnet (Montejo and Barnet 1966: 9) mentions in passing, "We also wanted to include a description of the methods employed by the informant [Esteban] to subsist in the most solitary conditions while in the hills, the techniques to obtain fire, to hunt, as well as his relationship to nature's elements, plants and animals, especially birds." Barnet's passage is in a purely curious register by a biographical interviewer. However, the fact is that, though no longer a fugitive nor an insurgent, Esteban once was both, and to the extent that he successfully continued to evade the state when he was both, the information provided regarding his existence as a fugitive and an insurgent, regardless of the prior state's legitimacy, is crucial for the present state to acquire. In this case, testimonio can be seen serving multiple functional roles for the state: in the formation and propagation of national identity and simultaneously in the accumulating of counterinsurgent intelligence to defend against subsequent external and internal threats. As such, Barnet's phrase "making the informant speak" no longer appears to be a felicitous metaphor for testimonio after all.

It will be interesting to those unfamiliar with *Biografía de un cimarrón* to know that Barnet's choice of Esteban Montejo as the subject for a testimonio was the product of a selection process. Very few have remarked on the fact that, initially, a man and a woman drew Barnet's attention as potential subjects for an ethnographic study. He explains:

> Two interviewees drew our attention. The first was a woman of 100 years of age; the other, a man of 104. The woman had been a slave; she was also a healer and spiritualist. The man, though he never directly discussed religious topics, his language nevertheless reflected an inclination to superstitious thought and popular beliefs. His life was interesting. He recounted aspects of slavery and from the War of Independence. However, what most impressed us was his assertion of having been a fugitive slave, a *cimarrón*, in the mountains of the province of Las Villas. We ultimately forgot about the old woman, and directed ourselves to the Veteran's house, where we found Esteban Montejo. (Montejo and Barnet 1966: 7)

Again, though our present notions of subalternity were beyond Barnet's theoretical horizon (and scope of interest), one has to insist on his decision to choose a man over a woman in this initial testimonial project, even when both subjects were black and former slaves. The passage suggests that Esteban's experience as a runaway slave and participation in the War of Independence led to Barnet's decision; however, the implications of that decision are significant to the extent that it signals a foundational (re) entrenchment of gender hierarchies in revolutionary Cuba's cultural and narrative self-fashioning. In this case, what has been reproduced is the insufficient representational value of women's social experience in Cuban history; both testimonio discourse and the new revolutionary subject are constituted via the subordination of a female former slave's biographical relevance. Like many projects of national or cultural emancipation in Latin America before it, the very process of representing the *raced* and *classed* subaltern subject constitutes itself in the reproduction of *gendered* subalternity.[15] From the outset of Barnet's testimonial output, the structural conditions sustaining the subalternization of women in narrative representation survives in the new state's forging of an emancipated, masculine, national identity.

In effect, Beverley's and Barnet's formulations of testimonio are neither mutually exclusive nor fully commensurate with each other's, and ultimately the most serious problems facing testimonio discourse (the literal and the literary, subaltern expression and de-subalternization) can be traced to their constitutive tension. The objective here is not to resolve this tension by privileging one term or one set over the other. Rather it is to consider the full implications of the ambiguous conceptual space lying between them— the threshold of signification that separates, divides, unifies, and sustains— which presents an altogether distinct and unpredictable space of theoretical reflection. Beverley and Barnet's discursive relationship is not solely born as a result of their political commensurability, nor necessarily out of moments of theoretical convergence; they come to constitute testimonio discourse as they represent each other's conceptual limits. It is from the vantage point of their mutual incommensurability, not their confluence, that the critical stakes of testimonio begin to arise, and where my discussion takes root.

Informed by these larger stakes in testimonio criticism, we can now direct our attention to *Me llamo Rigoberta Menchú*, this time, however, geared toward a critical reading of testimonio discourse's semiotic contradictions and breakdowns. Elizabeth Burgos's introduction to this testimonio provides a key point of entry, as it shows an uneasy and catachrestic adherence to Beverley's and Barnet's theoretical formalizations.

It is important to note that the structure of Burgos's introduction is not without precedent. In fact many of the methodological components of testimonio writing that we saw in Barnet's "La novela-testimonio" we also see outlined in Burgos's introduction, from Barnet's insistence on the writer's solidarity with the informant and knowledge of the geohistorical context to his assertion that creative liberties need to be taken in the transcription process as well as in narrative construction. It would not be accidental that Burgos, writing in the early 1980s, would rely on sources such as Barnet, as well as manuals from journalists like Margaret Randall (1983), to ground her testimonio writing.[16]

And this programmatic adherence is felt throughout Burgos's introduction. In the following excerpt she details the moment when she realizes she has gained Menchú's trust; while preparing a meal together, Burgos notes Menchú's rule of thumb regarding the issue of solidarity in testimonio production: "'We only trust people who eat what we eat,' she told me one day as she tried to explain the relationship between the guerillas and the Indian communities. I suddenly realized that she had begun to trust me. A relationship based upon food [*oralmente*] proves that there are areas where Indians and non-Indians can meet and share things: the tortillas and black beans brought us together because they gave us the same pleasure and awakened the same drives in both of us" (Menchú and Burgos-Debray 1984: xvi; 1983: 14).[17] This passage is significant to the extent that it establishes narratologically the solidarity between Burgos and Menchú. Moreover this moment enacts Burgos's "mirroring" of Menchú's identity; the creation of a literary "double" necessary for testimonial writing. For Barnet (1983a: 33), this doubling is a necessary condition, suggesting that "within this relationship between author-protagonist or investigator-informant, one must foster this doubling [*desdoblamiento*]. In other words, to try to live the other's life, to build a solid bridge of affects and dependencies."

This trust, and the mirroring capacity it is premised on, will find its payoff when Burgos discusses her conception of what the testimonio's narrative structure will look like. After describing the initial process of transcription and annotation, she begins work on a manuscript, giving it a form: "I soon reached the decision to give the manuscript the form of a monologue: that was how it came back to me as I re-read it. I therefore decided to delete all my questions. By doing so I became what I really was: Rigoberta's listener. I allowed her to speak and then became her instrument, her double [*doble*] by allowing her to make the transition from the spoken to the written word" (Menchú and Burgos-Debray 1984: xx; 1983: 20). Again Burgos's explicit use of the idea of the double should not surprise us. However, we should note the literary and cultural value this doubling brings about. It facilitates the creative appropriation of oral accounts in testimonio writing; however, understood within Barnet's literary program, it also signals a mode of solidarity formation that is incommensurate with the political conditions of the writing of Menchú's testimonio. In *Me llamo Rigoberta Menchú*, the relationship between Burgos and Menchú is not one between two members of a national, cultural, or ethnic community but rather one that Beverley (1989: 18) calls an *ideologeme*, "a figure denoting a union or radicalized intelligentsia and the poor and working classes of a country." We must remember that in Barnet (1983a: 34) we are dealing with a literary project focused on a singular national community and that this doubling acts as an instrument intent on consolidating a national "we": "I mentioned that this produced a self-detachment [*desprendimiento*]. It also produces a de-individualization [*despersonalización*]; one then becomes the other, and only then can one begin to think like him, talk like him, to intimately feel the knocks of life which are conveyed by the informant, to feel them the way he does. Therein lies the poetry, the mystery that this type of work brings. And, logically, this door opens to permit entry into our collective conscience, the 'we' [*nosotros*]." In Barnet's view, these features (the "poetry" and the "we") are inextricably woven into the fabric of testimonio writing. As a product of the writer's self-detachment and de-individualization, testimonio ultimately rests on the writer's ability to reproduce the cultural and social sentiments of the testimonial subjects and to constitute the ideals of their particular community through them. Consequently Burgos's adherence to Barnet's methodological principles results in a paradoxically heteroclite framing of Menchú's testimonio: a mode of testimonial production whose investment in authenticity and realism breaches the undefined limits of solidarity with both Menchú as an indigenous, social actor and the compiled, transcribed material.

The complications resulting from these critical investments are most clearly evidenced in Burgos's introduction. One such instance is her editorial decision to "correct" Menchú's grammar: "I also decided to correct the gender mistakes which inevitably occur when someone had just learned to speak a foreign language. It would have been artificial to leave them uncorrected and it would have made Rigoberta look 'picturesque,' which is the last thing I wanted" (Menchú and Burgos-Debray 1984: xxi; 1983: 21). To correct or not to correct? How are we to understand the "artificiality" Burgos invokes? Is she suggesting that Menchú's uncorrected grammar is too literal, and as such too unrealistic? As it seems to be understood here, this artificiality is located precisely in those textual moments that would normally be considered literal: the unmediated, uncorrected transcription of Menchú's recorded voice during the taped interviews. According to Burgos, it is the immediacy and rawness of the text that, if left intact, would reproduce such an artifice. This statement might seem counterintuitive to those who see the transcription of taped interviews conducted in Spanish as anything but a literary text. But in fact the reverse is true: within testimonial discourse, the literal becomes artificial. The poles between the literal and the literary, it seems, have been reversed, as have their conventional roles with notions of artificiality and authenticity. In this case, as in the case of indigenismo and the stylistic appropriation of orality we saw in chapter 2, the literal is surrendered, paradoxically, in favor of authenticity. Thus the decision to make the corrections to Menchú's grammar for the sake of avoiding artificiality and picturesque presentations positions the stamp of testimonial authenticity squarely in the hands of its "literariness."

If the literal is simply too inauthentic for Burgos, and if literal depictions are thus at odds with testimonio production, then to what extent is her anthropological introduction to the figure of Menchú—as both an authentic indigenous subject and one worthy of a testimonio—grounded along this disciplinary matrix? As we see here, the discourses of indigeneity and orality merge into an authentic voice that will speak truth and simplicity to our "inhuman" and "artificial" world. Further, Burgos presents Menchú as a subject who will be communicating with us orally, from that conceptual space where everything has meaning and where language remains authentic: simple, self-present, unambiguous, and true:

> That is why we have to listen to Rigoberta Menchú's appeal and allow ourselves to be guided by a voice whose inner cadences are so pregnant with meaning that we actually seem to hear her speaking and can almost hear her breathing. . . . Quietly, but proudly, she leads us into her own cultural world, a world in which the sacred and the profane constantly mingle, in which every gesture has a pre-established purpose and in which everything has meaning. Within that culture, everything is determined in advance; everything that occurs in the present can be explained in terms of the past and has to be ritualized so as to be integrated into everyday life, which is itself a ritual. As we listen to her voice, we have to look deep into our own souls for it awakens sensations and feelings which we, caught up as we are in an inhuman and artificial world, thought were lost for ever. Her story is overwhelming because what she has to say is simple and true. As she speaks, we enter a strikingly different world which is poetic, and often tragic, a world which has forged the thought of a great popular leader. (Menchú and Burgos-Debray 1984: xii–xiii; 1983: 9)

Burgos presents Menchú to the reader as a figure urging our attention, a "guide" who will narrate not only an individual's story but the story of an entire indigenous culture. Moreover, with Burgos's use of anthropological discourse ("sacred," "profane," "ritual") to conceive of Menchú's cultural grounding, not unlike Vargas Llosa's treatment of the same in chapter 2, she presents Menchú as coming from a culture where folkloric and traditional customs, and not writing, continue to provide that culture with meaning. In this passage, Menchú's nonliteracy serves as the foundation of her indigenous authenticity and the condition of possibility for the writing of the testimonio itself. We are presented with an indigenous figure whose voice is authenticated by her literary appropriation, but yet whose cultural authenticity is nevertheless grounded in her inability to either derive or produce meaning through writing. However, as we saw earlier, Burgos also chose to correct Menchú's grammatical mistakes—the "improper" but necessary inscription of Menchú's cultural authenticity—precisely because "to leave them uncorrected would have been artificial." So, once again, which one is it: the literary or the literal?

This simple question, though misleading (because it posits a choice), is significant because, taken together, these two contradictory instances of cultural appropriation place the very concept of authenticity into crisis. There is no either/or here. Only the multiple and contradictory attempts at authenticity in *Me llamo Rigoberta Menchú*—as a restitutive form of disciplinary practice—are revealed as at odds with themselves, in excess of themselves. Menchú's simultaneous and contradictory figuration within both literalness and literariness—to the extent that they are distinct categories and insofar as their categorical integrity can be maintained—neither establishes nor negates her cultural authenticity; instead this confrontation of oppositional reading codes disarticulates the possibility of authentication for either the object of representation (Menchú) or presumed disciplinary knowledge of the other (Latinamericanism) within testimonio criticism. Burgos's editorial choice between correcting an assumed nonliterate subject's grammar or emphasizing her oral cultural formation as radically other is not really a choice—upon which the redemption of Menchú hinges—but rather an irreconcilable symptom of what Alberto Moreiras (2001: 147–58) calls "restitutional excess." The issue here is not the authentic grammar through which Menchú will utter meaning but the assumption that there is authentic meaning to be had in the first place.

This collapse of authenticating—meaning-producing—structures is further illustrated later in the introduction, when Burgos issues a warning to the reader that during the testimonio-writing process she shared with Menchú, she had neither special nor prior knowledge of Guatemalan culture or society. It is important to note that despite Barnet's (1983a: 35) insistence on creative appropriation in testimonio writing, he also urges a focus on historical contextualization and accuracy: "With the informant in hand, one needs to take another step. The other is historical investigation, documentation, research, knowledge of the epoch and of its historical moments, social acts in which this subject found himself participating. A serious understanding of the period, scientific knowledge, is fundamental." In contrast, Burgos concedes her lack of knowledge of the Guatemalan cultural landscape in which Menchú's testimonio is grounded. However, more significant than this admission is her assertion that this testimonial disability actually worked to her advantage as it ultimately produced a more "realistic" portrait:

> I must first warn the reader that, although I did train as an ethnographer, I have never studied Maya-Quiché culture and have never done field work in Guatemala. Initially, I thought that knowing nothing about Rigoberta's culture would be a handicap, but it soon proved to be a positive advantage. I was able to adopt the position of someone who is learning. Rigoberta soon realized this: that is why her descriptions of ceremonies and rituals are so detailed. Similarly, if we had been in her home in El Quiché her descriptions of the landscape would not have been so realistic. (Menchú and Burgos-Debray 1984: xix; 1983: 18)

Burgos suggests that the "realism" gained from these interviews are a result of Menchú's perceiving that Burgos necessitated more detailed responses from her. But this statement also prompts a more critical question of location and cultural displacement. Might this statement also suggest that were it not for the fact that it was Menchú who was in a position of geographical displacement, and not Burgos herself, the testimonio would have been less "realistic"? In other words, would this testimonio in fact have been less realistic if it had been written in the province of El Quiché instead of Paris? Though we are familiar with the story leading to Menchú's and Burgos's encounter and why Menchú happened to be in Paris at the time, it behooves us to ask not whether Menchú's testimonio is sufficiently realistic but rather what is at stake in the claim of testimonial realism in *Me llamo Rigoberta Menchú*. Is this testimonio's greater or lesser degree of realism really what is at issue here? Would that lesser degree of realism be akin to the artificiality Burgos previously tried to avoid when deciding to correct Menchú's grammar?

As we have seen, Beverley (1989: 14, 15) argues that any critical stance with testimonio needs to begin with an emphasis on testimonio's real and anti-literary features, as noted in the following statements from "The Margin at the Center": "Unlike the novel, testimonio promises by definition to be primarily concerned with sincerity rather than literariness" and "[Testimonio] is not, to begin with, fiction. We are meant to experience both the speaker and the situations and events as real. The 'legal' connotation implicit in its convention implies a pledge of honesty on the part of the narrator which the listener/reader is bound to respect." Similar to Beverley's "promise" that testimonio be primarily concerned with "sincerity rather than literariness," Burgos also evokes an adherence to principles of authenticity and realism in the writing of *Me llamo Rigoberta Menchú*. Though they are not necessarily the stylistic qualities emphasized by Barnet, they are nevertheless realized through his programmatic insistence on the creative appropriation (erasure) of all that is literal (that is, artificial) in the published text. According to Burgos, the need to correct Menchú's grammar, as well as her acknowledgment of unfamiliarity with Menchú's culture, proved necessary to provide a more "realistic" account than it would have otherwise. Burgos's introduction thus becomes symptomatic of this genre's heteroclite and catachrestic nature: the extent to which testimonio is authenticated by assumptions of its "sincerity" and "reality" (the literal) but even more so by its poetic nature (the literary). In it one encounters a contradictory and strangely redundant problem: contradictory in that the literal and the literary are by all accounts (supposed to be) two distinct cognitive categories, and yet redundant in that neither Barnet, Beverley, nor even Burgos herself is able to prevent the two semiotic codes from seeping into each other. Instead they have served only to further entrench this foundational contradiction within testimonio discourse. But again, is realism ultimately what is at stake in testimonio production?

In Barnet, Burgos, and Beverley we see an insistence that testimonial signification is produced from the discursive consonance between writer and informant. The results of this conceptualization, however, have led to precisely the very tension I have been tracing: the irrevocable and irreducible tension between the literal and the literary. Instead we have seen that at the thresholds of testimonial critique lies a foundational fissure, a kernel of insignification and nonsignifiability between literal and literary codes. Does this tension represent the limits of testimonio discourse? Or does it instead signal its heteroclite conditions of possibility? Setting aside, for the moment, the discussion between Barnet, Burgos, and Beverley, I will attempt to show how Doris Sommer's essay "Rigoberta's Secrets," Brett Levinson's "Neopatriarchy and After," and Moreiras's "The Aura of Testimonio" opt for the latter possibility. These readings illustrate that the ground of testimonio discourse is not necessarily to be found in the literal or literary production of meaning, nor in some hybrid form or mixture of the two, but rather in the illiterate core that vouches for their semiological distinctness. As we will see, the governing principle within testimonio is neither literal nor literary, but entirely illiterate.

Doris Sommer's well-known reading of *Me llamo Rigoberta Menchú* is of critical importance to this discussion, and one that needs particular attention. Having appeared in many forms and phases, it was first published in 1991, has since been translated into Spanish (1992), appears in *The Real Thing* (1996), and subsequently appears as a chapter in her book *Proceed with Caution* (1999). Departing from the conventions that derive meaning from the writer and informant's assumed solidarity and theoretically unilateral utterance, Sommer's essay instead seeks out another pattern of signification that emerges from this always already fissured, problematic relationship. Sommer constructs a mode of analysis that reads meaning precisely in those moments where the writer and informant are at odds and not at all speaking in unison. In other words, "Rigoberta's Secrets" represents a critical analysis of meaning production in testimonio, premised not simply on Burgos and Menchú's solidarity but on the tensions resulting from the tenuous and limited terms of their solidarity.

In this essay, Sommer examines Menchú's appeals to secrecy as a self-reflexive form of resistance to unequal structures of power found within testimonial narrative, emphasizing the rhetorical role her secretive gestures plays not only in the upholding of cultural barriers and memory but also in the withholding of information, in marking the limits of reading practices that presume a totalization of knowledge from an inscribed, literate text. As a response to those moments when Menchú purposely withholds information, Sommer (1991b: 34) asks, "How then are we to take Rigoberta's protestations of silence as she continues to talk? Are there really many secrets that she is not divulging, in which case her restraint would be true or real? Or is she performing a kind of rhetorical, fictional, seduction in which she lets the fringe of a hidden text show in order to tease us into thinking that the fabric must be extraordinarily complicated and beautiful, even though there may not be much more than fringe to show?" With this series of questions Sommer begins an analysis of *Me llamo Rigoberta Menchú* in which she reads Menchú's resistance as the cause and not the result of a reader's interest in her cultural formation. What Sommer recognizes in this narrative dynamic between Menchú and Burgos is a rhetorical strategy deployed not only to keep hidden those secrets that Menchú cannot divulge but also, through its repetition, to further obfuscate the cultural depths of her secrecy. In other words, Menchú's every successive appeal to secrecy would safeguard against isolating and identifying information that is of actual, cultural significance by delimiting the space of secrecy to include information that might or might not be of equal importance to her community's continued survival. In this regard the preservation of memory is what is at stake in Menchú's secrets. This is preserved through a supplementing of subaltern memory with traditions, experiences, "secrets" that might or might not exist, have taken place, or have any cultural significance whatsoever.

Sommer's reading of Menchú's text, what in the introduction to *Proceed with Caution* (1999) she identifies as "particularist" rhetoric, while specifically examining the decisions Menchú makes with regard to disclosing or refusing to disclose important cultural details, is ultimately concerned with marking testimonio's interpretive limits, that is, to arrest tendencies in textual analysis that aim for complete exegetical mastery, which she calls "universalist" reading practice (xii). Because of this, "Rigoberta's Secrets" is one of the few contributions to survive the empiricist turn in testimonio criticism in the post-Stoll era. This textual strategy, which Sommer attributes to Menchú, ultimately makes it impossible for the reader to ascertain which of all the information is of any real value; these limitations therefore call attention to the secret as a site of the text's illegibility.

> My reason for posing the question of rhetorical strategy, about
> whether Rigoberta is persuading or troping, is to be able to read
> appropriately and responsibly this text which ceaselessly calls attention
> to its difference and to the danger of overstepping cultural barriers.

Personally, I prefer to think that her secrets are more "literary" than
"real." Let me explain why. Reading her refusal of absolute intimacy as
a deliberate textual strategy, whether or not much data come between
the producer and consumer of this text, makes the gesture more self-
conscious and repeatable than it would be if she merely remained silent
on particular issues. The gesture precisely is not silence but a rather
flamboyant refusal of information. Calling attention to an unknowable
subtext is a profound lesson, because it hopes to secure Rigoberta's
cultural identity, of course, but also because it is an imitable trope.
(Sommer 1991b: 36)

Sommer attempts to construct the means for an appropriate and responsible
approach to Menchú's testimonio. This is accomplished through a
reconceptualization of the terms that constitute the distance between
Menchú and her readers: from one of power and knowledge operating
unilaterally from informant to interrogator to one between coalitional
"allies." As Sommer's states, "Any way we read her, we are either intellectually
or ethically unfit for Rigoberta's secrets, so that our interpretation does
not vary the effect of reading. Either way, it produces a particular kind
of distance akin to respect" (36). For Sommer, the reader must contend
with the indeterminacy resulting from the logic of the secrecy rather than
the secrets themselves. To the "outsider," this indeterminacy determines,
metonymically, the nature and function of Rigoberta's secrets. More than
simply signaling the existence of culturally sensitive information, the secret
in this case also marks the impossibility of its textual ascertainment.

However, Sommer's assertion that Rigoberta's secrets are ultimately
"more literary than real" also destabilizes the conceptual grounds of
the testimonio itself, even those parts that are not necessarily deployed
as secrets. Though Sommer never contends that all of Menchú's secrets
are of dubious character, her charge is that some of them might be, and
this would be sufficient as an obfuscating rhetorical strategy. But aside
from the verifiability of this or that secret's content, secretiveness is an
epistemologically unsettling quality that often exceeds itself, particularly
when it is deployed as an authenticating strategy. Stoll's critique of *Me llamo
Rigoberta Menchú* illustrates exactly that: a charge of misrepresentation and
conspiracy resulting from statements made by Menchú uttered while under
the confidence of disclosure and not secrecy. In Stoll's case, statements made

under disclosure were read and treated as if they were one of Menchú's innumerable secrets. Therefore, in a discussion regarding her secrets, we assuredly cannot continue to limit our consideration to only those moments where she explicitly refuses to answer. By continuing to do so we would only reproduce the stability and plentitude of the rest of the text's nonsecret (real) parts.

This proves to be a particularly salient limitation in Sommer's essay. Her distinction between the secret (literary) and disclosure (real), deployed to reinforce epistemological and "respectful" barriers between testimonial subject and reader, ultimately reconstitutes the literal-literary tension yet again. For instance, if, according to Sommer, Menchú's appeals to secrecy are literary, then what are we to make of the rest of her testimonial text? Is it then, to use Sommer's oppositional category, "real"? Are the "real" parts of the text any more trustworthy and reliable than the secretive parts? Is not the real as indeterminate a category within testimonio discourse, if not more so, than the secret? Under these conditions, does not the secret actually become the less indeterminate of the two? Ultimately the secret in *Me llamo Rigoberta Menchú* functions as the absolute source of authentic signification from which the reader must turn away, not because it cannot be read but simply to maintain the reader's "respectful distance" from Menchú's culture. Or as Moreiras (2001: 231) suggests:

> A tenuous fetishization thus insinuates itself into Sommer's reading. Testimonio becomes the privileged site for the critical affirmation of an interpretive reticence in which radicalized restitution finds its own excess and passes over into criticism's self-redemption. Criticism is thus able to refigure its own aura at the expense of textual reticence and precisely in virtue of its relationship with it. . . . In Sommer's essay there is no prosopopeic chatter, but silence, identical to itself, and therefore in itself its own end, has here been made to speak, and thus also tropologized as that which is beyond the "impassible" limit. Spectacular redemption reaches thus its own specularity.

To read or not to read? This line of analysis—regardless of which of the two strategies is privileged—nevertheless continues to limit our discussion of testimonio to one between the literal (real) and the literary (secret) codes of meaning production. In this case, the latter is at the service of the former. The secret, Sommer's contribution to testimonio criticism, though it serves as a compelling instance of indeterminacy within testimonio, is nevertheless neutralized by the language Sommer uses to articulate its critical value (i.e., "literary" and not "real"). Instead, I argue, one must seek moments in *Me llamo Rigoberta Menchú* that signal another semiotic register of (in)expressibility, one not limited to the withholding or the disclosing of truth, as Sommer claims, but one that marks the uneven and incomplete processes of literacy within sociocultural conditions of nonliteracy and multilingualism. Here Sommer's (1991b: 43) remark on the text's play of orality and literacy proves crucial: "Beyond revealing the traces and scars of translation, as well as the liberating tropes that come from code-switching, the book retains an unmistakable oral quality through the edited and polished version that reaches us. As a device, the orality helps to account for the testimonial's construction of a collective self." Sommer conceives of the testimonio's oral quality as traces, scars resulting from editing and transcription. She conceives of this characteristic as a literary device, much like Menchú's appeals to secrecy, in the "testimonial's construction of a collective self." Sommer also asserts that these unmistakable qualities nevertheless appear "through the edited and polished version that reaches us." The question then is whether this oral quality appears *as a result* of the edited and polished version or *despite* the text's editing and polish. In other words, are the visible traces and scars of orality in this testimonio—minor imperfections that most assuredly guarantee a stamp of authenticity—the result of Burgos's correcting of Menchú's grammar, or do they appear despite them? Does the oral quality that appears in this text signal the source of a secret, the medium of the secret, or is it yet another instance of the rhetoric of secrecy?

Previous to this moment in Sommer's (1991b: 32) essay, she states, "What I find noteworthy here is that Rigoberta's refusal to tell secrets remains on the page after the editing is done. Either the informant, or scribe, or both were determined to keep a series of admonitions in the published text." Here Sommer suggests that regardless of the reasons why these appeals to secrecy remained in the finalized version, the secrets themselves represent a key point of entry into *Me llamo Rigoberta Menchú.* However, the "unmistakable oral quality" also evidenced in this testimonio signals another such critical aperture. Are these two characteristics related? To the extent that both the secretive and the oral qualities remained in the text's final form and are both articulated by Sommer as constitutive of this testimonio's literary apparatus, to what extent are these two dynamics determinate of each other's discursive function? Are they mutually exclusive or coterminous of testimonio's literal-literary tension? To what extent is Menchú's orality the cause or the product of her secrecy? Or perhaps to what extent is Menchú's secrecy the cause or the product of her orality?

Brett Levinson's essay "Neopatriarchy and After" (1996) provides a model with which to engage testimonio from the illiterate zone of indistinction revealed by this economy of reading —the literal and the literary, subaltern expression and de-subalternization, and the secret and disclosure—that both constitutes and unbinds it simultaneously.[18] His analysis culminates in the following assertion:

> All of this means, at bottom, that the ground of Menchú's discourse
> can only be an antinomy: the uncoupling of affliction and translation.
> Indeed, a "properly" indigenous discourse, *I, Rigoberta Menchú*
> shows us, is not one in which Western concepts are translated and
> transformed so as to reflect an indigenous "space." Nor does an
> indigenous discourse do the opposite: resist those Western paradigms.
> Within an indigenous discourse, rather, language cannot reflect its
> referent; representation is not even *like* the "territory"—agony—to
> which it bears witness. Suffering and injury, therefore, do not supply a
> foundation for a true understanding of this suffering; they do not yield
> or ground truth ("truth" understood as the adequation of language to
> reality, translation to a territory, thought to actuality, concept to the
> real) since the discourse that the misery "generates" is neither adequate
> nor inadequate to the misery itself but non-relational. In short, the
> "origin" and "essence" of indigenismo is neither language (testimony)
> nor the real (crime, oppression, death, suffering, silence) that precedes
> language but the incompatibility of the two. It is not the case that
> indigenous languages and discourses, necessarily caught up in the
> West, are incompatible with the actual indigenous situation. It is that
> the incompatibility is itself the indigenous situation. (46)

Levinson points to the productive, though debilitating, tensions in testimonio discourse, though neither to suggest a privileging of one over the other nor to propose a reading that reconciles them but rather to conceive of the two as mutually incompatible and inextricable formalizations. Seeing that testimonio's deployment of "non-rhetorical, non-aesthetic, non-fictional, direct, every-day" (47) language nevertheless exceeds literary adequation ("language cannot reflect its referent"), or that to privilege "the real" over the literary necessarily exceeds its textual limits ("Suffering and injury do not yield or ground truth"), Levinson instead offers an analysis conceived from the thresholds of their mutual exclusivity and inadequation, from the aperture revealed by the "non-relation" between the language of testimonio and its object. In short, he provides a reading that goes beyond the limitations of the literal-literary that unconceals testimonio's irrevocably illiterate ground. By radicalizing both the terms and the configuration of testimonio's (il)legibility, he reaches its vacuous, illiterate core. Specifying:

> Within indigenous circumstances, therefore, language and actuality
> *qua* agony form a discordant semiotics, one that is non-dialectical since
> the battle takes place neither between reality and discourse nor between
> two discourses, but between a single territory that is doubly informed:
> between a reality that is utterly linguistic, and between language that
> does not represent but includes the real (as pain and suffering) as one
> of its "signs." These components that make up the fragmented origin of
> contemporary indigenismo—testimony and oppression, translation and
> agony, speech and annihilation, communication and death—are not
> only incompatible, they are inseparable. (47)

Far from signaling a radical break between "the real" and testimonio discourse, Levinson proposes a reading of Menchú's testimonio from the fissures ("discordant semiotics") of its own discursive formalization, from the collapse of the two poles of testimonio discourse: literary language and the always already literary real. Which is to say, the real is no longer simply a referent subject to literary (in)adequation but itself another register of signification, though incompatibly and inextricably semiological. The tension therefore takes place not between two categories of literacy (the literal and the literary) but within the heteroclite nature of Literacy itself (illiteracy); "the foundational antinomy," he adds, "contrary to appearances, is not between discourse and a non-discursive topos, the antinomy is between discourse and itself" (46). Ultimately, the fact that testimonio's discursive grounds are of such a contradictory nature is neither accidental nor contingent; it is the very condition of testimoniality, what Moreiras (2001: 213) calls testimonio's "unguarded possibility." What is therefore at stake in Levinson's intervention is that the terms grounding testimonio discourse are themselves always already inextricably and incompatibly infused into the logic of its own (il)legibility, from within a "discordant semiotics" that not only is symptomatically inexpressible, silent, and illegible, but is itself the silence and illegibility of testimonio discourse.

While for Sommer interpretive reticence in the face of Menchú's secret becomes the lesson in *Me llamo Rigoberta Menchú*, for Levinson it is the secret's absolute reticence itself. Like Cornejo Polar, who saw in the indigenista novel a necessarily flawed and structurally inadequate narrative project, but who also saw its failures as its most critical contribution for Peruvian cultural politics, Levinson positions the incommensurability of the literary and the literal in testimonio in much the same way. However, unlike what we saw in indigenista narrative, where the particular dynamic exists between the discourse of orality and literacy, what we see here are the traces of illegibility signaled by the disjunction of the literal and the literary as competing and oppositional modes of representation: the (in)adequation of the language of testimonio and the illiterate semiology that is the real.

But what of this illegibility? What does Levinson mean by it? And what does Levinson attempt to do with it? His essay concludes with the following statement:

> As a book written in Spanish, mass-produced, easily translated and sent across the globe, *I Rigoberta Menchú* does something that other indigenous testimonies were never able to do: it renders both the destruction and appeal to justice (or the impossibility of that appeal) of the indigenous peoples *legible* to the West, although that legibility betrays the illegibility, the "secret" marks inscribed into the Quiché-Mayan experience itself. But *I, Rigoberta Menchú* is unique for another reason, caught as it is in a most traditional Western literary trope, the book or tome as tomb, signed (co-signed) by the author. Menchú's *testimonio* does not supply a voice for the voiceless, it supplies this voicelessness with something else entirely: a grave-site, an engraving, a name, an epitaph, a stone and a burial, however belated and improper. (1996: 48)

While Levinson provides no extended articulation of what he means by "illegibility" except as yet another "secret," he does conceive of it as the trace of the ultimately inexpressible condition of possibility for the legibility of Menchú's "appeal to justice." At the core of this legibility lies a kernel of insignification, of an inexpressibility that sustains the tension between the literal and the literary. As Levinson notes, Menchú does not "supply a voice for the voiceless"; she supplies yet another register of signification entirely illegible. This semiotic (in)expressivity is premised upon secrecy, nonliterality, and nonliterariness—an ultimately illiterate and unregistrable semiosis. The secrecy, in this case, represents what is inexpressible under any circumstances, whether through ethical or political impulses or whether because the secret is literally inexpressible.

In contrast to Sommer's conceptualization of Menchú's secretiveness, wherein she posits Menchú's moments of secrecy as the responsible limit to meaning, Levinson proposes these secrets as the cultural trace of the allegorically constitutive moment of Menchú's testimoniality, one that cannot be made legible or is rendered illegible at the expense of making legible her culture's appeals to justice. In other words, what Levinson's essay allows us to consider is whether, in her secrecy, her inability to express those key cultural codes, Menchú acts not in the role of individual agent, strategically withholding information to attain certain political (Beverley) and/or rhetorical (Sommer) objectives, and not from the transculturative effects of collective mourning where her silence acts as the "defensive foundation" of the "Maya-Quiché's cultural politics of resistance" (Williams 1993), but from testimonio's "unguarded" possibility: the threshold of illiteracy where orality, the literal, and the literary are revealed as refracted (artificial and contingent) relations generated from sheer relationality itself. As Moreiras (2001: 228) asserts, "I would claim that the secret, in Menchú's text, stands for whatever cannot and should not be reabsorbed into the literary-representational system: the secret is the (secret) key to the real as unguarded possibility." What if the secrets Menchú is beholden to are literally inexpressible? What if Menchú's secrets are unredeemable, even as secrets? And further, what if the secrets Menchú carries with her are ultimately secrets even to her?

An instance of this appears in the first few pages of *Me llamo Rigoberta Menchú*. In chapter 2, "Birth Ceremonies," Menchú recounts her community's cultural practices in preparation for the introduction of its newborn members. Some of the rituals she details include the mother and child's temporary isolation from the rest of the family and the binding of the child's hands for eight days, as well as other gender-specific customs for newborn babies. In addition, forty days after a child is born, a ceremony takes place in which the child is inducted into the indigenous community via a series of performative gestures, one of which is a public declaration from the parents that commits them to raise the child based on their indigenous traditions and to teach the child the importance of keeping the nature of these traditions hidden from the rest of the world. Menchú (1983: 48) writes, "The parents then make a commitment. That they need to teach the child . . . — referring most often to our ancestors—that the child learn to keep all of our secrets, so that no one can put an end to our culture, to our customs [Hacen un compromiso. Que los padres tienen que enseñarle al niño . . . — más que todo se refiere mucho a los antepasados—que aprenda a guardar a todos los secretos, que nadie pueda acabar con nuestra cultura, con nuestras costumbres]."[19] Here Menchú indicates that, as one of the most important customs the community needs to pass on, the child needs to learn to keep the secrets of her ancestors. However, this might mean not simply learning the secrets themselves but learning *how* to keep secrets secret. Reading this passage in the context of her entire discussion on maternity and parenting in indigenous culture, is it possible that she is performing exactly what she needed to learn how to do as a child? In other words, in the midst of her discussion of the rituals of childbirth and child rearing, in which a significant amount of culturally sensitive information is disclosed, she also evokes a child's necessary adherence to a principle of secrecy. Is she simply telling us that, in addition to all the other rituals and customs, the child needs to learn how to keep secrets, or rather, in a more self-reflexive gesture, is she *showing* us how the child learns to keep secrets? In other words, how can we be sure that the cultural information provided by Menchú in her testimonio is reliable and authentic, particularly when one of the characteristics of the community, of which she is a member, is learning how to keep secrets? Is she depicting actual birth ceremonies of her indigenous culture, or are they cultural inventions that might not have any cultural significance except as her own culture's form of preserving the actual secrets of their birth ceremonies? How would we know the difference?

Inadvertently or not, the text creates an illiterate tension between what the reader could take to be a description of actual indigenous customs or a series of ethnographical fabrications deployed to occlude them. From this there is no escape. This is a symptom, Moreiras (2001: 213) suggests, that results from what the testimonial experience necessarily brings about: "Testimonio provides its reader with the possibility of entering what we could call a subdued sublime: the twilight region where the literary breaks off into something else that is not so much the real as it is its unguarded possibility. This unguarded possibility of the real, which is arguably the very core of the testimonial experience, is also its preeminent political claim." Nowhere is this "unguarded possibility of the real" more clearly presented than in the passage cited earlier, where Menchú's simple description of indigenous customs could also be an enactment of the very measures she is describing. But further, Menchú's statement evinces a semiotic register that exceeds the restitutional distinction between authentic (literary) and counterfeit (literal) indigenous customs. Instead what one witnesses as the "unguarded possibility of the real" is the authentic breakdown of the literal and literary as modes of testimonial restitution. Evidence of the restitutional excess Moreiras diagnoses can be located in the passage's grammatical rendition. Looked at carefully, the first phrase of the second sentence begins "That they need to teach the child" but is immediately suspended by an ellipsis and followed by a phrase of differing sentence structure, one not in syntactical agreement with the initial phrase. While the subjects of the initial phrase are the parents ("they need to teach"), the subject in the second phrase transitions to the child ("that the child learn"). Meanwhile, separating these two statements is an ellipsis, signaling a pause, an interruption, a suspension of signification disconnecting the two syntactical arrangements.

Informed by the fact that this testimonio is a product of a transcription process, whereby Menchú's oral account is rendered in written, "grammared" form, the ellipsis, it seems, might not only represent Burgos's rendition of an intermittent silence in Menchú's vocally recorded utterance but might also signal Menchú's sudden reluctance to continue in the syntagmatic progression in which the statement was leading her. Under Sommer's analysis, the ellipsis might have signaled a moment in which Menchú recognized a syntactical danger, identified a potential fault line in her sentence structure that would have inadvertently disclosed information too sensitive for the Western interlocutor, that is, "what [exactly] the parents need to teach." Sensing this, she pauses, interrupts the signifying flow of the initial phrase, recalculates her syntax, and reframes the statement. The ellipsis might inadvertently mark Menchú's sudden realization that her diction was about to betray her cultural contract and thus disarticulates the information she was about to disclose with a sentence beginning "That they need to teach the child," instead providing us with what "the child needs to learn." To Sommer's reader, the ellipsis might confirm that Menchú is critically aware of the stakes of her grammar, of its capacity to produce signification despite the intentions of the uttering subject. It signals the possibility that whatever the secret at stake here, Menchú knows that it would be obfuscated and protected by a simple paradigmatic substitution of subjects (the parents, the child) and imperative verbs ("to teach," "to learn").

Nevertheless, though we are told that the child needs to learn to keep secrets, we are never told what exactly the parents must teach, what exactly the child must keep secret; we are never given the predicate for the statement beginning "That they need to teach the child" because the ellipsis interrupts what would have syntactically needed to follow ("that they need to teach the child x and y"). According to Burgos and critics like Beverley, what the parents need to teach, of course, is the very realm of orality: customs, folklore, ritual, in short everything assumed to provide indigenous ways of life with the appropriate meaning. On the other hand, "what the child needs to learn" constitutes the literate and literary strategies through which the child learns to hide and protect sensitive cultural content from the gaze and curiosity of the Westerner. What we are never given, however, is specifically "what the parents need to teach." Evidence of this culturally sensitive information is both signaled and forestalled by the ellipsis. The ellipsis thus marks not only the site of silence, pause, and interruption but also the space of her illiteracy, of her inexpressible secrecy: what is ultimately the semiotic threshold between what the parents need to *teach* and what the child needs to *learn*. But while this is simply, Sommer argues, Menchú purposefully withholding information too sacred to talk about, might it signal the possibility that, contrary to our assumptions about orality, secrecy, and indigeneity, the truth signaled by the ellipsis is ultimately inaccessible even to Menchú herself?

This critical revelation is not lost in Menchú, as it returns later in the narrative to reframe her own complicated indigenous subjectivity, as well as her relationship to testimonial production. This moment arises in her discussion over her mother's legacy and memory (chapter 30). In this chapter, Menchú laments over the fact that she did not learn as much from her mother as she now wishes she would have, that through the accidents of her family's life, many of her mother's lessons were in fact lost on her. Throughout the chapter Menchú's reflections signal a preference for her father and a profound disconnect between herself and her mother. On this point she observes, "As I said, my mother was brave but, nonetheless, I learned more from my father. I regret this very much now because my mother knew many things that I don't know, things like medicines and what she knew about nature. I know this as well, of course, but only on a general level, not at all profoundly" (1983: 340). And also "I love them both but I have to say that I grew up more at my father's side. My mother taught many people many things, but I didn't learn as much from her as I should have learned" (341). Menchú's assertion that she did not learn as much from her mother as she would have liked to, though evocative, nevertheless brings us back to the initial distinction between what needs to be *taught* and what needs to be *learned* in her culture. In this case, however, we are now shown Menchú coping with the secrets her now-deceased mother never taught her. And now, regretting her failure to learn them, and since the recuperation of these secrets is now an impossibility, Menchú, living under the cultural injunction to keep knowledge of her culture secret, finds herself in a position where she has to learn to keep secret those secrets she was never taught by her mother. Whatever knowledge has been lost between her and her mother is precisely the secret, precisely what cannot be known, even by Menchú herself. As such Menchú is not in possession of the authenticating knowledge that the discourse of orality assumes all oral subjects have. But further, neither is she in possession of the secrets that Sommer assumes she has. Ultimately the secrets Menchú keeps are secrets even to herself. Testimonio's real secret, understood here as the nonoral, nonliteral, and nonliterary—illiterate—conditions of secrecy itself, is signaled only by an ellipsis.

Moreiras (2001: 135) argues that Latinamericanism, of which testimonio constitutes a critical form, operates from a double injunction: "to reduce and preserve alterity." Testimonio criticism, as a particularly salient manifestation of Latinamericanism's discursive function, renders clearly visible the appeal and drive for the restitution of alterity, in this case the restitution of Rigoberta Menchú as an authenticatable, indigenous subject. What we see is that from the initial attempts at instituting the terms of her disciplinary appropriation into an object of study—the literal and/or the literary—something else transpires entirely, something that not only lays bare the contradictions of the literal and literary as an economy of reading, but that hastens its collapse. As a condition that Sommer reduces to the redemptive authenticity of Menchú's secrets, what Levinson calls "illegibility" and what Moreiras calls the "restitutional excess," what is ultimately revealed through the secret's inadequation to itself is the trace of the illiterate semiological exclusions that make testimonio even possible. The drive for meaning will always exceed itself, and, as in the case of Rigoberta Menchú, the attempts to extract restitutive meaning from her secrets—through oral, literal, and literary interpretive practices—simply confirms the vacuous core underwriting all claims to cultural authenticity, disciplinary knowledge, and narrative form.

Silence, Subalternity, the EZLN, and the Egalitarian Contingency

The Ejército Zapatista de Liberación Nacional (EZLN), a mobilized, intertribal association of indigenous peasants from the southern Mexican state of Chiapas, first appeared on the national and international political stage on January 1, 1994, when, on the very day the North American Free Trade Agreement went into effect, armed guerrillas stormed the municipal palace at San Cristobal de las Casas and issued the first Declaración de la Selva Lacandona (Declaration of the Lacandon Jungle).[1] In this communiqué, addressed both to the Mexican government and the public at large, the EZLN signaled its emergence as a militarized insurgency called upon to respond to the five hundred years of exploitation and injustice suffered by the indigenous peoples of southern Mexico, all of which the current government, as well as NAFTA, promises to perpetuate and intensify. Citing from Article 39 of the Mexican Constitution, which states, "The people have, at all times, the inalienable right to alter or modify their form of government," a clause also found in the U.S. Declaration of Independence, the EZLN declares an explicit issuance of war on the Mexican government "to restore legitimacy and the stability of the nation." The EZLN bases its demands that the Mexican government adhere to the rights of indigenous peoples as outlined in the 1917 Constitution, which the implementation of NAFTA in Mexico abrogates.

"Zapatista" in the group's name is a reference to the rebel leader Emiliano Zapata, a figure integral to the Revolution of 1911 and instrumental in the creation of the very 1917 Constitution that declared indigenous lands autonomous and set up the parameters for agrarian reform, and which is now threatened by NAFTA and the ruling Mexican political party. Linking its cause with the historical precedent established by Zapata (in the south) and Pancho Villa (in the north) during the Revolution, the EZLN justifies its existence as a continuation of their political legacy, stating, "We [the EZLN] are inheritors of the true builders of our nation [Zapata, Villa]. . . . Our struggle adheres to the [1917] Constitution and is inspired by its call to justice and equality." Registering not only as a call to arms but as a call for national and international solidarity, the slogan "Hoy decimos, ¡Basta!" (Today we say, enough is enough!) became synonymous with the EZLN's campaign not of independence but of a radical transformation of the Mexican state and national culture. In other words, and this is of paramount significance, the first Zapatista Declaración calls not for the creation of another state but for the restoration of a previous state in Mexican constitutionality.

The federal military in Chiapas was immediately mobilized in response to the attack at San Cristobal de las Casas, and violence erupted soon after. However, the huge outpouring of support for the Zapatistas, domestically and internationally, pressured the Mexican government to negotiate. A cease-fire was declared and cleared the way for negotiations, during which peace talks (*mesas de dialogo*) began. However, the EZLN soon abandoned the peace talks, but not before a minimal set of constitutional and economic agreements between the EZLN and the Mexican government, known as the San Andrés Accords, were signed by both parties on February 16, 1996 (Higgins 2001).

Of the many issues pertaining to the indigenous population in Chiapas, the San Andrés Accords contained the most crucial: recognition of the indigenous people's right to self-determination, regional autonomy, and recognition of the "community" as a political entity with legal status over municipal and agrarian matters. In addition, the 1992 amendment to Article 27 of the constitution that enabled foreign ownership of state lands previously allotted to indigenous communities was repealed. Though there were other issues drawn from the Zapatista list of demands to be discussed at these negotiations—including *mesas* on "democracy and justice," "well-being and development," "employment and housing," "reconciliation in Chiapas," and "women's rights in Chiapas,"—only the negotiations on indigenous rights produced this minimal accord. In short, what had initially begun as a regional declaration of war against the Mexican government had now, through a lengthy and tense negotiation process, resulted not only in a series of concessions by the state for the indigenous communities in Chiapas but also more sweeping reforms that affect the entire constitutional structure of Mexico and its population. The San Andrés Accords were not limited to reforms in the state of Chiapas, but ultimately, and more critically, they included significant changes to the Mexican Constitution's articulation of rights and land distribution. In other words, the reforms outlined in the Accords did more than promise restitution for the indigenous communities in southern Mexico; they promised a universal reconfiguration of democratic processes for all of Mexico's indigenous communities and citizens.

Meanwhile President Ernesto Zedillo, no doubt recognizing the full scale of the San Andrés Accords and the threat they posed to the current political system, refused to pass them into law, opting instead to increase the military presence in Chiapas to unprecedented levels. This led to the intervention by the federal government monitoring body, the Concord and Pacification Commission (Comisión de Concordia y Pacificación, COCOPA), to draft a new proposal as an initiative for constitutional reform. This proposal neglected to include many of the more crucial reform items originally included in the San Andrés Accords, such as those establishing land reform and distribution. The EZLN nevertheless accepted the terms proposed by the COCOPA proposal and were dealt an even stronger blow when the Mexican government then responded with its own counterproposal to the COCOPA resolution. Absent from the government's proposal now were numerous aspects related to Article 4 of the Mexican Constitution, the article relating to individual rights where the Accords relating to community rights were to be outlined. Also gone was the language relating to reform of Article 27. The EZLN ultimately rejected the counterproposal and abandoned the negotiating process altogether. The government's proposal was nevertheless included in the 2001 amendments to the Mexican Constitution, and since it contained none of the more critical issues previously addressed in the San Andrés Accords, it served merely to neutralize support for the EZLN by presenting an empty ceremony of constitutional reconciliation between the indigenous populations of Chiapas and the Mexican government.

Much has been written about the cultural and political impact of the EZLN's emergence since 1994, such as historicocultural analyses of the state of Chiapas that explain the formation of the EZLN (Collier and Quaratiello 1994; Montemayor 1997; Harvey 1998; Tello Díaz 2000; Higgins 2004), studies on Zapatismo's impact on antiglobalization and anti-neoliberal projects (Holloway and Peláez 1998; Holloway 2002; Irr 2003; Láscar 2004; Olesen 2005), and the EZLN's contribution to political theory (Wagner and Moreira 2003; Tormey 2006). Of course, an enormous amount of scholarship has also been dedicated to Subcomandante Marcos and his role in the EZLN, attempting to establish his real identity, speculating on the full extent of his leadership of the EZLN and his function as cultural intermediary, and literary analysis of his written work and interviews (Flores 1996; Sinnigen 1999; Steele, Corona, and Jörgensen 2002; Herlinghaus 2005; Ortiz Pérez 2003; Vanden Berghe 2005). But, of course, this is neither the entirety nor the end of the narrative. The EZLN has never ceased producing and disseminating language; since their emergence almost twenty years ago, and despite the state's sustained counterinsurgent efforts, they have issued a total of six declarations.[2] Despite these setbacks, the EZLN continues to show signs of life, or rather a demonstration of the ability to continue to produce language. The EZLN has been identified by Roger Bartra (2002: viii) as a "culture of ink," a sign of what he calls the "post-Mexican condition," of which he observes, "The Zapatista army threatened to wash the country in blood, but what it actually produced was a vast ink stain: fortunately, more letters than bullets came out of Chiapas." Unfortunately, what had initially begun as a local, insurgent revolt against the Mexican political system and transformed into a critique of global capitalism and neoliberal policy has now been overrun in recent years by the unrelenting, violent, and bloody reprisals by narco-gangs stemming from President Felipe Calderón's "war on drugs." Nevertheless, if the Zapatistas are still relevant and can offer anything toward the thinking through of the political in contemporary Latin America, and particularly if the lessons of Zapatismo are to gain purchase in other parts of the world, it is crucial that one remain attentive to the terms and limits of reading Zapatista speech and the notion of the political that can be ascribed to it. It is the wager of this chapter that they indeed still are and can.

In the previous chapters I have shown how the unpredictable effects of orality's figuration as semiological guarantee of alterity interrupts and serves to destabilize its categorical efficacy. Within twentieth-century literary and cultural discourse in Latin America, I have shown how orality and literacy—an inherited conceptual and representational system that not only constitutes cultural and racial difference but also serves as the dominant way to read and reinforce that difference—ultimately cease to function politically when they cease to function semiotically. The implications of this investigation signal the inextricability of orality and literacy to modern forms of governance and biopolitics in Latin America and the need to rethink Latin America's critical relationship to these cultural categories. Up to this point I have discussed the simultaneously constitutive and tenuous relationship between orality, literacy, and political narratology in a postcolonial Latin American context—how, for instance, illiteracy subverts both indigenista and mestizo cultural nationalism (i.e., Arguedas and Vargas Llosa in Peru) and how testimonial criticism, grounded as it was within strict indexical parameters of literalness and literariness, staked its disciplinary claim on a subaltern subject (Menchú) which it could not but restitute without excessive and contradictory meaning. I have not yet illustrated the extent to which illiteracy also manages to inform current and actual political realities. This chapter details just such a case through an analysis of the Zapatistas and their foundationally illiterate relation with the Mexican state, including La Otra Campaña (The Other Campaign), announced in June 2005.

In this chapter I examine the ways the EZLN conceives and deploys a language of radical political equality within Mexican constitutionality, how critics attempted to define the nature of this resistant discourse (silence and speech), and why the EZLN's initial engagement with Mexican political processes in the past decade established the need for a new program of action. I thus reflect on the critical implications of La Otra Campaña today and why it signals both a continuation and a radical transformation of the EZLN's discursive strategy of social mobilization and political participation in Mexico. I argue that though La Otra Campaña signals a new discursive relationship between the EZLN and Mexican political processes (a relation of nonrelation and withdrawal), it is also one that is, and constitutively so, grounded in the San Andrés Accords. As a consequence of both their production (inscription) and subsequent abrogation (erasure), the Accords come to function as a threshold of illiteracy within Mexican democratic logic: as the unlegislatable, legislated irruption of Mexican constitutionality's exclusions back into itself. In effect the EZLN both, and at the same time, demands its restitution within democratic forms while revealing the grounds of its impossibility; effecting the latter's now internal crisis of sovereignty at the moment strict constitutionality is insisted upon as the only mode of political restitution for indigenous people. So while La Otra Campaña will seemingly create the dialogic space where a heterogeneous and hence unregulated form of political discourse can emerge alongside Mexican state biopolitics, the Accords guarantee La Otra Campaña an always already inscribed relationship to it: the trace of exclusion and inclusion within Mexican constitutionality that simultaneously grounds it and renders it into crisis.

As such, this discussion aims to analyze the ways Latin American critics have approached the subject of the EZLN and how they have attempted to explore and understand the EZLN's impact on the contemporary Latin American social text. What I seek is a critical understanding of "silence" and "speech," and therefore of the notion of subalternity itself—the conceptual figure upon which governmentality, biopolitics, hegemony, and democracy rest. But first it is necessary to state that, and as noted earlier, despite the enormous scholarly attention given to Subcomandante Marcos, this study has very little to do with him specifically. Unfortunately, and contrary to what a number of studies devoted to Marcos would seem to suggest, all the emphasis on him simply confirms the public's curiosity about a Western man interested in indigenous issues, not the indigenous issues or indigenous people themselves. In other words, this investment in Subcomandante Marcos ultimately (and again, lamentably) reproduces the trope—foregrounded in my discussions of indigenismo and testimonio— that non-Western peoples simply cannot be understood without cultural mediation. As Analisa Taylor (2009: 79) understands it, "Ironically, Marcos's protagonism in the Zapatista struggle has itself served to reinforce this notion that indigenous peoples cannot speak truth to power, but must

rely on a non-indigenous interlocutor to do so." While one can appreciate how drastically different the EZLN's history would have been without
Subcomandante Marcos's involvement, it nevertheless certainly does not
follow that he is therefore the Zapatistas' "invisible hand." For while many
of the studies cited earlier tacitly suggest Marcos's larger and more critical
leadership role within the EZLN than publicly stated, only Brian Gollnick (2008: 166) has gone so far as to admit what many critics might have
wanted to say all along: "To avoid putting too fine a point on this issue, my
own sense is that Marcos is the author of all of the Zapatista communiqués,
both literally in terms of writing the final language in them and even more
importantly as the authorial signature whose connection to a style authen-
ticates EZLN discourse for dissemination." As my analysis demonstrates,
the truly radical nature of Zapatista speech is contingent upon neither Marcos's authorial nor his representational function. The notion of the political
at stake here is sustained by one foundational distinction: human speech
is either always already speech or it is not. Indigenous blabber does not all
of a sudden convert to speech with translation (or double translation) and
clever, charismatic, delivery, without also denying it the quality of speech
in the first place.

Having said this, it is equally important to say that what is significant
about Zapatista speech has very little to do with the cultural assumptions
of indigeneity and indigenous difference—linguistic, temporal, spiritual,
epistemological—that presents an alternative, cohesive, and superior-fash-
ioned worldview that the West has for too long suppressed and continues
to ignore at its peril. Fallacious reasoning plagues the hypothesis that the
cultural terms of a community's subordination are also (and have been all
along) the keys to resolving Western society's impulse to subordinate in the
first place. Undoubtedly this is not why social marginalization occurs, nor
can contemporary social problems find their resolution by simply reincor-
porating into the social fabric the very indigenous cultural traits and customs that were previously rendered folklore. As such, while it is one thing
to ascribe subaltern status to an indigenous group, it is another to say a
group is subaltern *because* it is indigenous, that is, to suggest that there is
something inherently subaltern about indigenous identity. Though related,
they are not mutually inclusive, nor should they be conflated. Such faulty
reasoning can no longer go unquestioned: we can no longer reproduce
the myth of the subalternized community that is itself immune from the

internal tensions and hierarchies that affect all others and which, through de-subalternization, represents the promise of the end of subalternity as such. Such a community quite simply does not exist, nor is it needed to motivate political work.

Given this criteria, one must consequently begin thinking about rewriting the EZLN's story. In "The Imagination to Listen" (2003), Mariana Mora acknowledges the necessary but insufficient scope of the conventional history of the EZLN I outlined earlier. Instead, she suggests, one must go further and deeper into this still unresolved narrative to see the Zapatistas' radical political effects in Mexico:

> One way to reflect on the past decade of failed negotiations with the State, dialogues with civil society, and low-intensity warfare would be to describe the transformations and challenges of Zapatista-State political relations. A reflection of this sort, one typically presented in the media, would simply narrate the interactions between the State and the EZLN by focusing on the suspended peace talks and on the eventual unilateral State-initiated constitutional reforms. Such a narrative would begin with the Peace Dialogues of San Andres Sak'amchen de los Pobres at the end of 1995, discuss the eventual signing of the San Andres Accords on Indigenous Rights and Culture on February 16, 1996, describe the reasons behind the suspension of any further negotiations, and finally conclude with the Mexican Congress approving constitutional reforms in 2001 that recognized a limited set of indigenous rights. A narrative of this sort would limit the understanding of all the practices of resistance, including mobilizations, *encuentros* (political gatherings), daily forms of resistance, and strategies employed to put pressure on the State, therefore reinforcing the State's centrality and authority as the most important terrain of political power. (18)

I would include in this conventional narrative Subcomandante Marcos's implied protagonism as well as the neocolonial assumption of a homogeneous indigenous culture. While I completely understand Mora's impulse to find a way to articulate the extent of the EZLN's resistant politics, it is important to point out that it is only through this very discursive context (i.e., the institutional relationship between the EZLN and the Mexican state) that her conceptualization of the "politics of listening" and my own analysis take root. Mora, while dismissing the sufficiency of this particular narrative, nevertheless includes its major points, if only to then dismiss them as insufficient to her alternative history. As much as her analysis wishes to resist "reinforcing the state's centrality and authority as the most important terrain of political power," any discussion of the EZLN would have to account for the state to mark and contain its biopolitical parameters, whether through unilateral negotiations and constitutional reform or low-intensity warfare. Though the historical narrative highlighted earlier has been the most conventional, it is also the least critically understood. It is, however, precisely within this narrative that the semiotic tensions between Zapatista and Mexican political discourse emerge and further refine the former's affectivity in Mexican national politics. For my part, I contend that the critical implications of La Otra Campaña cannot be understood without this historical context (as it is constitutive of it) and therefore continuously draw from it in my analysis. Having said this, however, any such discussion of the EZLN must first begin with the question of how to account critically for its language and signifying acts.

In chapter 1 I discussed at length the question of subalternity and elaborated on a certain tendency within Latin American thought to misread the finer points of Gayatri Spivak's celebrated essay "Can the Subaltern Speak?" Far too often (and consistently) the impulse is to respond to the rhetorical question her title invokes while failing to address the more critical intervention the essay actually provokes. In other words, the conventional response to Spivak's essay has been yes (the subaltern can speak) *and* no (we just don't listen), when in fact the actual question being posed is "Are we [intellectuals] assuming a pure of form of consciousness?" That the latter question has been answered unequivocally by the response given to the first—"Yes, we are assuming a pure form of consciousness"—is not accidental but rather is the result of misperceiving the formal aspects of subalternity itself and the intellectual's implicit and inextricable role in its reproduction.

In much the same way, scholarly thought on the EZLN has been guided by the view that the Zapatistas' historical and critical value is as subalterns who, through translation, can now be understood to speak (subalterns "that speak, know, and can *translate* their conditions"). However, and as we shall see, the result of such a claim within Zapatista critique (subalterns that can now *translate* their silence into speech) only further entrenches the double injunction of preserving and reducing alterity (yes, they can speak *and* no, we just don't listen) by providing the mechanism (translation) through which difference can be converted into sameness. In other words, it is through the deployment of translation that subaltern silence (understood within this rationale as that which is or can be *translatable*), posited precisely as a "pure form of consciousness" that the intellectual has access to, serves as the epistemo-ontological alibi of difference-as-truth that sustains hegemonic reproduction. Subalternity, I argue, can be interrogated not from fixed and transcendental binaries of orality-literacy and silence-speaking but from the historical effects of their categorical breaches, which is to say from the spaces of illiteracy that emerge from the inability to maintain strict semiotic compartmentalization, coherence, and order between them. Ultimately silence does not constitute the oppositional pole to speaking—just because the subaltern cannot speak does not necessarily mean it does not speak; silence (like orality) is contained within the semiotic system of Western literacy as a marker of subordination, nothing more. One must therefore look not to silence but to the thresholds of silence and speech to see the subaltern effects of an illiterate insurgency against "elite conceptualizations" (which orality and silence are and continue to be). In anticipation of what follows, I offer, as an elaboration of the notion of the political that both I and Gareth Williams (2007, 2011) are tracing, the following consideration from Jacques Rancière (1999: 32): "What makes an action political is not its object or the place where it is carried out, but solely its form, the form in which confirmation of equality is inscribed in the setting up of a dispute, of a community existing solely through being divided." For Rancière, an act is political when one group asserts its right to speak, not through some affirmation (via translation) of linguistic difference from the dominant group but precisely through the equality of their speech, precisely in their capacity to be understood through their equality as speaking beings. As we shall see, the appeal by critics to enlist translation as the political principle through which to validate the Zapatistas' colonial-Indian difference is fundamentally at odds with the latter's very invocation of the equality of speech and of speaking beings that serves as the ground of their critique. If translation surreptitiously conditions the very difference it seeks to neutralize—that is, if translation needs to occur before any understanding at all can take place—then translation quite simply cannot serve as a foundation for any progressive politics. The rest of this discussion aims to critically account for Zapatista language in the context of subalternity and this "confirmation of equality."

A significant attempt to engage Zapatista discourse can be seen in María Josefina Saldaña-Portillo's *The Revolutionary Imagination in the Americas and the Age of Development* (2003). Saldaña-Portillo addresses the Zapatistas' role in rewriting the stakes of indigenous subalternity and difference within a twentieth-century tradition of Latin American revolutionary practice that has historically only further subalternized indigenous peoples. One of the ways the Zapatistas have worked to reinscribe "Indian difference" onto the revolutionary map is through their deployment of "noisy" silence:

> But silence, as the quintessential marker of Indian identity in the subalternizing discourses of both North and South America, had been ruptured. The Indian silence enacted here was not the silence of the Indian in modernizing discourses—the silence of an absence, a lack, an incompletion. Neither was it the silence of the Indian in revolutionary developmentalism—the silence of incipient rebels, in waiting for leadership. Nor was it the silence of the Indian in Christian martyrdom—the silence of forbearance in expectation of eternal deliverance. It was a silence filled with noise, with planning, communication, movement, tactics, coercion, frustration, ties, networks, suffering, satisfaction—a silence so filled with activity that it ruptures from within, a truly deafening quiet. (194)

One gathers that Saldaña-Portillo conceives of at least two forms of silence within a dynamic interplay of differing silences. One she understands as absolute silence, indicative, for her, of the Indian in Mexican history; the other is constituted by noise, activity, biopower, emerging, she suggests, as a "methodology for interrupting the teleological discourses that have enabled twentieth century Mexican revolutionary nationalism" (196). For Saldaña-Portillo, the "noise" of Zapatismo constitutes a moment of rupture marking a historical transition between a *literally* silent subaltern form (in the figure of the Indian prior to the Zapatistas) and the emergence of a new "noisy" subaltern subjectivity in the Zapatistas. In other words, in the present moment a "noisy" and "truly deafening silence" emerges from the literal silence of the Indian in Mexican history, rupturing the formation of that silence.

However, one must note that within this articulation are contained a series of critical assumptions about subalternity, the most curious of which is the assumption that indigenous communities have actually remained silent for five hundred years and have only now, within the past twenty years, chosen to become "noisy." The contradiction that resides here contests the basis of not only many colonial scholars attempting to isolate moments of indigenous affectivity in the colonial and pre-independence periods but also those attempting to theorize subalternity as an effect of indigenous discourse (see Mallon 1995; Rabasa 2010; Bolaños and Verdesio 2002). In other words, a shift from a silent to a noisy subaltern form is not historically contingent; a historical transition from one to the other is simply not available. Consequently if the former, then the Zapatistas are still as literally silent as the Indian within modernizing, revolutionary, and Christian discourse, alluded to earlier; if the latter, then the Zapatistas are as noisy as the Indian has always been within Latin American cultural and political history. If the first, then Saldaña-Portillo's historicist reconfiguration (between a *then* when subalterns were inaudible, and a *now* when they're noisy) proves problematic from the start. The question that remains is not whether this noisy form of silence is audible, but whether it is productive of signification. And if so, how? As my analysis will bring to bear, the conceptual slippage between Saldaña-Portillo's use of subaltern silence and speech manifests a residual intellectual desire for semiotic plenitude (restitution) that extends beyond the interruptive and disruptive effects of silence implied by noise. Instead silence is posited as a positive language system (like orality) that competes for the hegemonic appropriation of democratic signification, and not its biopolitical suspension.

Saldaña-Portillo begins her discussion by recounting her participation in the Intercontinental Encounters for Humanity and against Neoliberalism in Chiapas in July 1996. According to her account, prior to commencing the Intercontinental, the Zapatista organizers insisted upon the attendees' complete and total silence, emphasizing that the event would not commence until that level of silence was obtained. The audience was forced to comply. Saldaña-Portillo (2003: 192) then notes:

> The performative act of silence imposed on our group that evening
> functioned as a political metaphor: if it was difficult for me, for us as
> a group of some five thousand people, to keep silent for ten minutes,

what had it been like for the members and supporters of the Zapatistas
to keep silent for ten years—one minute for every year? On another
level, however, the very content of the silence we experienced that
evening is a political metaphor for the fullness *and differentiation* of our
own community; more precisely, silence is the condition of possibility
for this differentiation and fullness. For it was in human silence that
we were able to recognize the musicality of noise, the seemingly infinite
possibility of differentiated sound, extending community beyond the
territory marked as human. How, then, to read the fullness of this
performative silence?

Saldaña-Portillo orients the reader into her glimpse of "the five hundred
years of silence imposed on indigenous peoples of the Americas" as well
as the active silence through which the Zapatistas first started organizing,
asserting that "silence is the mark of alterity, of Indian difference, in
subalternizing discourses of conquest, but also the mask of alterity, for in
'silence' the Zapatistas experience community and organize resistance" (193).
However, the account of her experience—the "fullness and differentiation"
while silent at the Intercontinental—could only have been figurative;
Saldaña-Portillo makes a point to emphasize the "musicality of noise" that
emerged amid the human silence. Noting the language used to describe this
scene and the silence that emerged ("fullness," "musicality," "noise"), silence
for Saldaña-Portillo is not a lack of sound but the poetic conditions of its
auratic fulfillment.

Zapatista noisy silence is therefore conceived by Saldaña-Portillo as fully
commensurate and productive signification and not unlike the discourse of
orality we have seen in previous discussions, figured as a musical and poetic
language form. Already visible here is the degree of conceptual slippage
within this critical discussion of subaltern speech in Latin America. This
time, however, we are seeing two conceptual systems overlap: orality-
literacy and silence-speech. While we can now see that Saldaña-Portillo's
analysis attempts to superimpose one onto the other (i.e., silence-orality
onto speech-literacy), it must be recognized that they are not mutually
inclusive formulations, and both are equally fraught with assumptions. In
other words, if her conceptualization of Zapatista silence, noisy silence,
is grounded in the discourse of orality, then, and as this study has been
attempting to show, appealing to the "musicality" and "sensuality" of

orality will not alter the relations of power within which these tropes are already entrenched.

Note, for instance, Saldaña-Portillo's analysis of an EZLN communiqué from February 1994, in which she activates the tropes of oral discourse that are used to domesticate and contain indigenous speech. I cite at length:

> The silence described in this communiqué is not the absence of sound but the condition of possibility for registering its *fullness*, for hearing the *musicality* of noise. Silence here is the backbeat or counter-time of noise. In the *sensuality* of silence, inanimate objects are animated, and the Zapatista community hears hearts pumping in the natural world around them. In the *sensuality* of silence, the Zapatistas hear the *fullness* of the pain and misery of their communal situation. . . . Silence is not the silencing of difference, but the *sensual* alertness that allows differences to emerge. Silence is the clearing that makes speech possible, not because it stands in a dichotomous relation to speech, as contentless space, but precisely because it is in the *fullness* of silence where differences take shape: "In silence, we were speaking." Silence is the noise of democracy. Thus the communiqués written in this voice are not only counterpunctual because they provide a folkloric accent to the communiqués written in the technical voice of guerilla action; they are counterpunctual because they emerge from the silence existing between the beats of the discourses of mestizaje and developmentalism. . . . While these communiqués register the musicality existing in the silence, they also make evident the processes of translation and transcription necessary for communicating the content of silence. (2003: 235, my italics)

As we can see, the tropes of poiesis invoked by Saldaña-Portillo to talk about her experience of silence at the Intercontinental also frame her analysis of an EZLN communiqué. By employing the same poetic discourse she used to reflect on her own experience at the Intercontinental (i.e., "musicality," "fullness," "sensuality") to now read the EZLN communiqués, is she not also positing that, beyond political metaphors, the critic and the subaltern ultimately speak and understand the same poetic language? Of silence? Of orality?

It is unfortunate that from a discussion of the political nature of subaltern speech in Zapatismo we are ultimately brought back to orality and literacy and all its attendant conceptual problems. However, there is still more to this. Though we see in Saldaña-Portillo's analysis an insistence on a silence-speech dichotomization that inevitably takes on the assumptions inherent in the orality-literacy binary, and though silence, like orality in previous chapters, is posited as an ultimately superior language form for democratic organization, she then also suggests that silence first needs translation in order to work ("processes of translation and transcription necessary for communicating the content of silence").

And it is at this particular point in Saldaña-Portillo's analysis, at the point where silence, noise, and democracy converge, where particular care must be taken. For if, according to Saldaña-Portillo, the Zapatistas' noisy silence interrupts the biopoliticized code of Mexican nationalism because it is grounded in the Indians' literal silence, and if it creates the conditions for an alternative, national identity constituted from the margins of the state ("Indian difference"), how exactly does she conceive of the necessary and the presumably revolutionary shift from noise to speech that would accomplish Zapatista de-subalternization? In other words, is Zapatista silence disruptive to hegemonic discourse because it has become noisy all of a sudden, or because this silence is actually an untranslated form of speech? What exactly constitutes the political kernel of Zapatista silence ("the noise of democracy"), suspended, as it is, within translation?

For Saldaña-Portillo, the force of Zapatista silence lies neither in what it does or precipitates but rather in what it holds and what is revealed in it when given consistency. In other words, for her the critical force of Zapatista silence—"the noise of democracy"—lies simply in its translatability. She argues:

> The EZLN's speech translates the silence into language, emerging as
> it does directly from the pain they register in the silent community
> existing in the counter-time of mestizaje and development. Pain
> is translated into hope, misery into dignity, death into futurity.
> We are still in an anthropological world of oral tradition, where a
> history of subaltern silence is handed down through parents and
> grandparents; however, this is not a passive exchange but a creative
> act of translation. Oral tradition requires actively taking possession of
> language through speech. . . . The act of recognizing the truth of their
> silence in their own words is also an act of re/cognizing the terms of

indigenous representation. . . . The EZLN translate their silence into
the conventions of folkloric speech to take possession of language as
a discursive system—they rewrite the representations of indigenous
experience in the twin discourses of mestizaje and development. . . . In
transcribing the content of their speaking among themselves, the
EZLN are actually involved in a double translation. They first
reconstruct their grandparents' and parents' experience in silence as a
history of never-ending struggle through the idiom of folkloric speech
and then translate it once again into the idiom of twentieth-century
revolutionary practice. . . . Silence is broken through this translation
and transcription. (2003: 236–37)

Saldaña-Portillo is concerned primarily with converting Zapatista "silence"
into speech, to account for Zapatismo as, ultimately, translated speech.
In other words, she is invested in a tactic of de-subalternization of their
discursive practice and seeks out translation as the vehicle that breaks the
silent mark of their alterity. However, what she concedes is that, because
this silence first needs to be translated, Zapatista silence was therefore never
speech to begin with. This concession strikes at the core of her analysis and
cancels out any notion of the political that can be ascribed to Zapatismo
itself. Given the conventional response to the question of subalternity—yes
(the subaltern can speak) *and* no (we just don't listen)—Saldaña-Portillo
seems here to be treading on similar ground (yes, they are noisy but no, they
can't speak without translation).

In other words, if, as Saldaña-Portillo proposes, translation (or double
translation) serves as the process through which noisy silence is converted
into intelligible and productive signification, this means that without
translation Zapatismo on its own cannot rupture the terms defining the
hegemonic articulation of signification that initially cathects their language into nonspeech. From within this position, the truth of Zapatista
silence is merely its difference as exteriority from speech (call it orality,
pain, misery, or death), its inherent translatability (like all good exteriority); hence the need for translation in order for it to become meaningful. In Saldaña-Portillo, then, we see no form given to Zapatista language itself that contests not only the silence but the discourse of speech
that constitutes it as silent in the first place. What we see is merely the
neocolonial gesture of "decrypting" subaltern silence (as a pure form of

consciousness) into the realm of hegemonic speech (as the "noise [and now pure voice] of democracy").

Ultimately what we have here is an analysis of subalternity in the Zapatistas that leaves silence and speech intact. It is an analysis grounded in a notion of the political that retains the hierarchy of silence and speech so as to effect and substantiate the transfer (via translation, like transculturation and mestizaje before it) of certain subalternities from one to the other. But again, it does nothing to alter the very terms of their installation as hegemonic articulation for language. If, as she argues, "silence is broken through this translation and transcription," then what is revealed to be of paramount political significance for her is the act and process of cultural mediation—translation—itself, not the Zapatista silence that first needs it to become speech. In this frame, Zapatista politics is reduced only to interactions and transactions from within this hegemonic articulation (from silence to speech), and thus is unable to conceive in it a trace of a critical beyond in the accounting of speech (neither silence nor speech), a suspension of this dialectic that can reveal its illiterate core.

Another significant and related attempt to critically engage Zapatista discourse can be seen in Walter Mignolo's "The Zapatista's Theoretical Revolution: Its Historical, Ethical and Political Consequences" (2011), a discussion that attempts to formalize Zapatista discourse within the frame of "diversality," or what he calls the diversity of universal projects emanating globally from the colonial difference.[3] As with Saldaña-Portillo, translation takes on even greater emphasis here. Mignolo sees the Zapatista uprising as an attempt to divest democracy of its "original," universal meaning and reinscribe its value and signification within the colonial difference (*Indian difference* in Saldaña-Portillo). In the following passage, Mignolo addresses the specific modality of "double translation" as the assertion of colonial difference where indigenous knowledges can now enter the discussion as productive agents:

> Double translation is then a key component of the Zapatistas'
> theoretical revolution. Double translation allows one to dissolve
> cultural relativism into colonial differences and to reveal the colonial
> structure of power (e.g., the coloniality of power) in the production and
> reproduction of the colonial difference. From the perspective of double
> translation there emerges an ethical and political imaginary that opens

up the gates for conceiving possible futures beyond the limits imposed
by two hegemonic abstract universals, (neo)liberalism and (neo)
Marxism. The theoretical revolution of the Zapatistas shall be located
in the double translation (and double infection) that makes possible a
double epistemic movement, framed by the colonial difference. That is,
forms of knowledge that had been discredited from the very inception
of modernity/coloniality enter into a double movement of "getting in/
letting in." This movement is allowed by the reversal of the power of
coloniality opened up by double translation. The theoretical revolution
grounded in double translation makes it possible to imagine epistemic
diversality (or pluriversality) and to understand the limits of the
abstract-universals that have dominated the imaginary of the modern/
colonial world from Christianity to liberalism and Marxism. (221–22)

As we saw with Saldaña-Portillo, Mignolo here appeals to the role of double
translation as the process that both enables and is enabled by the reversal of
"colonial structures of power" (colonial difference). However, what remains
unclear is what exactly "the reversal of the power of coloniality" looks like
and whether this "reversal" is the result of double translation or its impetus.
In other words, to what exactly does Mignolo attribute to the Zapatistas'
"ethical and political imaginary": the reversal of coloniality or double
translation? The nature of the relationship between the two is critical, for
if, as Mignolo argues, this reversal is rendered visible ("opened up") *by*
double translation, then there is simply no theoretical revolution to speak
of, for as saw in Saldaña-Portillo, translation (even double translation) is
incapable of generating such critical possibilities. That is, within the realm
of the translatable, no assumption of equality exists; rather translation, even
double translation, affirms the very dis-equality that translation is deployed
to render commensurate. If translation continues to serve as the means by
which the West captures its outside as difference, then double translation
(translation of translation) does little to undermine this history of socialized
capital; in fact it reaffirms the very logic and value of Western thought
(identity and difference) that is implied in the Zapatistas' "getting in/letting
in" (subalterns "that speak, know, and now *translate* their conditions"). In
short, any previous inscription of equality (the heterogeneous assumption
of the equality of one speaking being with any other speaking being)
marking the scene of a dispute is immediately foreclosed at the very

moment translation (even double translation) is invoked as the means for a democratic "opening up."

But further, Mignolo's very notion of "getting in/letting in" obscures a conflation of representational categories (proxy and portrait) that double translation only makes more pernicious. As we saw in Spivak's (1988a: 276) discussion of *Darstellung* (portrait) and *Vertretung* (proxy) in "Can the Subaltern Speak?," wherein she warns, "they are related, but running them together, especially in order to say that beyond both is where oppressed subjects speak, act and know *for themselves*, leads to an essentialist, utopian politics," for Mignolo (2011: 250), the "getting in/letting in" (proxy and portrait) is equally fraught with such dangers ("the getting in/letting in is indeed the strength of Zapatista discourse and the grounding of their theoretical revolution"). For if "getting in/letting in" signifies the process by which Amerindian knowledges appropriate the West, transform and return it (253) in/as subaltern speech, then "getting in/letting in" signifies for Mignolo nothing other than transculturation at its most spectacularly Western (i.e., the West reflecting on itself as Other reflecting on the West).

Consideration of one of Mignolo's key examples will do much to substantiate the case. One of the more striking pieces of analysis he provides is of Major Ana María's speech given at the Intercontinental of 1996. Mignolo seeks to highlight in this part of the discussion precisely how his notion of double translation works. In particular he aims to illustrate how Tojolabal language structure forms the basis for indigenous political critique that translates, transforms, and reintegrates conventional Western critical forms. Mignolo makes a series of statements that seek not only to mark Tojolabal's radical linguistic difference from Western languages but to assert its exceptional capacity to think through or from the limits of democracy, the "people," "rights," "justice," and "equality." Specifically he posits Tojolabal's missing subject-object correlation as a crucial linguistic feature that enables in the Zapatistas' double translation the promise of a theoretical revolution: postrepresentationalist politics. A summary of Mignolo's (2011: 226–27) argument runs something like this: Tojolabal has no subject-object correlation; therefore Tojolabal does not engage in acts of representation; therefore Western theories of language could not have been formulated by anyone thinking from Tojolabal; therefore democracy could neither have been formulated by anyone thinking from Tojolabal; therefore speakers of Tojolabal, through an irreducibly postrepresentationalist linguistic structure, speak (and know themselves) beyond the limits of both senses of Western representation. As such, Mignolo asserts, Tojolabal's distinctive linguistic features function in a critical capacity within indigenous political critique. He points to the nonexistence of subject-object correlation in Tojolabal, which in Major Ana María's speech enables an indigenous articulation of political reality that both transforms and is transformed by conventional Western linguistic structures of governmental signification. Instead, Mignolo argues, what the absence of subject and object modes enables is a language form that privileges "intersubjective enactments" and hence a reconceptualization of political communities within a strict "I/You" pronominal structure rather than "I/They" or "We/Them," which syntactically reproduces an "I/It" correlation. Thus Tojolabal—due specifically to this missing subject-object correlation and therefore its postrepresentationalist structure—serves as the primary vehicle for Zapatista "double translation." And according to Mignolo, what emerges through this language is an expression of democratic logic inscribed from within the colonial difference. In other words, democratic discourse "could not have been formulated by anyone thinking from Tojolabal," but yet, as expressed within double translation, one arrives at a postrepresentational articulation of democracy that can only emerge from the colonial difference.

However, even if, as Mignolo argues, no Western theory of language could have accounted for Tojolabal's missing subject-object correlation, it simply does not follow that it can therefore be taken as the grounds of what he calls the EZLN's "ethical and political imaginary." Why not? Because one cannot, without contradiction, assert a politics of equality based on the divergences between historically contingent language forms throughout the world nor from the normative and universal system of grammar that governs the very criteria used to measure them. As such, to read Tojolabal's *missing* subject-object correlation, what appears to Mignolo to be an uncontested and entirely conceded claim, as a manifestation of colonial difference in effect concedes the point of politics from the very start. What exactly is Mignolo saying when he argues that democracy "could not have been formulated by anyone thinking from Tojolabal"? If he is suggesting that, because of this missing correlation, which is nothing more than an accident of history, thinking of democracy as *Vertretung* (proxy) would have been impossible, is he then not also saying that, as *Darstellung* (portrait), democracy would be impossible to understand by anyone thinking

from Tojolabal? Once again, Spivak's (1988a: 279) intervention is of critical value: "[Intellectuals] must note how the staging of the world in representation—its scene of writing, its *Darstellung*—dissimulates the choice of
and need for 'heroes,' paternal proxies, agents of power—*Vertretung*." In
other words, what we see deployed in Mignolo's "getting in/letting in" of
those for whom democracy would not or could not have been formulated in
Tojolabal simultaneously excludes them from the realm of equal speaking
beings that is the ground of all politics. So if, for Mignolo, double translation and "diversality" are understood as the means by which "formerly"
subaltern groups can now enter the discussion, it is only after they admit
that they are simply unable (due to the particular nature of their language's
grammatical structure) to understand the "abstract universals" that otherwise, and in the first instance, confirm the equality they ultimately seek. In
effect, "getting/letting in," far from representing a revolutionary epistemic
movement, constitutes instead a relinquishing of the very terms that grant
their speech equality to all others, ground their equality as speaking beings
to all others, and guarantee their right to act politically, terms that nullify
from the start the question of necessary mediation.

Furthermore, and this point needs to be emphasized, if Western language does have a subject-object correlation, and if Tojolabal doesn't, and
if Tojolabal's missing subject-object correlation becomes constitutive of its
identity, then its identity is precisely (and still) its grammatical and representational difference (lack) from Western language. Ultimately this suggestion changes nothing; Tojolabal's missing grammatical component was
no doubt first discovered by colonial missionaries and nevertheless used to
justify its cultural and pedagogical subordination to Spanish. However, to
now assert that Tojolabal's grammatical structure is postrepresentationalist (because of this same lacking subject-object correlation)—an attribute
occurring nowhere else in the world that would make it immune from the
problems of representation and ideology that have plagued the West since
the Greeks and that can thus now, perhaps for the first time in history,
be harnessed for its exclusive truth-bearing (nonrepresentational and nonideological) potential to critique this very West—accomplishes nothing but
confirms an unyielding and irreducibly Western desire for logos and the
neocolonial fantasy of finding and unconcealing evidence of such logos in
previously colonized space. Of course, there is no such thing as non-Western logos either. Unfortunately one does not simply counter the narrative of

Western exceptionalism with a reverse-ethnocentric narrative of another's. To critique the West from the assumption of difference, even colonial difference, as Mignolo does here, willfully disavows all critical insight gained on the foundation and workings of Western thought itself (based precisely on such assumptions of difference as lack). In effect, such a pronouncement only reinforces Western modalities of knowledge production and cannot therefore serve as any ground for politics. As Spivak (1988a: 285) carefully reminds us, "There is no unrepresentable subaltern subject that can know and speak itself."

But that is not all. This passage also suggests that a certain knowledge of Tojolabal's linguistic and syntactical features becomes a necessary instrument in the framing of Mignolo's analysis of Major Ana María's speech. On more than one occasion we have seen Mignolo remark on the model of translation used by colonial missionaries to both catechize and write grammars for the indigenous peoples. In each case he asserts the monological and unilateral function of translation whereby religious and political control of an Indian community is established from a systematized understanding of their language (2011: 251, 255). But while he argues that a Western theory of language could not have accounted for the missing subject-object correlation in Tojolabal—"this is what the missionaries who wrote grammars of Amerindian languages never understood"—he nevertheless seems to agree with the principle, deployed by these same missionaries, that a systematized grammatical understanding of Tojolabal will yield or predispose the production of meaning in that language. In other words, as Mignolo's analysis of Ana María's speech demonstrates, a grammar of Tojolabal renders meaning for those who do not speak it.

Ultimately Mignolo's analysis defers to the knowledge base gained through the colonial accumulation and systematization of indigenous linguistic systems in order to illustrate the colonial difference in the Tojolabal language. In this case it is the presumption of complete knowledge of an indigenous language that he uses to provide meaning from a subject (Major Ana María) who speaks Spanish but who "thinks from" the Tojolabal language.[4] However, the effects of colonial difference and double translation can only emerge under conditions of complete linguistic systematicity, the ultimate meaning of which is contingent upon the accuracy of Tojolabal grammar. Unfortunately, assurance of such accuracy can be guaranteed only from those who continue to insist on the grammaticity and commensurability of Language, and therefore of all languages.

In a previous chapter we saw an instance in which the grammar of an indigenous language serves as the guarantee of translatable and commensurate meaning within an oral-literate conjuncture. In *Los ríos profundos* we are provided an etymological survey of two Quechua suffixes (*-yllu*, *-illa*) that supplements narratological meaning to the reader about the protagonist Ernesto. In particular the etymology provided (which, Cornejo Polar [1973: 106] warns, might be false) is used to establish a semiotic connection between the Quechua word for a spinning top, *zumbayllu*, and Ernesto's almost mystical attraction to it. However, the point here is not the accuracy of the etymology but the very suggestion of a philological approach to indigenous traditions and oral expressional forms. As it turns out, Ernesto's analytic approach to a Quechua word for which he has no referent—to separate and identify prefix, suffix, and root—enabled in him the grammatical terms to derive meaning from the unknown word *zumbayllu* and to establish a particularly intense and significant relationship to it, with a zeal no other child in the novel manifests. It proves critical that the philologically based understanding he derives from the word will actually determine the form, function, and beauty that the top holds for him (even if completely and utterly incorrect). This lettered approach to the word *zumbayllu* ultimately determines his fetishistic relationship to this object, even if (or precisely because) the meaning derived is etymologically inaccurate or epistemologically indeterminate. In that discussion I argued that in the episode of the zumbayllu we see an instance in which an indigenous, oral expressional system, to the extent that the suffix -ayllu provides Ernesto the means to understand word *zumbayllu*, is presented as already systematized into a literate, etymologized, and grammared form. In short, we see Quechua presented here as an already incorporated and consistent language form, where, like Western languages, Quechua too can be rendered and broken down into grammatical and etymological units (even inaccurate ones) and where these structural units can be used to provide meaning from unknown words.

In Mignolo, as in Arguedas, indigenous languages are presented as coherent, systematized semiotic systems such that literate, translatable meaning can be derived from their grammatical units. He cites the missing correlation of subject and object in Tojolabal as the semantic grounds upon which to center Ana María's speech, and hence the underlying logic of Zapatista discourse. However, Mignolo's analysis ultimately rests on the assumption that knowledge of Tojolabal grammar is complete and systematized to such an extent that it can serve as the arbiter of Zapatista meaning. I insist that the main object of my critique is not Mignolo's positing of Tojolabal as a legitimate language system, but rather that he defers to the ideological value of grammar both to legitimate Tojolabal and as the means to render meaning from it. In doing so, and by grounding Tojolabal's missing correlation between subject and object as the only necessary distinction between it and Western language, Mignolo safeguards the primacy of Western interpretive forms by guaranteeing Tojolabal's (and therefore every language's) inherent translatability and complete grammatical reducibility.

What results therefore in both Saldaña-Portillo's and Mignolo's analyses of Zapatismo is a notion of silence (as the interiorization of speech's exterior as difference) that is itself *neither* a "pure form of consciousness" nor a linguistic bedrock that, without translation, can signify on its own. Instead its ascription as "noise" or "silence" in the face of (double) translation confirms its exclusion from the realm of equal speech; that is, it wasn't speech in the first place. Like Marx's notion of class, silence is heterogeneous and artificial, and therefore neither the voice for Zapatista appeals nor something (class consciousness) whose translation from silence to speech would eradicate the ground of Western thought (identity-indigenous or colonial difference). Silence represents neither that incommensurate utterance of "truth" in exteriority nor the name of its resistant, authentic embodiment. Its critical value lies beyond the hegemonic-counterhegemonic articulations of silence-speech, identity-difference that both Saldaña-Portillo and Mignolo employ and are limited to. Another critical path must be sought.

The nature of the crisis the Zapatistas' silence provokes—at once a crisis of Mexican democracy and the "crisis" that is democracy itself—is most clearly revealed through Rancière's notion of *politics*, which I read as the contestation over the understanding and definition of political objects that reconfigures the rationality of the speaking situation upon which governance is enacted (i.e., between beings who are able to speak and those who are not). For Rancière, politics constitutes a semiological confrontation over the very terms of the current social order (which he calls *police*), a critical emplotment where the capacity for speech—that is, the distinction between "noise" and "discourse"—is revealed as constitutive in or of political life.

In order to find a critically legible demonstration of the EZLN's confrontation with police logic one need only return to the initial communication report broadcast by the state government of Chiapas after the EZLN's uprising on January 1, 1994. The very first paragraph of the communication reads:

> Various groups of Chiapan peasants, numbering close to 200
> individuals and consisting mostly of monolinguals, have carried
> out violent, provocational attacks in four districts within the state,
> including San Cristóbal de las Casas, Ocosingo, Altamirano, and Las
> Margaritas. (my translation)
>
> Diversos grupos de campesinos chiapanecos que ascienden a un total
> de cerca de 200 individuos, en su mayoría monolingües, han realizado
> actos de provocación y violencia en cuatro localidades del estado que
> son San Cristóbal de las Casas, Ocosingo, Altamirano y las Margaritas.
> (Díaz Arciniega and López Téllez 1997: vol. 1, 106)

It is curious that the one of identifying markers used to characterize the actors who have seized control of government buildings throughout the state of Chiapas is "monolinguals." Quite curious because, given that the rest of the report indicates that the "monolinguals" in question were a group of indigenous peasants, this means that the designation *monolingual* was chosen specifically to convey some additional, not previously given or connoted meaning in its connection with the identity of these actors. Monolingual peasants are Indians, according to state officials; it's that simple. Except this connection doesn't just go without saying because they just now had to say it, they just now had to draw a connection that hadn't been made and therefore could not go without saying. It is perplexing that, despite the ethnoracial context in Chiapas, the report takes the opportunity at this moment to equate and substitute (metaphorically? metonymically?) indigeneity with monolinguality, especially given the need for communications of this level of seriousness to use the simplest, most direct language possible—especially descriptions and identities of the actors involved in the uprising—in order to avoid confusion and/or misunderstanding by the public. Nevertheless the connection between monolinguality and indigeneity remains strangely infelicitous, catachrestic. Since when has monolinguality ever functioned as a trope for indigeneity? Orality certainly has, but not monolinguality. Of all the tropes used to express the condition of indigenous subordination to Spanish or creole lettered culture (since the fifteenth to the twentieth century), monolingualism was never one of them. So of all the possibilities afforded to the state officials drafting this report, why "monolinguals" as the defining characteristic (after "peasant")? What motivated state officials in charge of the report to employ "monolinguals" at all, instead of, say, "insurgent peasants" or simply "insurgents"? Why, when they have at their disposal an entire arsenal of tropes of indigenous peasantry that the Mexican public would recognize immediately, would a state-issued news bulletin choose the most forced and ill-fitting characterization of these actors? In other words, why the rhetorical stretch? What is actually in play here?

As early as 1997 Carlos Montemayor had taken note of this very report and its obtuse characterization of these actors and pointed out how the deployment of the word *monolingual* confirms two unfortunate things simultaneously: the racism of Mexican society that ascribes monolinguality to indigenous peoples who do not speak Spanish and the spectacularly quixotic deduction that suggests that all Mexican hispanophiles are therefore multilingual:

> The report did not specify the quality of "monolinguals" to refer to
> this group's linguistic universe but rather to emphasize their distance
> from that civilization that expresses itself in Spanish. At that time, to
> consider the EZLN insurrection as an indigenous rebellion amounted
> to a disqualification of the movement itself. The governor's racist vision
> had overlooked that on our continent, the monolinguals tend not to
> be the Indians: monolingual is the typical Mexican, as he only speaks
> Spanish, as is the typical North American, who only speaks English.
> Mexican Indians, in addition to speaking their language, often have
> knowledge of another, neighboring, indigenous language as well as
> Spanish. (my translation)

> El comunicado acentuaba la calidad de "monolingües" no tanto por
> el mundo lingüístico de los grupos, sino por su distancia respecto a la
> civilización que se expresaba en la lengua española. En ese momento,
> considerar la insurrección del EZLN como una rebelión indígena
> favorecía la descalificación del movimiento mismo. Esta visión racista
> del gobernador olvidaba que en nuestro continente los monolingües
> suelen no ser los indios: es monolingüe el mexicano promedio, que sólo

habla español, como el norteamericano promedio, que sólo habla inglés.
Los indios mexicanos además de hablar su idioma suelen conocer otra
lengua indígena vecina y también el español. (38)

Montemayor succinctly addresses the poorly veiled racial implications
stemming from the report, maintaining that the enlistment of *monolingual*
was to highlight not a lack or insufficiency in linguistic capacities but the
figure through which to foreground the insurgents' existence lying outside
the limits of Hispanic world. The condition of monolinguality, it appears to
go without saying, suggests that the insurgents are therefore beyond reason
and understanding. But once again this is a stretch, and it is beginning to
reach its figurative limit, and Montemayor quickly moves to restore the
qualification of monolinguality to its literal, denotative state. He argues,
again quite reasonably, that the use of *monolingual* in the report ultimately
reveals a crucial sociohistorical contradiction: to wit, that if anyone is more
likely to be monolingual, it is the typical Mexican Hispanic, who would
know only Spanish, whereas typical indigenous Mexicans know not only
their own language but would have at least a rudimentary knowledge
of Spanish as well. Montemayor thus makes quick work of this report:
according to him, the report's problem is that it simply confuses the
meanings of *monolingual* and *multilingual,* and its bigoted charge emerges
from this confusion. The report, he concludes, is not only incorrect, but it
is so in the strongest possible sense: *monolingual* was simply the absolutely
wrong designation to use, for *multilingual* is the most accurate description
of these actors.

Yet while Montemayor is right to to critique the report for these
reasons, one must admit that his analysis remains far from sufficient.
Whereas his reasoning here is both sound and incontrovertible—arguing,
in effect, that "we" are the monolinguals, not they—one gets the feeling
that there is still something else being actualized, that something else is
going without saying. Montemayor demonstrates that one can very easily
critique a forced metaphor by grounding it within a discussion that (re)
appeals to the literal meanings that make it up, but this does nothing but
reprioritize literal meaning over figurative and forecloses any ability to see
the semiologically constitutive dimension of sovereignty and order at play
here. For Montemayor, the central problem with the report is quite simply
that it willfully misidentifies who is in fact multilingual. Such a reading

obstructs from view the political sequence just opened up by the EZLN's emergence. In short, Montemayor's critique proves unable to account for how the report functions in the setting in motion of yet another field of intelligibility, and how the report itself serves as an announcement of a confrontation between an egalitarian contingency and the police order. I wish to reside a bit longer at the core of this contradiction, at this fundamental misapprehension of monolingualism, within the torsion of a catachrestic figure that posits monolinguals as external, irrational otherness beyond human communication. It is here, at this threshold, where the dispute between the Zapatistas and the Mexican police order run up against each other.

Within his understanding of the police, Rancière (1999: 22) talks about a "symbolic distribution of bodies" that is divided between "those that one sees and those that one does not see, those who have logos—memorial speech, an account to be kept up—and those who have no logos," between those who have a name and the "lowing of nameless beings" who cannot speak. Between them, Rancière asserts, "no situation of linguistic exchange can possibly be set up, no rules or code of discussion. . . . The order that structures . . . domination recognizes no logos capable of being articulated by beings deprived of logos, no *speech* capable of being proffered by nameless beings, beings of no ac/*count*" (24). What Rancière means by this, of course, is not that those without names are incapable of speech but rather that they are made to appear as nameless beings that, as such, have been given no space from which to speak: "There is no place for discussion with the plebs for the simple reason that plebs do not speak. They do not speak because they are beings without a name, deprived of logos—meaning, of symbolic enrollment in the city. . . . Whoever is nameless *cannot* speak" (23). As such, what the police order conditions is a symbolic distribution of speaking bodies wherein some are ascribed the capacity for speech and others are not, the latter relegated as "beings of no ac/count," "the part of no part."

Informed by this political topography, one can see that the distinction between monolinguals and multilinguals in the drafting of this report is not arbitrary but rather performs a very specific function, as this duality ultimately serves as the semiological economy that instantiates the symbolic distribution of speaking bodies through which the Mexican public will receive the first news of the Zapatista takeover in Chiapas. In other words, it is clear now that by *monolingual* the Chiapan state officials are not referring to the peasants' orality, but to their *nonliteracy*, that is, their incapacity to read or write in Spanish. The "beings of no account," the "part of no part" are thus monolingual to the extent they are nonliterate in Spanish. This distinction is crucial as it announces, for the first time, the critical conditions determining inclusion and exclusion and figures as the means by which "monolinguals" are made to appear (as excluded from the human community); in effect this ascription aims to disqualify their speech in advance of their speaking. It is through this report, the first to describe the Zapatista uprising, that *multilinguals* and *monolinguals* serve as terms to distinguish between those one can see, those with names, those who can speak, and those one does not see, those without names, those without speech.

Given, therefore, this specific emplotment of the police order in the early hours of the Chiapas uprising, it becomes plain to see that the political sequence has nothing to do with correctly assigning designations to the appropriate groups ("Indians are not multilingual"). If *monolinguals* is the specific form through which the Mexican state deprives the Zapatistas the capacity for speech, then it accomplishes nothing to simply invert this economy. Political activity in this scenario does not consist of assigning designations to certain groups, such as determining which group is more accurately monolingual and which is multilingual. Rather political activity commences with the assumption that the police order (both those that form a part and "monolinguals") consists entirely of bodies that could speak all along, which is to say that the designation of *monolingual* is arbitrary and contingent. Rancière (1999: 22–23) adds, "Politics exists because the logos is never simply speech, because it is always indissolubly the account that is made of speech: the account by which a sonorous emission is understood as speech, capable of enunciating what is just, whereas some other emission is merely perceived as a noise signaling pleasure and pain, consent or revolt." In other words, the critical value of the political moment is not simply about the choice and the choosing of whether a certain group is making monolingual noise or is indeed speaking. This simply reproduces the police order currently in play. If, as we saw with Saldaña-Portillo and Mignolo, politics is not about translating silence into speech, then neither is it about choosing between monolinguality and multilinguality, as Montemayor does, but about asserting the fundamental equality of the nameless and logos-less who can speak all along. As Rancière again notes, the political act is precisely in the manner in which this assertion of equality destabilizes the reduction of choice—between noise-discourse, silence-speech, monolingualism-multilingualism—to something altogether different:

> The problem is not for people speaking "different languages," literally or figuratively, to understand each other, any more than it is for "linguistic breakdowns" to be overcome by the invention of new languages. The problem is knowing whether the subjects who count in the interlocution "are" or "are not," whether they are speaking or just making noise. It is knowing whether there is a case for seeing the object they designate as the visible object of the conflict. It is knowing whether the common language in which they are exposing a wrong is indeed a common language. The quarrel has nothing to do with more or less transparent or opaque linguistic contents; it has to with consideration of speaking beings as such. (50)

Informed by this, and looking back at Saldaña-Portillo's and Mignolo's analyses, it becomes evident that they have remained stratified within the contingency of semiotic choice—between noise and discourse—that the political moment they are analyzing has already rendered into crisis. While Saldaña-Portillo's analysis privileges the Zapatistas' "noisy silence," Mignolo opts instead to posit Zapatista discourse (Tojolabal) as already, and fully, incorporated into the democratic order through double translation. In other words, the political moment of the EZLN's emergence has already put into crisis the very categories (and their choice) both Saldaña-Portillo and Mignolo (and even Montemayor) use to talk about them. So although the political in Rancière constitutes a radical redistribution of semiotic categories, they are no longer (to be understood as) the same categories that existed prior to the EZLN's emergence. For it is precisely the contingency of such a distinction as "that which had no business being seen." In effect the EZLN's political wake is not even over yet; the potential grounds of a new semiotic ordering in Mexico are still to be determined. Framed within Rancière's notion of the political, what we must insist upon is not the either/ or of the EZLN's noise and discourse that acts against the lettered city but rather the illiterate speech that emerges when the EZLN threatens them with indistinction.

The political moment, in other words, suspends the distinction between noise and discourse and conditions the possibility for the emergence of an other semiotic ordering. As understood by Rancière, if, as the Zapatistas contend, "peace can be affirmed, demonstrated and convincing in silence," it is not because *silence* is itself an alternative language system that seeks to correct the deficiencies of democratic logic in Mexico with positive sig-nification; *silence* is neither the answer to the Zapatista's problems, nor is it the kernel of radical "truth" upon which democracy must be re-erected to resolve them. Instead, given that the critical implications of Zapatismo and the crisis they provoke in modern Mexico are locatable neither in nor as noise or discourse, one must trace the threshold of illiteracy that binds them together as a hegemonic economy of signification. As *monolingües*, the Zapatistas are themselves that threshold, as they assert their equality as speaking beings within a political system that refuses to admit it has under-stood their speech all along.

Consequently what the Zapatistas ultimately bring to bear is that the state of exception upon which Mexican governmentality is grounded is in the exclusion and inclusion of indigeneity. We must therefore consider that despite the appeals of the EZLN for a more inclusive democratic system, what they are provoking is not an appeal to a better, more ideal form of democracy but rather democracy's irreversible legitimization cri-sis, one in which the relation of exception, outlined by Agamben, would become reversed (bare life as sovereign). That is, by demanding a "bet-ter" or "truer" democracy, the Zapatistas only further point to its impos-sibility as an ideal form of social organization in Mexico. One need only look back to the failed negotiations between the Zapatistas and the Mex-ican government to illustrate this. In this case, it lies between the resti-tutional form of Zapatista democratic discourse as conceived from the Indian-colonial difference and the "impossible" form of Zapatista dem-ocratic discourse emanating from the unlocalizable space of "bare life" within Mexican constitutionality. While the former articulates a vision of a better democracy that would ultimately include those who have been historically excluded, the other articulates the exact same thing, but only in order to suspend and rupture democratic discourse from within and to quicken its collapse.

Early on, many critics were able to point to the Zapatistas' indetermi-nate and ambiguous posture. These critics, far from suggesting that the Zapatistas no longer consider democracy an option, were also careful not to promote their cause as restitutional of its logic. Note, for instance, John

Holloway's (1993: 187) reflection on the uncertainty of the Zapatistas' revolutionary goals:

> An uncertain revolution is, however, an ambiguous and contradictory revolution. Openness and uncertainty are built in to the Zapatista concept of revolution. And that openness means also contradictions and ambiguities. At times it looks as if the EZLN might accept a settlement that falls short of their dreams, at times the presentation of their aims is more limited, apparently more containable. Certainly, both the direction and the appeal of the uprising would be strengthened if it were made explicit that exploitation is central to the systematic negation of dignity and that dignity's struggle is a struggle against exploitation in all its forms. The very nature of the Zapatista concept of revolution means that the movement is particularly open to the charge of ambiguity.

And also José Rabasa's (1997: 424–25) contention that

> in reflecting on Zapatismo, we ought to avoid reductive readings of folklore and retain the impossible as a utopian horizon of alternative rationalities to those dominant in the West. . . . The impossibility of speaking and the eminent folkorization that has haunted the discourse of Zapatistas at every stage of their dialogue with the government—exchanges that could very well be understood as colonial encounters caught in a struggle to the death—do not manifest subalterns who "know far better" and "say it well," but a clear understanding that the possibility of their call to justice, liberty, and democracy resides paradoxically in the impossibility of being understood. The point of departure is not that "subalterns speak very well," but that they "cannot speak" and "choose not to learn how"—indeed, they demand that the discourse of power "learn how to speak to them."

Holloway and Rabasa make clear that it is impossible even today to determine what the Zapatistas are proposing, even if one can understand the democratic discourse deployed in their statements. This is the problem we saw in Saldaña-Portillo's and Mignolo's analyses, which allowed, one could say, absolute counterhegemonic productivity to Zapatista discourse. In other words, what Saldaña-Portillo and Mignolo deferred to was the restitutive appeal to democracy as an end and not as a means by which the

EZLN can effect further crisis, while inhabiting both the inside and outside of the philosophical groundings of modern sovereignty and law. Zapatista discourse cannot be limited to democratic logic—either as an object of critique or appeal—but rather is the site of a radical, persistent interrogation of the grounds of modern governmentality and the foundational exceptions and inclusions upon which it is established. Nowhere is this rendered more visibly than in the EZLN's Sixth Declaration of the Lacandon Jungle (2005), and in the announcement of the group's latest phase, called the Other Campaign (La Otra Campaña). And it is to this pronouncement that we now turn our attention.

The Sixth Declaration of the Lacandon Jungle is a document composed of six parts: "I—What We Are," "II—Where We Are Now," "III—How We See the World," "IV—How We See Our Country Which Is Mexico," "V—What We Want to Do," all of which serve as a preamble to the final section, specifically entitled "Sixth Declaration." It marks the lengthiest of all their pronouncements thus far, as it speaks to both the history of the EZLN since its emergence as well as the reasoning behind their new phase, the Other Campaign. It seems that even for the EZLN, the Other Campaign cannot be understood without first reflecting upon the events preceding it. Prior to the Sixth Declaration, the Zapatistas witnessed the relative failure of several institutional attempts to integrate themselves into the democratic machine— the National Democratic Convention (1994), the Movement for National Liberation (1995), the Zapatista National Liberation Front (1996, dissolved in 2005)—culminating, of course, in the unilateral move by the Mexican government to pass, in 2001, the severely impoverished constitutional reforms on indigenous rights and culture. Unlike previous formal pronouncements by the EZLN regarding the state of its agenda, the Sixth Declaration now reveals a tone cognizant of and critically suspicious of certain limitations of democratic logic. This is new. Unlike many revolutionary groups, which opt only for armed conflict, the EZLN opted for integrative negotiations instead, and, as the Sixth Declaration suggests, this strategy resulted nevertheless in reinforcing its status as a foundational biopolitical exclusion ("bare life") within the state of exception that is Mexico.

> And then we saw quite clearly that there was no point to dialogue and
> negotiation with bad governments of Mexico. That it was a waste of
> time for us to be talking with the politicians, because neither their

hearts nor their words were honest. They were crooked, and they
told lies that they would keep their word, but they did not. In other
words, on that day, when the politicians from the PRI, PAN and PRD
approved a law that was no good, they killed dialogue once and for all,
and they clearly stated that it did not matter what they had agreed to
and signed, because they did not keep their word. And then we did not
make any contacts with the federal branches. Because we understood
that dialogue and negotiation had failed as a result of the political
parties. We saw that blood did not matter to them, nor did death,
suffering, mobilizations, consultas, efforts, national and international
statements, encuentros, accords, signatures, commitments. And so
the political class not only closed, one more time, the door to Indian
peoples, they also delivered a mortal blow to the peaceful resolution—
through dialogue and negotiation—of the war. It can also no longer be
believed that the accords will be fulfilled by someone who comes along
with something or other. (EZLN 2005)

For the first time the EZLN seems cognizant of certain structural (and
not simply historical) obstructions impeding its full political integration
within the democratic state. And this understanding seems to have
emerged precisely from the failed attempts to implement the Accords as
part of a constitutional reform in Mexico. The Sixth Declaration and the
Other Campaign are thus the result of and the point of departure for the
Zapatistas' reconceived understanding of the Mexican state's biopolitical
foundations.

The most revelatory statement in this passage is the one in which the
EZLN consigns the hard-fought San Andrés Accords to oblivion: "It can
also no longer be believed that the accords will be fulfilled [by anyone]." It
can be argued whether the San Andrés Accords would have been sufficient
to the Zapatista agenda, but what cannot be disputed is their importance to
the political resolution of indigenous autonomy within democratic political
systems. However, as Rabasa (2005: 197) notes, one must be wary of state
processes that attempt to resolve political conflicts through the institutionalization of autonomy, for as a form of political status denoting independence from particular state structures, it does not exist outside of sovereign
law but is rather entrenched in it: "The danger is not the implementation
of the Acuerdos of San Andrés nor that there should be laws recognizing

Indian autonomies, but the reduction of the accords to a constitutional resolution of the conflict that would domesticate the constituent power of the multitude. For the crisis of constituent power to be productive, it must retain the will not to be resolved. This, of course, requires a multitude ready to assert its force, its practice of autonomization." As Rabasa notes, the practice of autonomization requires a "will not to be resolved," which is to say a positing of the San Andrés Accords as politically unrecognizable: a legislative pact caught in a state of suspension, whose implementability, as legislative language, cannot be denied, but whose implementation, as legislation, would collapse the grounds of sovereign law in Mexico. And this is precisely where the San Andrés Accords fall now. In other words, in the rush to "resolve" the constitutional crisis implied by the Accords, the Mexican state ultimately betrayed the grounds of its own sovereignty as it concretized the Accords in an affirmative relation of exception to the Mexican Constitution and as it managed to preclude the EZLN's approval and consent to institutionalized forms of autonomy. Thus, aided by the Mexican state's urgency to "resolve," the Zapatistas' abandonment of the San Andrés Accords as a legislative goal—a signed set of documents that signal their one and only link to full democratic integration and autonomy—signals a critical shift in their understanding of political forms, particularly in the ways one can see that the failure of the Accords are now used to further ground their critique.

From now on, according to the Sixth Declaration, no longer do the San Andrés Accords signify the possibility of indigenous integration into the democratic state; rather they now come to signify indigeneity's impossible (yet irrevocable) status within it, in a relation of *nomic* exception. And it is precisely the "impossible" status of the San Andrés Accords that now serve as the threshold of illiteracy (between indigeneity and sovereign law) and the source of "autonomization" that threatens the formal efficacy of democratic distribution of rights. As a result, and as a theoretical point of departure for the Other Campaign, the San Andrés Accords are still a functional and determinant aspect of the EZLN's agenda; however, they now assume a new form and are conceived differently: not as a legislatable agreement, the goal of which would be a change in the constitutional status of indigenous people (recognition and autonomy), but as an illiterate challenge to constitutionality as a sovereign form (illiteracy and autonomization): "The Constitution is all warped [*manoseada*] and changed now. It's no longer the one that had the rights and liberties of working people."

Consequently what we see in the Sixth Declaration is the ushering in of a constitutionality of its own, one grounded not in the exclusion of "bare life" but in the San Andrés Accords: the threshold of illiteracy signaling the irresolvable and irrevocable rupture within the Mexican constitutional form. More than simply a restitutional, counterhegemonic constitution, the Sixth Declaration pronounces an illiterate constitutional accord with "the simple and humble people of Mexico," one that exists in an affirmative relation of exception to Mexican constitutionality and hence one that irrevocably runs parallel to its irresolvable crisis. The Declaration itemizes its own accord with the people of Mexico in the following manner:

1. We are going to continue fighting for the Indian peoples of Mexico, but now not just for them and not with only them, but for all the exploited and dispossessed of Mexico, with all of them and all over the country. And when we say all the exploited of Mexico, we are also talking about the brothers and sisters who have had to go to the United States in search of work in order to survive.

2. We are going to go to listen to, and talk directly with, without intermediaries or mediation, the simple and humble of the Mexican people, and, according to what we hear and learn, we are going to go about building, along with those people who, like us, are humble and simple, a national program of struggle, but a program which will be clearly of the left, or anti-capitalist, or anti-neoliberal, or for justice, democracy, and liberty for the Mexican people.

3. We are going to try to build, or rebuild, another way of doing politics, one which once again has the spirit of serving others, without material interests, with sacrifice, with dedication, with honesty, which keeps its word, whose only payment is the satisfaction of duty performed, or like the militants of the left did before, when they were not stopped by blows, jail or death, let alone by dollar bills.

4. We are also going to go about raising a struggle in order to demand that we make a new Constitution, new laws which take into account the demands of the Mexican people, which are housing, land, work, food, health, education, information, culture,

independence, democracy, justice, liberty, and peace. A new
Constitution which recognizes the rights and liberties of the people
and which defends the weak in the face of the powerful. (2005)

Like the San Andrés Accords' legislative suspension within Mexican
constitutionality, the Sixth Declaration, insofar as it simultaneously
rehearses this critique, also points to its own programmatic impossibility
within the constitutional form. In other words, as illustrated in item 4, to
erect a new democratic constitution on the illiterate grounds of the Accords
is to collapse the grounds of democratic constitutionality as it suspends
it in potentiality. What the Zapatistas demand is ultimately not simply
counterhegemonic but impossible, and whether they are aware of this or not
is beyond the point; their demanding of the impossible threatens the sheer
contingency of the Mexican social order itself: between noise and discourse.

This critical path has been traced by Gareth Williams in his essay "The
Mexican Exception and the 'Other Campaign'" (2007) and most recently
in his book *The Mexican Exception* (2011), in which he elaborates, from
within the Zapatista' Other Campaign, a notion of the political grounded
in the possibility of language beyond silence or speech as hegemonic
articulation. As distinct from Saldaña-Portillo's and Mignolo's reliance on
the translation of Zapatista silence to speech, Williams (2007: 143) instead
points toward an inscription of the confirmation of equality in the Other
Campaign that reveals

the possibility of an egalitarian language that emerges in the wake
of, and in spite of, the state's biopolitical calculations and administra-
tive pacts. . . . It emerges in the name of something other than sovereign abandonment to life in the state of exception, or to the law-pre-
serving violence of an increasingly flailing juridical and political
order. . . . This is a campaign not for electoral victory (that is, not for
hegemony, counterhegemony, consensus, or homogeneity) but for a
life-giving communication in the wake of ruin. Indeed, it is a campaign for just language itself.

As a call for another language, an ordering of social realities beyond noise-
discourse and silence-speech, Williams conceives of Zapatista language
as a semiotic withdrawal from the matrix of sovereignty, as the EZLN's
subtracting itself from the configuration of the formal order of democracy

in Mexico. In short, it is a critical tracing of a beyond to the hegemonic articulation of signification as silence-speech and noise-discourse. It is a call to a beyond to *both* silence *and* speech, noise *and* discourse, identity *and* difference.

In Williams withdrawal and subtraction, as opposed to translation and transculturation, signal the radical grounds of a politics based on the confirmation of the equality of all speaking beings to each other. It is a matter of the form in which the Zapatistas present an accounting of themselves as "the part of no part," as speaking beings who wish to transform the social field by withdrawing from it. Or, again, as Williams (2011: 40) argues, "Withdrawal and subtraction are the first political steps in the EZLN's proposed challenge to the reason of nation-state sovereignty. Withdrawal in this context is not just a negative force fully dependent upon, and circumscribed by, the characteristics and maneuvers of its negated object. It is the advent-word for the possibility of an infinitely preferable police to come; that is, for the possibility of an affirmative suspension of the current state form in the name of freedom." As the *monolingües*, the "part of no part," the Zapatistas assert their equality as speaking beings through the simultaneous assertion of and withdrawal from democratic logic's inability to include them as speaking—and hence equal—beings in the first place, a confrontation in which, for Williams, democracy "is both the adversary and the unconditional promise of a new foundation of social life" (37). In other words, what the crisis of Mexican governmentality that this "politics to come" reveals is the dissolution of (and the very choice between) silence-noise and speech-discourse monolinguality-literacy as biopolitical categories. This emergent language (the accounting of speech) does not seek incorporation into already established allotments within the social field ("noise" for "discourse"), but rather, as Williams emphasizes, this "advent-word" will emerge neither from the discourse of hegemony (neither as "diverse" speech *nor* the "monolinguality" of subalternity) but from a threshold of illiteracy between (that which both joins and separates) noise and discourse, silence and speech, inclusion and exclusion.

However, the formal aspects of Zapatista withdrawal that Williams sees in the Other Campaign can be traced back even further. There was precedent. Until the issuing of the Sixth Declaration and the Other Campaign in 2005, 1998 marked the last declaration the EZLN would make for seven years. In fact the time elapsed between the group's previous declarations has never been greater than the years that separate the fifth from the sixth. For the EZLN this was a period marked by a series of setbacks and unforeseeable complications resulting from their negotiations with the Mexican state: from the breakdown of talks at the Mesas de Dialogo in 1996, the intervention of the *ley* COCOPA initiative, the massacre at Acteal in 1997, and, immediately following Vicente Fox's election as president in 2000, Congress's unilateral passing of the Law for Indigenous Rights and Culture (a heavily amended version of the ley COCOPA which the EZLN rejected as a "betrayal of the San Andres Accords"). To be sure, this period marked a most critical moment in their history since their emergence in 1994 (see Higgins 2001). Given its immediate historical context, the Fifth Declaration, issued on July 19, 1998, remains one of the most significant of the EZLN communiqués, not only because its drafting was entrenched in the then ongoing though unsuccessful campaign for constitutional integration, but because it simultaneously (and implicitly) enacts a short-circuiting of the signifying structure that radically transforms the very terms of the speaking situation between the Zapatistas and the Mexican state.

Indeed, the Fifth Declaration is the most interesting because, as indicated, it foreshadowed the EZLN's subsequent failure to secure constitutional reforms for the San Andrés Accords. The Fifth Declaration is an acknowledgment that while the Zapatistas' initial foray to effect changes in Mexican national politics managed to alter the party landscape, it was insufficient to shift the grounds of the Mexican political system itself. Reflecting upon the Fifth Declaration, it is difficult not to perceive a tacit shift in their language from previous communiqués. On the one hand, the EZLN uses the Fifth Declaration to respond to the state's deployment of the usual measures of counterinsurgency: stalled negotiations and low-intensity warfare, denouncing the government's violation of the cease-fire agreement and thus the terms of negotiation. But on the other hand—and more critically—the Zapatistas employ this same declaration to respond to these immediate events by not responding: a response of nonresponse, illiterate speech.

> While the government piled up hollow words and hastened to argue with
> a rival that constantly slipped away, the Zapatistas made a weapon of
> struggle out of silence, which [the government] did not understand and

against which [the government] could do nothing, and time and time
again they opposed our silence with sharp lies, bullets, bombs, blows. Just
as we discovered a weapon in words after the combat in January 1994,
now we did it in silence. While the government offered everyone threats,
death and destruction, we were able to learn from ourselves, teach ourselves, and teach another form of struggle, and teach that with reason,
truth and history, one could fight and win . . . through silence. (1998)

What is striking in this passage, and something that runs through the entire
Fifth Declaration, is a certain deployment of silence as the heterogeneous,
non-All of speech. This declaration effects a staging of the transposition of
their silence into speech not through "words" but through the torsion that
reveals the very "word's" difference from itself. To wit, where the Zapatistas
once had "discovered a weapon in words," the word itself—the void upon
which the hegemonic articulation of signification is established—is now the
object of the very disagreement between the contingencies of silence and
speech for which Zapatismo is a name.

What, for the Zapatistas, initially began as an insurgent declaration of
war against the state (First Declaration) and which subsequently shifted to
a discourse of negotiation with the same (Third Declaration) has, in the
period between the Fourth and Fifth Declaration, been reinscribed onto a
terrain of silent engagement, one no longer grounded on guerrilla warfare
("we did not know them") nor the "police" logic of constitutional reform
("double translation," "getting in/letting in") but rather as the unconcealing
of the void that inhabits the very core of hegemonic signification in
postrevolutionary Mexico.

We saw that our silence was shield and sword which wounded and
exhausted those who want to impose war. We saw our silence make the
power which simulates peace and good government slip time and again,
and make their powerful death machine crash time and again against
the silent wall of our resistance. We saw that with each new attack
they won less and lost more. We saw that by not fighting, we were
fighting . . . and we saw that the will for peace can also be affirmed,
demonstrated, and convincing in silence. (EZLN 1998)

For the EZLN of the Fifth Declaration, silence is installed as the non-
All of the word, the irreducible gap between the word and itself, the

threshold of illiteracy that responds neither with declarations of war nor with pleas for negotiation—with words—but rather with the silence brought about by irreducibly heterogeneous signification. Neither noise nor discourse but beyond both, Zapatista semiosis constitutes the inscription of equality that makes visible the "sheer contingency of the [police] order" in Mexico.

Ultimately the heterogeneity of Zapatista silence, "which [the Mexican government] did not understand and against which they could do nothing," represents neither an utterance of "truth" nor the presentation of a subaltern language through which it is voiced. Rather silence is the form in which the Zapatistas present an accounting of themselves as "the part of no part," as speaking beings who have effectively transformed the social field by speaking silence. As it is conceived in the Fifth Declaration, silence, simultaneously spoken and inaudible, illiterate and illegible, not only serves to mark the EZLN's withdrawal from the Mesas de Dialogo but also signals the semiotic irruption of a silent "magnitude that escapes ordinary measurement, this part of those who have no part that is nothing and everything" (Rancière 1999: 15).

Therefore, if, as Rancière (1999: 30) argues, "political activity demonstrates the sheer contingency of the order, the equality of any speaking being with any other speaking being," then the political effect of illiterate Zapatista semiosis is a suspension of the distinction between silence-noise and speech-discourse, the conditions of which potentialize the emergence of another semiotic ordering that Williams reads in the Other Campaign. Therefore, and as we see in both Rancière and Williams, the critical value of the irruptive moment is not simply about the choice and the choosing of whether a certain group is being "noisy" or is indeed speaking. Nor is it about simply translating noisy silence to "diversal" speech, nor about correctly determining which group is more monolingual. Rather it is the very manner in which the political situation destabilizes the reduction of choice—between silence-speech, noise-discourse, monolinguality-literacy—to something else altogether. Therefore as a critical accounting of "those who are of no ac/count," what Zapatista silence thus makes visible is "what had no business being seen" in Latin American disciplinary practice: namely, the weakness and ultimately conservative nature of the persistent appeal to translation and transculturation as the grounds for politics.

Again, translating, transculturating—that is, sublating—subalternity into counterhegemonic ideological production does nothing but concretize as truth or Being what is otherwise the artificiality, "the sheer contingency" of subalternity itself. Instead, following Williams, what Zapatismo attests to is the crisis of silence-speech as hegemonic articulation, and this through a notion of the political grounded in the inscription of equality as speaking beings—the heterogeneous assumption of democracy—that their silence renders both visible and irrevocable.

Hinging on Exclusion and Exception:
Bare Life at the U.S.-Mexico Border

In 2002 Debra Castillo and María Tabuenca Córdoba published *Border Women: Writing from* La Frontera, a book featuring select readings of women's writing from and about the U.S.-Mexico border. *Border Women* is presented as a properly binational study of U.S.-Mexico border literature. That is to say, it is conceived with the specific and explicit intention to include border writers from *both* Mexico and the United States. According to these authors, there is a reason for such attentiveness, emphasis, and specificity in including writers from *both* sides of the border, and this reason governs the principal disciplinary intervention they seek to make: to complicate and challenge the predominance of Chicano and U.S.-based scholars (over their Mexican counterparts) in critical discussions of U.S.-Mexico border writing and culture.

In the introduction Castillo and Tabuenca Córdoba work to unconceal a foundational tension that exists between the ways the border is conceived, elaborated, and deployed in U.S. and Mexican cultural spheres. While a

stated goal of their book is to "develop a coherent perspective on the prolif-
eration of border theories and practices" on and about the U.S.-Mexico border (2002: 5), Castillo and Tabuenca Córdoba nevertheless seek to assert a
fundamental discord, a fault line, another critical border lying between the
U.S.-Mexico border itself, a discursive fissure persistently disjointing efforts
at disciplinary convergence and straining otherwise assumed notions of solidarity between them. For critics working on either side of the U.S.-Mexico
border, they contend, though they are allied through a mutual and simultaneous engagement with the critical realities of this border, no "convincing
critical framework" has been established between them. As a result, what
we have is a region of study programmatically and ideologically at odds
with itself: "Despite the numerous elements that would seem to suggest
the affinity between U.S. and Mexican border theories and literatures, the
asymmetry between the United States and Mexico also marks the differences between the two cultural projects. The border as perceived from the
United States is more a textual—theoretical—border than a geographical
one" (6). Here Castillo and Tabuenca Córdoba appeal to the history of economic and political inequalities between the United States and Mexico as
conditioning the emergence of the divergent disciplinary projects each side
of the border now inhabits: a textually and theoretically conceived border
from the North and an irreducibly material ("geographic") border from the
South.

However, that cultural production from the South continues to occupy
a marginal, dependent, and resistant intellectual status to those from
the North is not necessarily what is at issue here. Castillo and Tabuenca
Córdoba's argument runs deeper. They insist that as the southern side of
U.S.-Mexico border always, as its own predetermined condition, suffers
from asymmetrical power relations with the United States, so too have their
own intellectual contributions over this very border been subordinated and
marginalized by those emanating from their Chicano and border studies
counterparts in the North. What this means is that the effects of such
asymmetrically grounded historical and political relations at the U.S.-Mex-
ico border are further constitutive of that border. In other words, the border
both marks the source of the asymmetry and is simultaneously governed
by it.

For Castillo and Tabuenca Córdoba, this ideological tension at the
border is laid bare by the confrontation between competing disciplinary

figurations over it. Since the mid-1980s, they contend, the border itself has become the site of an entrenched (and again asymmetrically given) conflict between two seemingly exclusive interpretive practices (i.e., "theoretical" *or* "geographical") emanating from two distinct cartographies (i.e., the United States and Mexico) and constituted by two disciplinary camps: Chicano scholars and border theorists in the United States[1]— whose disciplinary and theoretical mapping of the U.S. Southwest and Mexican American culture has "effectively captured the bulk of the attention" and therefore come to predominate most discussions of this border (Castillo and Tabuenca Córdoba 2002: 5)—and northern Mexican *fronterizo* critics and writers for whom "the borderline itself retains a stronger materiality" than for Chicano studies and for whom the border is very real and "difficult to conceive" as "metaphor" (3). They thus ascribe a political foundation to the relation between "the ways in which the Northern Mexican border serves from the one side as a definitive barrier and from the other as an inconsequential (immaterial, metaphorical) line" (2) wherein predominant structures of knowledge and power in the United States results in the northern Mexican border region as a form of colonialism. They argue that "the intellectual colonialism from which the Mexican border has suffered to this day will be perpetuated to the detriment of both its primary referents—the people in general or flesh-and-blood artists—and its literature" (4). Given these terms, it is not difficult to see that what is most at stake for Castillo and Tabuenca Córdoba within such textually based, intellectually "colonialist" projects is that they constitute critical work whose "efforts to erase the borders and the appropriation of categories such as that of the migrant, and even of the border itself, facilitate the erasure of the physical border, along with its flesh-and-blood migrants, writers, and readers, as well as the artistic expression that is produced on the Mexican side" (13). Consequently the predominance of such "border-as-metaphor" theory figures in Castillo and Tabuenca Córdoba as a "colonializing gesture" (13) that effectively subordinates and obscures—erases—the northern Mexican border's very materiality and referential status. Therefore what Castillo and Tabuenca Córdoba conceive at and as the U.S.-Mexico border is an irreducible and asymmetrically given tension between the colonizing aspects of the "metaphoricity" of theoretical borders and this "other" border's very material, literal, and resistant positivity.

Before going further, it must be mentioned that neither the form nor the terms given in the staging of this dispute over the U.S.-Mexico border—the assertion of competing (literal *or* metaphoric) conceptualizations of the border emanating from its sides—are unusual or surprising. In fact highlighting an opposition and hierarchy is, after all, the process and formula by which all counterhegemonic ideological practice inserts itself into the discursive field of an established order. In this discussion we are pointed to marginalized and subordinated formulations of the border coming from Mexico (understood as *Fronterizo*), which confronts and defines itself against its more prominent—metaphoric, theoretical, textual—disciplinary articulation in the United States as ascribed to Chicano studies. Nevertheless simply highlighting this difference, particularly in order to affirm the positivity (the materiality) of the subordinated term, only reproduces this economy and does nothing to alter the logic that sustains it. Nevertheless we must not fail to note that despite their critiques, Castillo and Tabuenca Córdoba's proposition is ultimately a modest one: they urge us to recognize that there are two sides to this border, each with disciplinary contributions over it, neither of which one should marginalize, homogenize, or be forced to disavow. Only by recognizing and informing one's work with perspectives from *both* sides can real transborder work be accomplished: "It is important either to take both sides—the United States and Mexico—into consideration or to be specific about which side one is going to talk about or study and recognize the material and metaphorical differences involved in such transnational analyses" (4). In short, they insist, there is a *real* difference between the sides of this border, they should be understood as *equivalently* different, and the maintenance of their irreducibility is a necessary precondition for any truly meaningful engagement with the U.S.-Mexico border.

However, it should be clear that the impulse to seek an articulation of the border devoid of ideological attachments, immediate and identical to itself, to which all groups could and should subscribe without conflict, is itself such an attachment. If the border is made visible, conceivable—as object in representation—only through existing and conflicting claims over it, then what should concern us most of all are the form and terms of the dispute itself. For, as Rancière (1999: 27) argues, "parties do not exist prior to the conflict they name and in which they are counted as parties. . . . [The conflict] it[self] concerns the speech situation itself and its performers." That is, while attention is given to the sociocultural processes and parties between these "sides" of the border, the very border itself continues to evade scrutiny and assumes a dangerous transparency. Given their disciplinary mapping of the field, and if the study of the U.S.-Mexico border should indeed continue to mean anything at all, Castillo and Tabuenca Córdoba seek to establish, in unequivocal terms, the assumption of difference that inheres on, at, or from the border: that differences exist, that those differences are irreducible, and that those differences are nonhomogeneous but nevertheless equivalent differences. Under such conditions, and verging on tautology, study of the U.S.-Mexico border can be nothing other than the exploration and understanding of the border as the site of (dis)equivalent differences amongst its "sides," and only even and equal consideration given to both "sides" will serve to promote and maintain it. In short, within Castillo and Tabuenca Córdoba's discussion, the border itself is taken only as an algebraic relation expressing a state of entropy ($A \neq B$) where there *should* be equilibrium ($A = B$). However, in either case (entropy *or* equilibrium) the border is deployed simply as a formal sign structure used to express these relations, and nothing more.

From this it is not difficult to see that the principle quality of U.S. border work being contested here, as that which "has effectively captured the bulk of the attention" and to which is attributed an effect of "intellectual colonialism," is precisely the intrusion of theory at the U.S.-Mexico border. What is tacitly being asserted is that U.S.-based border theory has come to intrude and lay claim to discussions of the border in Mexico—onto a side of the border that is not proper to it—from where the border is otherwise conceived in more literal terms. However, one must be careful not to confuse Castillo and Tabuenca Córdoba's critique of the hegemony of U.S. border theory with Scott Michaelsen and David E. Johnson's critique of the same in *Border Theory: The Limits of Cultural Politics* (1997). While Chicano studies' specific relationship to the border serves as the discursive index in both critiques, they do not emerge from the same critical position. According to Michaelsen and Johnson, for Chicano studies the U.S.-Mexico border obtains "as a place . . . of a certain property, and of a certain properness," through which a specific and exclusively border-forged form of hybrid identity (Chicano) emerges and keeps intact (15). As a critical practice engaged in U.S. cultural politics and identity, Chicano studies constitutes the southwest border within a "narrative of possession, a genealogy of occupation" that, inscribed as a "right of property" and exclusive "birthright" of Chicano identity, has resulted in "a certain legislation that governs access to culture and cultural identification": "the policing of the border of culture and of the borderlands in general as the location of Chicano culture" (16, 21). In short, the problem with Chicano studies' relationship to the border, they contend, is that the U.S.-Mexico border is ultimately inscribed as a ("theoretically impossible") desire for hybridic purity: a geopolitical discourse of identity formation that, while pointing to itself as the very product of heterogeneity, actually, and by necessity, disavows it, and that, while conceived as or within a politics of inclusivity, actually, and by necessity, founds itself through exclusions.[2] What Michaelsen and Johnson's critique of Chicano studies ultimately means to this discussion of U.S.-Mexico border theory relations will soon become apparent. If their critique of Chicano studies is that it engages in exclusionary, identity-based thinking and politics, then the question we inevitably have to entertain is the degree to which Castillo and Tabuenca Córdoba manage to avert this in their own (counter)elaboration of the border.

Unfortunately they don't. The oppositional qualities Castillo and Tabuenca Córdoba ascribe to this intellectual border—metaphoricity and literalness—seek not only to posit and designate the northern Mexican border's proper and more immediate relation to its "primary referent"—the border itself—and its materiality but also to displace the theoretical and "colonial" hegemony of the United States over the border as mediated, secondary, exterior. At the core of this discussion is the (re)partitioning of the study of the border, between that based in the United States whose work is "textual" and "theoretically" oriented and that based in Mexico for whom the border retains a "material," "geographical," "flesh-and-blood" referentiality. But further still, it is precisely against the theoretical "colonialism" of U.S. border work that the literal, physical, and material grounding of the U.S.-Mexico border is both installed and affirmed.

Nevertheless Castillo and Tabuenca Córdoba's oppositional categories—literal *versus* metaphorical—are neither sustainable nor without critical precedent. Otherwise known as logocentrism, metaphoricity and literalness, when taken as oppositional, axiomatically bound terms, cannot but produce undesired results, and further obfuscates the principal task which "is not a matter of inverting the literal meaning and the figurative meaning but of determining the 'literal' meaning of writing as metaphoricity itself" (Derrida 1976: 15). What is more, as Derrida goes on to note, "all that functions as *metaphor* in these discourses confirms the privilege of the logos and founds the 'literal' meaning then given to writing. . . . This metaphor remains enigmatic and refers to a 'literal' meaning of writing as the first metaphor" (15). In short, in Castillo and Tabuenca Córdoba's ascription of metaphoricity and literalness onto what they perceive as a mutually exclusive intellectual relation between theoretically and materially based work on the U.S.-Mexico border, they appeal to the metaphysics of presence that assigns and confirms verity to "literal" expression, and thus to the material ground of the border. However, what is fundamentally at stake in this border, what is at stake between any and all borders, is not a dispute over the relationship between words and things but rather the always already mediated relation between words and referentiality itself.

At work in Castillo and Tabuenca Córdoba is the very process through which the assignment of metaphoricity to U.S.-based border work "confirms the privilege of the logos and founds the 'literal' meaning" then given to the Mexican-based border. What gets obscured in all this is the metaphoricity of the literal itself, as first metaphor: the metaphoricity of the literal border as first metaphorical border. Consequently, these partitions do not stand up to scrutiny; the material, geographical, and flesh-and-blood side of the U.S.-Mexico border is ultimately no less metaphorical and textual than the "theoretical" border work it opposes itself to. As such, in the attempt to reinforce the intellectual partition that exists between U.S. and Mexican scholars working on the border by appealing to the primacy, immediacy, and self-identical referentiality of the material border, Castillo and Tabuenca Córdoba ultimately ground themselves within the very metaphoricity the border itself is presumed to ward off. Therefore if the principle charge against U.S. border theory is its "intellectual colonialism" over the Mexican side of the border, it is not because the former is any more metaphorical than its fronterizo formalization. This always already displaced and distantiated condition at the U.S.-Mexico border forecloses in advance the grounds of dispute they seek to engage in with their northern counterparts, for it reveals that the Mexican side of this border, the side onto which is ascribed primordial materiality and flesh-and-blood referentiality, is instead the very first metaphor—the inescapably and irreducibly figural foundation of all geopolitical borders and of all border writing.

Therefore, even though Castillo and Tabuenca Córdoba were right to finally bring to the fore the dynamic and critical function of the

relationship between the material and the metaphorical in the ideological formation of sociocultural realities along the U.S.-Mexico border,
they are nevertheless hasty in their assumption that the material and the
metaphorical are mutually exclusive categories that can be harnessed to
identify, circumscribe, and neatly segregate sides of the border from each
other, and ultimately mistaken to suggest that what is otherwise an ideological effect of a historical contingency between the U.S. and the Mexican state is instead a dispute over naturalized cultural essences that, on
the one hand, are deployed as preexisting the erection of this border but,
on the other hand, further serve to justify and legitimate the need for
maintaining the existence of it. Castillo and Tabuenca Córdoba make
this position explicitly clear in their evaluation of Gloria Anzaldúa's *Bor-
derlands/La Frontera* (1987). It is precisely through such a text, wherein
hybridity (racial, cultural, linguistic, and epistemological) is deployed and
formalized as the essential grounds of a border cultural identity, that Castillo and Tabuenca Córdoba (2002: 15–16) identify the former's effects as
the principal danger of border-as-metaphor discourse:

> In the Chicano/a attempt to decolonize the border, there is still a
> trace of "a longing for unity and cohesion," as can be noted in Gloria
> Anzaldúa's search for a mythological space in *Borderlands/La Frontera*.
> In the same way that [Guillermo] Gomez-Peña has been legitimated as
> "the migrant," critics have made Anzaldúa "the representative" of "the
> border." In Anzaldúa's work the border also functions primarily as a
> metaphor, in that the border space as a geopolitical region converges
> with discourses of ethnicity, class, gender/sex, and sexual preference.
> Nevertheless, Anzaldúa's book, despite its multiple crossings of cultural
> and gender borders—from ethnicity to feminisms, from the academic
> realm to the work of blue-collar labor—tends to essentialize relations
> between Mexico and the United States. Her third country between two
> nations, the borderlands, is still a metaphorical country defined and
> narrated from a First World perspective. Her story is less ludic than that
> of Gomez-Peña, and more anchored in real referents, but these referents
> are defined solely in terms of an outcast status. Anzaldúa's famous
> analysis does not take into cognizance the many other othernesses
> related to a border existence; her "us" is limited to U.S. minorities; her
> "them" is U.S. dominant culture. Mexican border dwellers are also

"us" and "them" with respect to their Chicana/o counterparts; they can
in some sense be considered the "other" of both dominant and U.S.
resistance discourses. . . . Anzaldúa speak[s] from the interstices of U.S.
dominant culture and [she] ha[s] self-authorized [her] hybrid discourse
in the social construction of that difference.

Anzaldúa was never "authorized" to speak. We are made to understand by
this passage that while not having the authority to speak she nevertheless did,
and as a result of her disregard for this authority—in "self-authorizing"—she
spoke out of turn, out of line, out of place. This passage in effect constitutes
an act of censure for speaking beings along the border, not only of Anzaldúa
but of all Chicano thought as well. As an act of censure, it is important to
keep in mind it ultimately has very little to do with this or that aspect of
Anzaldúa's text; rather, and more fundamentally, it is over Anzaldúa's very
right to speak in the first place. Speaking solely "from the interstices of U.S.
dominant culture," Castillo and Tabuenca Córdoba contend, Anzaldúa
had no authority to speak on, from, or about the U.S.-Mexico border, and
thus disrupted a field of intelligibility that had previously regulated both
speech and speaking beings at this border, radically reconfiguring its terms
and scope in the process. For from Anzaldúa's improperly exercised—"self-
authorized"—right to speak emerged a "hybrid discourse" that effectively
and perhaps irrevocably "essentialize[d] relations between Mexico and the
United States" and by means of which has been established as "representative
of the border." Ultimately what Castillo and Tabuenca Córdoba challenge
is the legitimacy of this disciplinary outcome, given the illegitimacy of
Anzaldúa's speech.

To be clear, Anzaldúa's principal infraction here is not that she conceived metaphorically what one should instead conceive literally; it is not
that her formalization of the borderlands is utterly "mythological" when the
urgency is to speak of the materiality of U.S.-Mexico geopolitics; in short,
it is not that she essentialized what should not be essentialized. Rather the
problem for Castillo and Tabuenca Córdoba is that Anzaldúa spoke, literally, out of place, that in Anzaldúa's "self-authorization" to speak from more
than one side, in her breaching of proper protocols of place that would permit her to speak in line, she misspeaks, misapprehends, and thus ultimately
mis-essentializes the U.S.-Mexico border as hybrid what is otherwise, to
"authorized" parties, simply *entropic*. In other words, the problem is not

that Anzaldúa's borderlands are too metaphorical for the U.S.-Mexico border, but rather that they are an unsanctioned metaphorics and therefore
the *wrong* kind of metaphoricity. In the "social construction of difference"
along the U.S.-Mexico border, the asymmetrically governed, entropic, cultural ground of fronterizo identity is the one seen defining itself against an
unauthorized and entirely mis-essentialized form of equilibrium.

Before I move on, I must state that I am not concerned with ascertaining
the degree to which the critiques against Anzaldúa's *Borderlands/La Frontera* are warranted or not; I do not intend to carry out an analysis of nor seek
to resolve the legitimacy of the disciplinary dispute between these actors.
What I am interested in are the critical realities that are revealed through
their very confrontation and the contradictions that result from the terms
and conditions by which this dispute is installed in the first place—in the
dispute itself as a precondition of the U.S.-Mexico border as object of study
and ground of cultural identity.

One can now see how Castillo and Tabuenca Córdoba's assertion of a
logocentric economy immediately confronts itself at its own epistemological threshold, and the resulting critical effects weigh heavily and precipi-
tously on their subsequent identitarian claims. For if the purity or unmediated properness of the Mexican side of the border is the primary contention,
and if the speech that emerges from within this field of intelligibility is
therefore assumed to be a direct and entirely unmediated relation between
things and words, then what is ultimately being asserted about the category of speech, of speaking beings (that which counts as speech and who
counts as a speaking being) and of their allotment along that other, metaphorical or mythological side of the border that is ascribed to Anzaldúa's
borderlands? What kind of counterhegemonic appeal is being struck here
in the name of fronterizo-ness when it is defined in (literal) opposition to a
metaphorical Chicano border identity, narrative of possession, and "mestizo
aboriginality" (Michaelsen and Johnson 1997: 17)? In other words, what
do Castillo and Tabuenca Córdoba mean to suggest by the literal or material when the foundational tropes of Chicano discourse, against which *lo
fronterizo* is being defined, are nothing if not mestizo and hybrid spatial
and identitarian constructs? What, specifically, are they reacting against
in this dispute if not the impurity and improperness of both speech and
speaking beings encroaching from the non-Mexican side of this border?
If, as Michaelsen and Johnson argue, Chicano identity (like all identity) is

ultimately based upon exclusivist politics, then Castillo and Tabuenca Córdoba, who are defining *lo fronterizo* against both it and its cultural hegemony at the U.S.-Mexico border, exhibit nothing else than a more forceful articulation of this very same practice. How can one come to terms with this disciplinary dispute when an appeal to purity—a reactionary implication to be sure—is used to substantiate claims of the northern Mexican border's marginalized and irreducible materiality?

Given these terms, it is clear to which of the aforementioned assumptions Castillo and Tabuenca Córdoba subscribe (the material-literal and the metaphorical-theoretical; fronterizo-entropy and the Chicano-hybrid), and neither, it must be stated, presents us with a direct path to trace the critical impasse faced at this border. To the extent that these positionalities are each defined against the other—each asserting identity from the other's difference and exclusion—these analytic assumptions come to constitute the very impasse they themselves were deployed to resolve. Or as Michaelsen and Johnson (1997: 18) suggest, "to the extent that various 'studies' take sides, occupy one side of the border against another—engage in resistance against assimilation or collaboration—they all share in the same problems." In other words, border studies—as the preconstituted tension between the need to reduce and the need to sustain borders as a principle of identity—is itself the impasse that it cannot but disavow and that cannot but continue to reproduce its own impassibility as tautological grounds for existence. As Michaelsen and Johnson insist, "one must mark an other relation to [the border]," "an other way of thinking [that] produces defamiliarizing border readouts without the possibility of laying it on the line," one "which presupposes and circumscribes nothing . . . one in which differences mean nothing, add up without sum," and one that "can never be totalized to account for identity . . . in which there would be no (question of) identity" (22, 15, 4). In short, they reason, the flaw in reading borders through a principle of identity ($A = A \neq -A$) or through a logic of equivalent differences ($A = B$) is that they obscure, by necessity, the assumption of heterogeneity ($A = -(-A)$)—and the radical principle of equality that is inscribed in it—that serves as the constitutive, foundational exclusion for both.

In this discussion I understand border studies the way Moreiras (2001: 129, 135) positions the discourse of Latinamericanism: as a disciplinary practice through whose "double injunction to reduce and preserve" borders serves as an "apparatus of mediation for transcultural social relations."

Within such an approximation, U.S.-Mexico border studies serves not only as a mechanism that "expresses and regulates relationships between groups with conflicting claims over it" (127) but also as the preconstituted set of parameters through which the border itself "come[s] into light as object through representation; [as] the object is not given except as an always already socially articulated phenomenon" (127). As such, border studies itself cannot but posit its object of investigation in or through representation: as always already mediated, necessarily dissymmetrical, and hence contested by competing claims over it. What is at stake here is determining whether or not one can divorce the U.S.-Mexico border from "groups with conflicting claims over it," whether the representation of a border over which there is no conflict is even thinkable, and whether the representation of the border itself "could be taken as the alterity on which a new form of epistemic appropriation needs to occur, whereby the possibility would be released of an alternative politico-epistemic dispensation—'another lease of life . . . so as to change life itself'" (133). These pages constitute just such an attempt.

And it is precisely from the irreducibly representational nature of the border within border studies that Castillo and Tabuenca Córdoba reveal, through tautology, the epistemological limit that both enables and forecloses its very possibility. To the extent that their use of the border remains nevertheless a figure of equivalency through which they define their cultural project against those on the other side, there is no object outside of its disputation in representation. For if scholars from both sides of a border are among the groups with "conflicting claims over it," then neither has a proper claim over it, and thus no ground to stake identity on nor control over the forms of alterity that assert themselves from its restitutional excess. As Moreiras (2001: 130) contends, "Alterity is always present within every given group and contact only happens at the unrepresentable border or outer edge of the groups themselves." In other words, alterity is not to be found on the other side of the border but rather at the threshold of illiteracy that is the border itself. Such is the case here that one does not have the luxury to choose between Castillo and Tabuenca Córdoba's either/or; however, it is a choice that must nevertheless be attended to as a predicament within hegemony itself, as its limit, as the trace of its necessary insufficiency, as the opening to the irruptive potential of alterity that this either/or seeks to keep hidden from view.

Therefore, in the critical tracing of the partition that both binds and separates U.S.-Mexico border work from each other, the task becomes to explore how this critical disjunction among scholars working on both sides of the border preconstitutes the border as an object of dispute, that is, how the terms themselves condition its representation as always already asymmetrically and unevenly given. But further, and more important, to understand how, through inclusive-exclusion, this dispute is constituted upon and opposes itself against a negative territoriality—bare life—that both conceals and reveals a zone of double exclusion from those conflicting cultural spheres staked out by groups with existing claims over it. So it is precisely to the necessarily contradictory, oppositional, and irreducible figuration of the border that we must direct our attention. For it is only through this figure that one can explore the critical aperture revealed by border studies' implicit and foundational injunction to both reduce and preserve borders and as the very means by which to trace the illiterate ground upon which competing claims over the U.S.-Mexico border hinge: the sovereign ban of border crossing, the abandonment of border crossers to the state of exception, and their irreducible alterity as a negative community through whose exclusion both Chicano and fronterizo identities can take root.

Given the cultural and identitarian stakes of this border dispute, one must turn to what is presented as the outermost limits of this field of intelligibility, an examination of how this exteriorization manifests itself as irreducibly heterogeneous, and why instead this exteriority actually constitutes the radical and contingent core of any and all discussions of identity at the U.S.-Mexico border. To do this one must mount a form of critical engagement (always speculative and provisional) into the juridico-political figuration of crossing state borders, one that both informs and is informed by a philosophical grounding of sovereign power and the figure of *Homo sacer* as the discursive threshold upon which the border rests. What I seek is a biopolitical figuration into how the U.S.-Mexico border coincides with and lays bare a topological ordering of the state of exception.

On May 23, 2001, along the Arizona-Mexico border, between Yuma and Nogales, a tragic though ultimately unsurprising event occurred. Arizona Border Patrol units discovered a group of five disoriented border crossers stumbling across a main road. Again, this is not unusual. Discoveries of five- to ten-man groups like this happen all too often along the U.S.-Mexico border. Most recently a group of more than one hundred migrants was apprehended by Arizona Border Patrol agents along a mountain range just southwest of Tucson.[3] However, what made this such an exceptional case is that when questioned, the apprehended migrants informed the Border Patrol agents that they didn't remember how many of them there were at the start of their attempt to cross the border, that they had became lost, were separated from the others soon afterward, and did not know of their whereabouts or condition. Within minutes the entire Border Patrol fleet was engaged in rescue operations. By the end of the next day, fourteen bodies were recovered and twelve more migrants rescued. This incident would later be determined to be the worst death event in U.S.-Mexico border history, with fourteen of the twenty-six migrants dying in the Arizona desert. This group would later be remembered as the Wellton 26, so named after the town whose Border Patrol station provided first response.

The story of the Wellton 26 was written soon afterward. In 2004 Luis Alberto Urrea published *The Devil's Highway*, a narrative reconstruction of the group's journey, originating in Veracruz, Mexico, leading all the way up to their discovery by Arizona Border Patrol and its political aftermath. Urrea attempts to piece together everything that can be known about this group—their names, their families, their reasons for leaving Veracruz, family and local networks that put them in contact with migrant smugglers, and so on——in order to reconstitute, with varying degrees of probability, the rationale for every decision taken by them on this journey, most particularly of those final and ultimately lethal decisions while lost in the Arizona desert:

> The group's condition deteriorated dramatically. . . . The aliens began
> to consume cactus and their own urine in an attempt to sustain
> themselves and to fend off the effects of heat exposure and dehydration.
> As individual members weakened and succumbed, the group splintered
> into several smaller groups. During the evening of May 21, 2001,
> several group members demanded that Jesus Lopez-Ramos [their
> coyote] depart their location in search of water and transportation
> for those that remained alive. Lopez-Ramos agreed, collected $90.00
> from the group's members, then set out with "Lauro" . . . to locate
> water. . . . Coyotes always collected the money from their pollos

[immigrants that pay coyotes for guided transport across border] before
leaving them to die. They always said they were going for help. They
always said they would be back shortly, then failed to return. They
always demanded dollars. (153–54)

Fashioned from journalistic, testimonial, governmental, and forensic
accounts of this event, *The Devil's Highway* is at once a narrative
representation of the sociopolitical conditions necessary for an event of this
magnitude to occur in the first place, a reading of the tracks and traces—
"sign-cutting"—left by the Wellton 26 as they crossed the desert, and a
description of the political, legal, and diplomatic effects this event left as
aftermath between Mexico and the United States and of the very border
that both binds and separates them.

It bears repeating that, although exceptional, this incident was not
unimaginable. Critics have known for years that the major objective of border lockdowns and militarization at major entry ports in San Diego, El
Paso, Laredo, McAllen, and Brownsville through operations Gatekeeper
(1994) and Hold the Line (1993) was to redirect and rechannel smuggling
routes precisely across the Arizona border, precisely between Yuma and
Nogales, precisely through one of the most inhospitable climates and ter-
rains on the continent. (Urrea [2004: 85] calls it "the deadliest landscape
on earth.") This funneling of routes through the southern Arizona desert
was designed to act as its own deterrent against illegal entry; despite little
to no Border Patrol presence in many of these areas, migrants would nevertheless avoid crossing through it. Needless to say, research into the tally
of border-related deaths in Arizona since these measures were adopted has
concluded otherwise (Rubio-Goldsmith et al. 2006): these operations did
not deter those seeking entry into the United States. In fact most migrants
would not know they were being actively deterred as they would not know
their arrival was already anticipated and their passage redirected. However,
smuggling routes did continue to follow the funnel through Arizona as
these policies intended. Urrea remarks:

The hundreds of walkers who once ran this gauntlet are now forced
to move east. They rarely try to swim around the western barrier, and
if they do, they land in a state park where "fishermen" casting into
the surf are often armed feds. The only way to go is out there, back of
beyond, away from civilization. And if you go far enough, the fence

devolves into a two-foot-high road barrier you can step over. Farther still, and you're in territory much like Sasabe. There are approximately two thousand miles of this kind of terrain to enter. . . . This new paradigm—walkers crossing Desolation in place of urban fences—has made Altar [Valley, Arizona,] the largest center of illegal immigration on the entire border. (59–60)

It should surprise no one to learn this was the very route that the Wellton 26 embarked on. This is one of only a few indisputable facts surrounding the Wellton 26 and the events leading up to their demise. Beyond speculative efforts issued by Border Patrol trackers, forensic examiners, government agency reports, and even Urrea himself, which seek to account for the nature and timeline of this event, the narrative of the Wellton 26 remains irrevocably foreclosed.

As such, despite Urrea's intentions to bring the story of the Wellton 26 to the light of history, one is faced with the fact that *The Devil's Highway* is by necessity uneven and incomplete. The book is replete with instances of narrative indeterminacy, ambiguity, and, in certain moments, Urrea's sheer conjecture. Seemingly narrating its own inability to fully narrate, *The Devil's Highway* incessantly divulges its lack of specific or reliable information regarding the details of certain events, and this narrative "resistance" is often attributed to the twelve surviving members of the Wellton 26, who cannot seem to remember, agree upon, or speak about many of these events with any degree of certainty: "As they walked, they started to lose themselves. Their accounts of the following days fade into a strange twilight of pain. Names are forgotten. Locations are nebulous, at best, since none of them, not even the Coyotes, even knew where they were. Nameless mountains loomed over them, nameless stars burned mutely overheard, nameless demons gibbered from the nameless canyons" (Urrea 2004: 108).

It can be argued that too little is known of the Wellton 26 and too many of them died to fully reconstruct this historical narrative of failure. After all, while the narrative acknowledges that twenty-six bodies (alive and dead) were recovered, the size of the original group to this day remains unknown. Furthermore, the surviving members themselves were of little value to this investigation: "They're in shock. They can't spell their own names. They can't spell the names of the villages and ranches they came from. They look to the deputies, as if the Americans can help them remember the letters.

They don't know what day it is. They don't know the name of where they were" (Urrea 2004: 71–72).

For the surviving members of the group, this illiterate resistance is quite unintentional and literally meaningless; they are unable to spell and therefore unable to create the necessary meaning. One must contend with the possibility that all the desired information, even if discovered and decipherable, would still prove inadequate to the task of recovering the hidden history of the Wellton 26 that explains, once and for all, how their journey ended in utter catastrophe and why it could *not* have ended in any other way. "There was no thinking evident, no reasoning process at all," Urrea (2004: 139) suggests of their final moments. For the question *The Devil's Highway* ultimately poses, inscribed within and throughout this account, is not why the events had to happen, but rather—in a more critical fashion—why events like this have not happened more often. "For a long time, the Border Patrol had worried that something bad was coming," Urrea reminds his reader; and on that day, upon the Wellton Border Patrol station's receiving the call for immediate search and rescue support, Urrea discloses what to the Border Patrol was an already acknowledged, though heretofore unguarded, fear: "The guys at Wellton knew the apocalypse had finally come" (18). Therefore as a narrative reconstruction of the unguarded "worry" that ultimately, and forcefully, presented itself as sheer contingency in the Wellton 26, *The Devil's Highway* will always fall short of its aims; it begins and ends as narratological impossibility, much like the Wellton 26 journey ended in failure and much like the Arizona Border Patrol's charge to prevent events like these from happening ended in failure. Nevertheless *The Devil's Highway* itself demonstrates that the urgency to narrate this event (even inadequately) persists, and further, perhaps, that the critical lessons sought from this historical event might only ever be revealed from this very exercise in narrating this impossibility.

In "The Impossibility of Subaltern History" (2000: 288), Gyan Prakash conceives of subalternity as the figure for internal disciplinary contradictions resulting from the double register through which an object of study is first constituted, where, "on the one hand, it projects the subaltern as an irrational other beyond authoritative reason and understanding; on the other hand, it claims that the subaltern is completely knowable and known as an embodiment of irrationality." The question of the subaltern therefore is not about the relation of an object's "pure externality" to dominant systems of

knowledge and its disciplinary incorporation and containment as difference but rather how the subaltern figures internally within disciplinary formations as externality itself. Thus "as an abstraction used in order to identify the intractability that surfaces *inside* the dominant system, the project
of writing of subaltern histories . . . has always carried with it an awareness
that it must fail to satisfy the discipline's desire for completeness and posi-
tivist reconstruction. It is the refusal to accept the dominant construction
of the subaltern as a radical exteriority (beyond reason, rational causality,
etc.) that permits the subalternist scholar to question the writing of history
as the march of reason, the narrative of progress, and the biography of the
nation" (294). It is in this precise, critical sense of subaltern history that I
see in *The Devil's Highway* the necessarily impossible venture of bringing
to light that which the dominant discourse cannot appropriate completely,
that otherness that resists narration—the Wellton 26—as the impossibility
of inscribing consciousness to a moment of contingent historical failure. In
this regard Urrea makes much of the group's unavoidable mental and physical debilitation as they continued to walk long after their recognition of
being lost and aimless. Urrea (2004: 120–29) further emphasizes the degree
to which the six stages of hyperthermia that results from extended exposure
to this climate compromise everyone's ability not only to act but to think.
As such, when Urrea's reconstruction of this journey culminates in the diag-
nosis, "They were beyond rational thought. . . . They walked west, though
they didn't know it; they had no concept anymore of destination" (3–4),
one can perceive that though the Wellton 26 constitute an integral aspect
of this narrative, the contingency they have been attributed has less to do
with the assumption of consciousness that determines collective action and
thought than with consciousness's very unsustainability ("irrationality") as
an assumption and the interpretive limitations over their decisions resulting
from their exposure to this climate. Urrea's acknowledgment of this foundational limitation permits him to offer a historical account of the Wellton
26 while simultaneously insisting on the fact that he, as Spivak (1988a: 9)
has argued of the South Asian Subaltern Studies Collective, "is engaged in
an attempt at displacing discursive fields, that [he himself] 'fail[s]' (in the
general sense) for reasons as 'historical' as those [he] adduce[s] for the heterogeneous agents [he] stud[ies]."

   Thus I read the *The Devil's Highway* as a subaltern history that, in
seeking to narrate a tragic scene of radical contingency, exception, and

abandonment, begs its own question. Ultimately Urrea's narrative constitutes a provisional attempt to glean from the biopolitical formalization of
this particularly crucial stretch of the U.S.-Mexico border the state of exception that constitutes it, the negative territoriality of its topological ordering,
and the negative community abandoned within it. And it is here, at the
zone of irreducible indistinction between inside and outside, inclusion and
exclusion, zoe and *bios*—what Agamben calls the state of exception—where
I position *The Devil's Highway* as a critical response to the juridical status
of the U.S.-Mexico border, its disciplinary staging as object of study, and its
deployment as ground for a signifying economy that regulates its cultural
intelligibility.

In *Homo Sacer: Sovereign Power and Bare Life* (1998: 1), Giorgio Agamben traces the critical importance of *zoe* and *bios*, two distinct yet inextricable formulations of life as the conceptual ground of the modern state: "*zoe*,
which expresses the simple fact of living common to all living beings (animals, men, gods), and *bios*, which indicates the form or way of living proper
to an individual or a group." Zoe, which is translated here as "bare life,"
functions in Agamben as the radically negative terrain upon which bios is
established; the figuration for the "exteriority that," through its exclusion,
"animates *bios* and gives it meaning." As the effect of the sovereign structure of law, the opposition between zoe and bios is ultimately where one's
humanity, or participation in the community of "Men," is determined. If,
as Agamben notes, in the "politicization of bare life the humanity of the
living man is decided" (8), it is because zoe, or bare life, is only posited
against bios to the degree that it is also—and necessarily—excluded from
the sphere in which bios is to emerge.

Consequently what for Agamben constitutes sovereignty's critical role
in contemporary political life is the conceptual logic of inclusive-exclusion
by which bare life and politically qualified life are distinguished, opposed,
and managed. However, the foundational biopolitical borders between zoe
and bios—nature and culture, inclusion and exclusion—are not so easily
maintained. In fact, Agamben argues, it is at their point of intersection, at
the topological limit between the zoe and bios, where a zone of indistinction emerges, "a threshold in which life is at once both inside and outside
the juridical order" (27). And far from signaling the weakest point at which
this biopolitical frame breaks down, it is in fact its most pronounced focus
of power. It is here, existing within a state of exception, Agamben argues,

where the two limit figures of the juridical order are inscribed: the sovereign exception, and *Homo sacer*.

If, for Agamben, the sovereign constitutes the point of indistinction between zoe and bios because they are both incorporated within a state of exception (i.e., the juridical order as both the inside and outside), for *Homo sacer* the effect is inverted: *Homo sacer* belongs to neither the sphere of zoe nor the sphere of bios (neither inside nor outside the juridical order). In other words, *Homo sacer* represents the limit figure in which zoe and bios constitute each other in including and excluding each other. As a result of this doubly exceptional status, *Homo sacer*, being neither animal nor citizen, lives in banishment amid the juridical order, as life belonging neither to zoe nor bios, as a form of life that can be killed but not sacrificed.

Thus conceived, the events named after the Wellton 26 reveal a critical demonstration of the U.S.-Mexico border's juridical form; their errant itinerary serves to trace this border's innermost workings and processes. Urrea's narrative thus doubles as an attempt to critically grapple with the state of exception that exists along the southern Arizona border, where abandonment and not the application of law is sovereign, ultimately resulting in the deaths of the Wellton 26, for whom and without whom this juridical field would have remained hidden from view. Through this subaltern history of the Wellton 26, Urrea (2004: 19) attempts to direct our attention not to the secondary and more visible manifestations of sovereignty along the border zones many come across on a daily basis, in San Diego, Nogales, El Paso, Laredo, and McAllen, the ones with "bigger fences, floodlights, sensors, infrared spy videos, night vision cameras, and more agents," but to the foundational structure of exception grounded in those sparse, rarely witnessed zones where the only thing a crosser will see is a fallen, rusted, barbed-wire fence and a sign that simply warns "Prohibido." It is along sites like this—what Agamben (1998: 9) reveals as "the hidden foundation on which the entire political system rests"—that the conditions for radical rupture of sovereignty itself present themselves. Or, as he goes on to say, "when borders begin to get blurred, the bare life that dwelt there frees itself in the city and becomes both subject and object of the conflicts of the political order, the one place for both the organization of State power and emancipation from it" (9).

Much like Agamben's articulation of the state of exception, the Devil's Highway is not a line that divides inside and outside, inclusion and exclusion; it is the point that marks their indistinguishability from each other, a terrain into which one is irreducibly abandoned between both, one in which the only laws that govern are those pertaining to biological life exposed to severe desert climate. Urrea provides several names for the vast desert region in southern Arizona, including, naturally, the Devil's Highway, or simply Desolation; however, he is very precise on a point he repeats on various occasions: "In the desert, we are all illegal aliens" (2004: 120).

Thus conceived, the biopolitical structure Urrea presents constitutes a radical unworking of a conventional and uncomplicated colonial binary, one in which Mexico constitutes the outside/zoe to the United States as inside/bios. Rather *The Devil's Highway* figures as a doubly marginal void of political space in which both the United States and Mexico, individually and internally, manifest their own topological ordering and exclusions. The distinction is crucial. For, as Urrea (2204: 48) contends, the U.S.-Mexico border is, after all, a geopolitical intersection between two historically delimited frontiers:

> In North America, the myth tends west: the cowboys, the Indians,
> the frontier, the wild lands, the bears and wolves and gold mines
> and vast ranches were in the west. But in Mexico, a country narrow
> at the bottom and wide at the top, the myth ran north. The Mayas
> pushed north, and the Aztecs pushed north once they'd formed an
> empire. Later, the Spaniards pushed north. The wide open spaces lay
> northward. The cowboys and Indians, the great Pancho Villa outlaws,
> the frontier, lay north, not west. That's why norteño people are the
> cowboys of Mexico—not westerners. The Spanish word for "border" is,
> after all, *frontera*. The frontier.

What Urrea ultimately asserts here is that the border is not a seamless and uninterrupted transition between two political orders. Rather the U.S.-Mexico border is constituted through the tangential relationship between the outermost limits of each sovereign sphere, one meeting the other at the most uneven and incomplete margins of the other's own territorial claims. The border, understood by Urrea as the threshold between two frontiers, is thus presented as a doubly exceptional figure. If the frontier always already signifies those margins of indistinction within a given state—between inside-outside, inclusion-exclusion, zoe-bios—then the border is constituted by nothing less than that exteriority that has been excluded from both frontiers. Like a demilitarized zone, it is a space that is neither inside nor outside the juridical order, neither inside nor outside the sovereign claims of Mexico or the United States, but instead is a doubly constituted state of exception existing between both.

Most remarkably is that historically Urrea is absolutely correct about this proposition. Mary Pat Brady, in her book *Extinct Lands, Temporal Geographies* (2002: 18), reminds us that this particular stretch of the U.S.-Mexico border, the one between Yuma and El Paso, began as a cartographical mistake:

> Southern Arizona was not part of the land ceded by Mexico in the
> Treaty of Guadalupe Hidalgo. Instead, it was purchased in a separate
> agreement worked out years later. What happened? While the
> boundary survey commissioners were working to establish the post-
> 1848 border near El Paso del Norte, they discovered a problem: The
> Disturnell Map used during treaty negotiations incorrectly located
> both El Paso del Norte and the Rio Bravo. The difference between the
> "material" and the "metaphorical" was not insignificant.

The critical significance of this origin cannot be underestimated. Between 1848 and 1854—that is, between the signing of the Treaty of Guadalupe Hidalgo and the Gadsden Purchase—the territory today known as southern Arizona came into being as an exception, as a confusion between the material and the metaphorical, as a critical error over where sovereignty along this region was to be bound. From an error on a boundary-determining map more than 150 years ago emerged the state of Arizona, the Arizona-Mexico border, and consequently the enlisting of the Devil's Highway to deter the human- and drug-trafficking problem that was already being channeled in its direction. No clearer illustration of the Arizona border's exceptionality can be made than Urrea's (2004: 55–56) description of what walkers risking entry on the Devil's Highway actually encounter when they arrive: "There is no real border here, just a tattered barbed wire fence, a dusty plain, and some rattling bushes. . . . No matter where they entered, they had only to step over a dropping bit of wire fence, or across an invisible line in the dust. Near the legendary crossing at El Saguaro, there is often no fence at all."

"An invisible line in the dust," it seems, is all that separates, in many places, the United States from Mexico; it is a border completely devoid of the law's application but not devoid of the law's inscription. It announces that at the innermost core of sovereign territorial limits one will see no border at all, a border invisible even to its artificial and contingent self, a field of invisibility that suggests not that one is at the threshold of abandonment but rather that one entered it long ago, that one is always already within it. There is nothing hidden, nothing to unconceal, but nothing is ever disclosed in advance. The Devil's Highway—abandonment itself—Urrea suggests, in declaring nothing of itself, announces nothing other than its own abandonment, its state of silence, voicelessness, and stillness: there is no law here, there is only the Devil's Highway. You may enter—no one will stop you—but only at your own peril. One must ask therefore if a border left unguarded is failed government policy or its very reason for being.

In *Targeting Immigrants* (2006), Jonathan Xavier Inda also takes up the case of the Wellton 26 as an example of the human consequences related to recent shifts in the terrain of governmentality through an intensification of security and immigration policy in the post-9/11 United States. As an exhortation against the sanctioning of rising migrant deaths along the U.S.-Mexico border in the name of peace and security, Inda concludes, "the fact is . . . that immigrants are dying. And they are dying as a consequence of an anti-citizenship technology that has propelled them to cross through dangerous terrain. When all is said and done, then, the border has turned into a zone of abandonment. It is a place where immigrants are being channeled into danger. It is a place where their lives are being forsaken: where their death is being disavowed" (174). Inda is right about the consequences of what he calls "anti-citizenship technology"—Operations Gatekeeper and Hold the Line, the absorption of the Immigration and Naturalization Service into the Department of Homeland Security in 2003, among others—that have "propelled" migrants toward "dangerous terrain." He is right about the "forsaken" and "disavowed" status of migrants that continue to die along the U.S.-Mexico border. Where he falls short, however, is in his assertion that, sometime between a before and an after, "the border has *turned* into a zone of abandonment" and that it could, and therefore should, be reversed.

Urrea and Brady suggest something radically different: not that the Arizona border has turned into a zone of abandonment but rather that its origins lie precisely in having always been one. While I too am suggesting that the Wellton 26 figures as the very name for the forsakenness and disavowal of migrant deaths at the Arizona border, it is not because it serves as the name for the collateral effects of the shift in immigration and security policy in the United States. Rather the Wellton 26 emerge as exceptional because it is only through their narrative impossibility that the Devil's Highway is rendered visible, for the first time, as a state of exception. The assignment of contingency here is crucial. If the principal question, as I am suggesting, is not how this incident could have happened but rather why events of this magnitude do not happen more often, then the more critical revelation from this event is not only that the Wellton 26 were victims of failed immigration policy and enforcement but that their journey—and its impossible narrativization—reveals that the U.S.-Mexico border is in fact perfectly in line with the grounds of the sovereign exception that constituted it in the first place. It can be argued that current Border Patrol and Homeland Security policy in Arizona is perfectly consistent with the border's history as a state of exception from which it emerged, where it is simply law abandoning the life that belongs neither here nor anywhere, life that is neither animal nor citizen (*Homo sacer*), that may be killed but not sacrificed. It is because of this that when the Wellton 26 found their lives "forsaken" and "disavowed" it was not due to the direct application of either Mexican or U.S. law—or through their negligence—but rather due to the law's absolute abandonment of life along the Devil's Highway. As such, no mere change in border policy can effect a reversion to a previous unabandoned state of sovereignty because, in this case, no such reversion is available.

Consequently the "invisible line" signaled by Urrea does not separate Arizona from Mexico; rather it unconceals the very gap that exists between them. It demarcates the zone of indistinction revealed by the Disturnell map's contradiction between the metaphorical and the material. A similar proposition may be made in relation to the grounds of identity and culture at the U.S.-Mexico border discussed earlier. Whereas in Castillo and Tabuenca Córdoba the material and metaphorical are conceived as mutually exclusive categories and deployed to condition and structure the field of intelligibility along the sides of the U.S.-Mexico border, Brady issues an altogether more productive and critical relationship between these categories and the "politicality of space" through which a border first emerges: one that departs not from the confrontation between these oppositional categories but from their point of indistinction. She argues:

> Arizona began as a mistake. The United States government used a
> mistake on a map to take what is now called Southern Arizona from

Sonora, Mexico—to abscond with it. This far-from-innocent (mis)
taking emerged out of contradictions and shifting interpretations; the
mistake showcases the seeming aporia structuring the distinctions
between the metaphorical and the material, the real and the mapped.
Consideration of this particular (mis)take also exposes the politicality
of space, revealing a battle over how to characterize space and how
to produce places that then almost magically become background or
setting, and thereby hide space as a formative, intimate participant in
the pleasures and work of sociality and subject formation. Unpacking
that mistake, resignifying a dubious nineteenth-century error, requires
beginning with contrasting accounts, not of the mistake exactly, but of
the spatial work that evolved from it. (2002: 13)

The primary (mis)take, Brady suggests, lies precisely in the overlooking
of "the aporia structuring the distinctions between the metaphorical and
the material, the real and the mapped," which is to say, as in the case of
Castillo and Tabuenca Córdoba, it is the (mis)taking of the aporia that
is the U.S.-Mexico border itself for a clear, definable, and stable one that
defines its material status by disavowing its irrevocably metaphorical
foundation. As such, Castillo and Tabuenca Córdoba's (mis)take constitutes
not an unearthing and discovery of this foundational aporia but a further
compounding of it. Brady urges that if one is to critically understand the
historical conditions that ground the Arizona-Mexico border, one cannot
avoid reflecting on this foundational (mis)take that is its absent cause. In
short, the "politicality of space," though intimately linked to this border's
exceptional structure, emerges only out of the latter's foreclosed status. Of
the "mistake exactly," it will remain invisible, absent, aporetic; the politics
of space at the U.S.-Mexico border therefore, in its most critical form, can
only ever be the radical unworking of both the "spatial work that evolved
from it" and the narrative of reality it establishes as normative.

The Devil's Highway, on the other hand, works precisely to unconceal and
inhabit this state of exception, the result of which is a rendering visible of the
contingent and conflict-ridden nature of the "politicality of space" between
fronterizo and Chicano thought at the U.S.-Mexico border. In ascribing
sovereign exceptionality to the Devil's Highway, Urrea simultaneously
acknowledges the heterogeneous element that irrevocably and irreducibly
presents itself when the politics of space at the border is reduced to competing

hegemonic and counterhegemonic claims. Indeed the Wellton 26 are the very confirmation of this. It must be remembered that for the Wellton 26, this would not have been their first experience with the sovereign logic of inclusive exclusion. Urrea informs us that the group originated from Veracruz, Mexico. With this he renders a perfectly clear articulation of the marginal status the Wellton 26 held not only while crossing into the United States but previously while in Mexico, as subjects constituting the same exteriority, but this time to an altogether different bios:

> The Mexican mestizos south of the border, who traditionally lack
> our nostalgia for the "Indian past," call the walkers "Oaxacas," from
> the name of the Mexican state that houses one of the largest Indian
> populations. "Oaxaca" is a code-name for Indian, usually Mixtec.
> The women are often ridiculed as "the marias." The majority of the
> group came from Tropical Veracruz. . . . Most of them had never
> seen a desert. What we take for granted in the United States as
> being Mexican, to those from southern Mexico, is almost completely
> foreign. . . . They were aliens before they ever crossed the line.
> (2004: 39–40)

In this passage Urrea presents us with yet another critical reality of this particular border. Not only were the Wellton 26 not *fronterizos* (northern Mexican border inhabitants), but they were not mestizos either (in official national terms); instead they were constituents of the bare life that is excluded from both (i.e., the still-living indigenous figure that disrupts and betrays the historical legacy apportioned to *La raza cósmica* and frontier mythology). The point is that the Wellton 26 would not have called themselves "Oaxacas," though, in a relation of inclusive exclusion, they came from a bios that does. The Wellton 26 are thus presented in a doubly exceptional status, inhabiting the disavowed core of Mexicanidad (to be at least mestizo) while simultaneously tracing the threshold of illiteracy between the United States and Mexico (neither fronterizo, Chicano, nor Anglo). Urrea insists that the Wellton 26 "were aliens before they ever crossed the line," which is also to say they were *bare life* before they even left Mexico.

This proposition is of equal significance to the first. For what we are here presented with is a critical articulation of the Wellton 26 as a part of those who have no part, as the uncountable element without whose exclusion no community can be founded. In other words, the Wellton 26 embody the figure of heterogeneity that disrupts any and all claims to identity and difference staked along this border. In this context I am speaking not only of Chicano identity's dependence on the discourse of mestizaje and the assumption of cultural and linguistic hybridity in the U.S. Southwest but also of northern Mexican, fronterizo identity and its reactionary (and again, compounding) affirmation of homogeneity and properness. The Wellton 26 are included in neither but are simultaneously excluded from both. As such, what the Wellton 26 offer, as the trace of radical negativity and negative community along the U.S.-Mexico border, is to unconceal the desire for purity each of these competing border identities inhabits. If in the name of hybridity, as Michaelsen and Johnson assert, Chicano identity is founded in certain exclusions, we also see, in Pablo Vila (2000: 26–27), a very similar dynamic underwriting fronterizo identity:

> Here it is important to remember the presence of a powerful regional
> hegemonic discourse that claims that the North was almost untouched
> by *mestizaje,* and that Northern Mexico tends to be "white," whereas
> Central and Southern Mexico tends to be "Indian" (or lat least,
> mestizo), that is, dark-skinned. . . . Therefore, the Chicanos' search for
> their Indian heritage is totally at odds with Fronterizos' (and Norteños')
> search for their heritage. Many Fronterizos and Norteños pride
> themselves on being "whites," and on lacking Indian blood.

This passage does much to crystallize the stakes of the discussion at hand, the implications of which can no longer be evaded or subordinated. If Vila is right to suggest that "Chicanos' search for their Indian heritage is totally at odds with Fronterizos' (and Norteños') search for their[s]," then the fundamental ideological difference separating Chicano and fronterizo cultural projects at the U.S.-Mexico border is the inscription of race.[4] In other words, what was, for Castillo and Tabuenca Córdoba, a difference between the privileging of the material or the metaphorical along the border can now be read otherwise: as a difference between competing ethnic claims of birthright (white or indigenous) for which the U.S.-Mexico border is the territorial stake. As a result, the terms of Castillo and Tabuenca Córdoba's disciplinary dispute over the study of the border cannot be disentangled from this regionalist, fronterizo mythology of racial purity. One can see now that Castillo and

Tabuenca Córdoba's deployment of a logocentric economy—material versus metaphorical—to account for the divergence and opposition of border-centered cultural projects is ultimately a reencoding (and subordinating) of socioracial mixedness as metaphorical, "mis-essentialized," "out-of-place," entropic. Metaphoricity, it turns out, was itself a metaphor for the undesirability of hybrid forms along this border. Whether in their critique of Anzaldúa's *Borderlands* as a "metaphorical country" or of her speaking-out-of-place ("self-authorized hybrid speech"), Castillo and Tabuenca Córdoba's implicit appeals to whiteness are most pronounced when, in the name of fronterizoness, they assert the naturalness and properness of the materiality of the border over which they lay claim.

But this is not only an "external" matter, for this distinction also pertains to the formal aspects of the Wellton 26—the "Oaxacas"—who, Urrea asserts, were themselves "aliens before they ever crossed the line." The extent to which the Wellton 26 constitute the bare life through whose exclusion is conditioned the very fronterizoness that would call them "Oaxacas" cannot be dismissed. In this regard fronterizo identity is defined not only against the indigeneity claimed by Chicano critics in the United States but also against the very migrants from southern Mexico and Central America who flock to the border in countless numbers every year seeking entry. The sheer heterogeneity of the figure of the migrant is irreducible, even to those asserting the constitutive materiality of border identity. As such, fronterizoness can exist only to the extent that a multitude of the countless and the indeterminate—always already exogenous to the region—continue to amass at the border, whose objective is not to remain and settle there but to traverse it altogether, hoping never to have to return or repeat the journey ever again. Fronterizoness—all border identity, for that matter—can only ever be asserted via a demarcation with this itinerant form of bare life.

Unsurprisingly this irreducibly heterogeneous figure of the migrant as presented in *The Devil's Highway* constitutes a critical problem for Chicano territorial claims as well. Let me first state, however, that though they ultimately constitute two distinct critical projects, I see both Anzaldúa's *Borderlands* and Urrea's *The Devil's Highway* as critiques of the very deep, formal aspects of border politics. The former seeks to present and affirm a form of cultural identity that emerges from within this region simultaneously with a type of consciousness that both appropriates and resists dominant structures of race, gender, and sexuality in the United States and Mexico.

Urrea, on the other hand, seeks to tease out the formal implications of the very act of crossing the U.S.-Mexico border, what this means for the subjects attempting it, and what that means for all of us when they do not survive it. So while the former attempts to forge a (mestizo, gendered, and queer) epistemological base onto the insider-outsider subject of the borderlands (zoe), the latter seeks to unconceal the sovereign foundation of the border itself (bios) through a critical tracing of the subject subjected to the sovereign ban of crossing it. What is of critical interest here, however, is that both projects are grounded from and within a primordial scene of border crossing.

Having said this, and seeking to further tease out the critical threshold that is revealed only in their juxtaposition, there is one productive tension between Anzaldúa's and Urrea's reflections on border crossing to which I wish to draw attention: the ascription of language attributed to the act of border crossing, or rather how crossers themselves become semiotically iterative of the very border they attempt to cross. For Anzaldúa, the borderlands are themselves the site of productive signification in which are contained variants of both English and Spanish and from which emerges their linguistic plurality—what she calls "el lenguaje de la frontera." Note, for instance, the way Anzaldúa's (1987: 78) border crosser is also inscribed as an active semiotic smuggler in the borderlands: "From *los recién llegados* [recently arrived immigrants], Mexican immigrants, and *braceros*, I learned the North Mexican dialect."

From this short sentence we can infer many things, for instance, that in the borderlands the northern Mexican dialect forms an integral part of "el lenguaje de la frontera," that "los recién llegados" are among the ones who bring it with them when they cross, and that by doing so, in the trafficking of both their very selves and the semiotic registers through which they speak, los recién llegados contribute to the formation of Anzaldúa's borderlands as a site of bare life that is nevertheless productive of its own signification. However, this very statement implies simultaneously a certain number of conditions and exclusions. The first of these is that unless one is already a legal Mexican immigrant to the United States or comes from a family with a multigenerational history of living and working in the U.S. Southwest without legal status, a recién llegado is the only other thing one can be. As such, because *recién llegado* becomes the name given to those who successfully crossed the border in any other way, it constitutes a rather empty category, propertyless, amorphous, having nothing that would positively define it in relation to the other categories, except for one thing: that it is from los recién llegados, among others, that Anzaldúa learned the "North Mexican dialect." This statement presents us with even further complications, the most important of which relates to how, exactly, one figures the category of the recién llegado and what is at stake when they—named for the nameless, characterless, propertyless mass of migrants—must then also bring with them a northern Mexican dialect.

Ultimately only those who have successfully crossed the U.S.-Mexico border—by any and all means—can find belonging in Anzaldúa's borderlands. However, though crossing is a necessary condition, it is nevertheless insufficient. To gain semiotic purchase they must also bring with them the northern Mexican dialect; in order to find inclusion within the zoe of the borderlands, in order to be heard, read, or understood there, one needs to be a *recién llegado del Norte* and from nowhere else. Those who do not bring with them the northern Mexican dialect, have failed to *llegar*, or who have died *llegando* fail to gain entry to the borderlands because they remain illegible, unintelligible, and radically incommensurate within it. The latter—*los que nunca llegarán* [those who will never arrive] and/or those who do not bring with them a northern Mexican dialect—come to inhabit the bare life of the borderlands itself, its constitutive outsides, "the part of no part." Or as Urrea insists, "aliens before they ever crossed the line."

Nevertheless los que nunca llegarán never go without leaving a sign, a trace, an (il)legible marker of their never having made it. Whereas in Anzaldúa the semiotic contributions made only by those who have already successfully made it past the border (los recién llegados) become constitutive of the borderlands, *The Devil's Highway* reflects upon the residual though empirically relevant signs left by those who will have never made it, an investigative technique the Border Patrol calls "sign-cutting," the act of tracking migrants by the forensic trail left behind as they walk through areas known as "drags" or lines of smoothed-over sand which, when traversed, are inscribed by the very act of traversal, of its trespassing, the trace of *recién pasados*. Urrea (2004: 29) remarks, "Cutters read the land like a text. They search the manuscript of the ground for irregularities in its narration. They know the plots and the images by heart. They can see where the punctuation goes. They are landscape grammarians, got the Ph.D. in reading dirt."

In the case of the Wellton 26, the group of twenty-six originating from Veracruz, Mexico—neither fronterizos nor recién llegados—the signcutters were there to finish the story for them:

> From the Vidrios Drag, the signcutters started back into the wasteland, cutting, cutting. They read the ground and found, after an amazingly long haul, where the journey had all gone so wrong. Some of the illegals had walked over sixty-five miles—a couple of them fell in sight of the freeway. All you can do . . . is cut sign, cut sign, cut sign. The sign tells the story. The sign never lies. And the whole investigation became a series of drag-cuts. . . . The footprints wrote the story. And after the footprints ran out, it was a trail of whispered stories and paper sheets. It was the big die-off, the largest death-event in border history. (Urrea 2004: 31)

"Reading dirt" "like a text," until "the footprints r[u]n out." Sign cutting, in other words, is the critical tracing of the limits of the field of cultural intelligibility in *The Devil's Highway*. It is not only the name for the forensic practice of reading tracks but also the way to reveal the semiotic disjunctures that foreclose the ascribing of consciousness to los que nunca llegarán. In short, a threshold of illiteracy obtains between Anzaldúa's recién llegados and Urrea's Wellton 26, an irreducible narratological gap between signification and meaning that any and all claims to identity and knowledge are forced to disavow. Unlike what we saw in Castillo and Tabuenca Córdoba, this is not an either/or; rather it is an acknowledgment that even the most inclusive of conceived spaces—the borderlands—cannot ever come into being without a previous and foundational demarcation with its own, internally constituted figuration of bare life. A juxtaposition of *Borderlands/La Frontera* and *The Devil's Highway* renders this economy perfectly clear: the northern Mexican dialect brought by los recién llegados and the footprints, discarded items, and bodies themselves left in the desert by los que nunca llegarán; the cultural imaginary that assumes the only border crossers are northern Mexicans, and the fact the Wellton 26 originated from Veracruz; the assertion that only those recién llegados are productive of frontera signification, while the signs left behind by los que nunca llegarán remain radically illegible, incommensurate, intractable, and consequently suspended in the state of exception that is the Devil's Highway. Despite appeals to the contrary, Anzaldúa's borderlands are a homogeneously constituted site of enunciation, one that requires, indeed reproduces its own form of subalternity. As such, one must confront the possibility that the contradictions that emerge from this are irresolvable and irreparable; as with lo fronterizo, los que nunca llegarán represent the radical exception upon which the borderlands rest, without whose inscription of externality it cannot take form. Ultimately los que nunca llegarán remain, to the degree that they are excluded, neither inside nor outside; they remain the trace that both binds and separates, the sign that threatens inside and outside with indistinction, the conceptual figure that ultimately ruptures the idea of a seamless and borderless borderlands.

I have been insisting that the sheer heterogeneity of the present-day border crosser—and therefore of the U.S.-Mexico border itself—forecloses the ability to serve as grounds for any identity-based affirmation of border culture, particularly when border crossers themselves serve as the very objects of play between groups with conflicting claims over it. Like Marx's notion of class, community is equally heterogeneous and contingent. Instead, through the figure of the Wellton 26, one sees how in either form—through a relation of inclusive exclusion ("Oaxacas") as we see in fronterizo identity or through a relation of exclusive inclusion (recién llegados) that we see in Anzaldúa—*los que nunca llegarán* becomes the name for radical, critical inquiry into the nature, state, and culture of the U.S.-Mexico border. Therefore, as a politics of reading resistance, sign cutting will always assert the contingency and irreducibility of the subaltern form inscribed along *all* sides of the U.S.-Mexico border, irrupting into the very "politicality of space" that had previously regulated its meaning (i.e., as between fronterizos, Chicanos, and Anglos).

Afterword: Illiteracy, Ethnic Studies, and the Lessons of SB1070

Above all, what I hoped to accomplish in this study is to make visible, and glean, the possibility of an ever more vigilant approach to cultural and critical practice in Latin America. While my analyses focused on discrete though interconnected scenes of contingent semiological upheaval that betray conventional—dominant and resistant—assumptions of coherence, order, and progress, my aim has been to fashion a mode of critique that accounts for the contradictory dynamics and tendencies within disciplinary reading practices.

But much more than that, I would argue that *Thresholds of Illiteracy* is an attempt to demonstrate how—through the crises, impasses, and deadlocks arising from prominent resistant claims, that is, from the critical realization, long overdue, that the programs and theories of cultural difference we have come to rely on most ultimately share in the same appeal to an all-encompassing One-All—a truly progressive politics can finally emerge. In other words, as opposed to seeking and ascribing resistance among opposing and competing views, the shift from one to another makes visible, even momentarily, resistance as a thing itself, a thing that is both the object *and* what prevents access to the object. As such, ontological failure, the impossibility of filling the gap with substance, is precisely the outcome we should have been seeking all along. In the shift from one to the other, and in the semiological breakdown that results, one sees antagonism as such. Illiteracy *is* that shift, and it bears the name of *el hombre natural, aclimatados, colonos, monolingües,* and *los que nunca llegarán.*

Nevertheless while this project is a sustained reflection on contemporary understandings of democracy, power, and resistance in Latin America, it is one that can also serve as a model for other social contexts wherein such phenomena seep into cultural practices. One such scene of disruption to the social order is found in the state of Arizona, where recent anti-immigration and anti-education legislation have reignited a veritable culture war between various competing social groups that shows no sign of abating or resolution. I close this book with a brief illustration of how illiteracy can and must be brought to bear in all cultural disputes, even those transpiring closest to home, irrupting right in one's midst, including those within which local popular support appears incontrovertibly and overwhelmingly one-sided.

In April 2010 the state of Arizona became embroiled in nationwide controversy as a result of two pieces of legislation signed into law: Arizona Senate Bill 1070 and House Bill 2281. The former, signed by Governor Jan Brewer on April 23, 2010, ascribes criminal status (as an "unlawful entrant") to persons unable to provide proof of registration documents enabling them to reside in U.S. territories and mandates enforcement of this law by local and state government agencies. The signing of SB1070 has elicited enormous and heated reaction not only in Arizona but throughout the country; proponents appeal to the strictest adherence to legal status for all residents, while critics argue that SB1070 will foster the institutionalization of racial profiling as the primary means of enforcement by local agencies, thereby infringing on and inevitably violating the right of U.S. citizens against search and seizure without probable cause. HB2281, signed three weeks after SB1070, has received less widespread attention than the first, though many critics conceive of HB2281 as an ideological extension of the anti-immigrant agenda laid by SB1070. Signed on May 12, 2010, HB2281 prohibits state-funded schools from including classes in their curriculum that are conceived, in the language of the bill, as courses that (1) promote the "overthrow" of the U.S. government, (2) promote "resentment toward a race or class," (3) are designed exclusively for students from a particular ethnic group, and (4) "advocate ethnic solidarity" over student individualization. This legislation would lead to the effective deinstitutionalization of Mexican American (*raza*) studies but also African American studies and Asian American studies from the public education curriculum.[1]

Though the fate of this legislation remains to be seen[2]—as I revisit these pages the case itself is being heard by the Supreme Court—what is clear is that the form, terms, and stakes of the U.S.-Mexico border are being reconfigured by these laws as the platform for a new political order and rationality. In other words, regardless of the outcome of these laws, their very passage into law has already—unilaterally and irrevocably—altered the "politicality of space" for which the border is an ethnocultural center. An overarching effect of the passage of both SB1070 and HB2281 has been the self-identification of one particular ethnic group as the legislation's primary and intended target. By and large, many critics in Arizona have asserted that together these two laws constitute a concerted and *specific* targeting of Mexicans and Mexican Americans alike, culminating in the attempt to eliminate from the public education system classes focused on the history of Mexicans and Mexican Americans in the region. This reaction by the Mexican American community against these laws is not without justification; in fact this is a population (30 percent of the total population in Arizona) all too aware of and still determined by a long history of discriminatory immigration, labor, and racial policies in the U.S. Southwest, and these laws simply constitute its latest manifestation. Furthermore the very program of study that would provide young students with the historicopolitical context necessary to perceive this legacy of discrimination at work in these laws has effectively been banned by one of them. However, and as is wont to occur in moments of upheaval such as this, what we are seeing is the emergence of a subhegemonic cultural minority in whose name, history, and identity the conflict takes exclusive shape (i.e., Mexican American vs. Anglo). In other words, what we are seeing here, in the name of diversity, is an appeal to the logic of hegemony—the very logic used against the Mexican and Mexican American community—that subsumes and subordinates the interests of other ethnic groups to the interests of the most populous of them.

While one can perceive quite clearly that this legislation will have a direct and deleterious effect on the sizable Mexican American community in Arizona, one must also account for the fact that this community will not be the only one affected. Just as those crossing the U.S.-Mexico border into the United States will not all be from Mexico itself (fewer and fewer are), neither is Mexican American (raza) studies the only ethnic studies course in danger of being shut down for violating HB2281. The stakes of HB2281 are therefore much larger than simply one group's right to curricular representation; *every* group's right to assert the right of representation is on the table. As such, the discourse that facilitated the establishment and institutionalization of (certain) ethnic studies in the United States more than forty years ago can no longer be appealed to as a defense against this new law. A more radical form of political engagement is warranted. This critical shift in focus, I suggest, is necessary in both formal and historically salient ways, particularly as it relates to the Arizona anti-immigration laws and the refashioning of the border that serves as its (absent) cause. It must be remembered at all times that it is not only one group (or even two) that is affected by these new laws but rather all groups. What remains to be seen is the degree to which the future of these laws (and/or future laws) will either intensify the cultural politics between the Mexican and Mexican American and Anglo communities or instead, and more productively, open up and redirect the discussion toward an ever more radical and diverse critical practice. For these reasons, one must at all costs avoid framing the Arizona laws as being anti-Mexican because their reach will extend (and already has extended) far beyond this self-limiting ascription. Rather a response informed by, inclusive of, and *in the non-name of All* obtains now as a most critical and historical imperative: that regardless of population size or history in the area, *every* minority group has the right to assert the right to representation *anywhere*—even against the most traditional and predominant among them. In other words, we are witness to a moment in time in which one is faced with exigency to go even against one's own name in the interests and aspirations of an ever more inclusive and progressive politics. I submit that the fate of SB1070 and HB2281, and their future impact nationwide, will be determined by the degree to which challenges to this law by the Mexican and Mexican American communities in Arizona adhere to this principle of radical diversity and the assumption of heterogeneity inscribed within it.

These statements should not be understood as disavowing the history and legacy of Mexican and Mexican American struggle in the U.S. Southwest, nor as a misapplication of concepts to a political context with which there is no sociocultural relation. For this community, the U.S.-Mexico border has long served as the ideological ground zero of Mexican American cultural nationalism and as the symbolic kernel of social and political resistance against the United States. However, critical reflection on the grounds and effects of such claims of resistance at the U.S.-Mexico border instead reveals that it is the figure of the present-day border crosser, of those who, regardless of their point of origin or entry, "were aliens before they ever crossed the line"—The Wellton 26, "Oaxacas," and "los que nunca llegarán"— that unconceals the sheer heterogeneity of border space; they make up a subaltern itinerancy that destabilizes and interrupts the very narratives of originary cultural difference and resistance long associated with the U.S.-Mexico border. Indeed this very border, inscribed as a state of exception and therefore the ground of nonidentity as such, is instead the site of the irreducibly and irrevocably heterogeneous amassment of itinerant bare life that displaces all—dominant *and* resistant—political claims of origins, foundation, and belonging. It is this critical reality, I argue, that both binds and separates the U.S.-Mexico border from itself, eroding the misgrounded narrative of history that backers and opponents of SB1070 and HB2281 take as a precondition. Ultimately it is this threshold of illiteracy that insists on a fundamental reevaluation of conventional political strategies used to challenge these laws.

Together SB1070 and HB2281 constitute an event that—with conventional oppositional tactics—will culminate in nothing more than an exhausted rehearsal of identity-laden hegemonic-subhegemonic politics. These pages advance the possibility that the outcome in Arizona can still be otherwise. The Wellton 26 provide a critical precedent by which to (re) map the politics of resistance at the U.S.-Mexico border, as they constitute the figure of sheer subordination that radically reconfigures the field of its cultural intelligibility, freeing this border from all competing claims of property, properness, and belonging. Indeed the Wellton 26 remind us that this border belongs to no *one* and that instead of constituting a deadlock, this proposition can become the basis for a truly progressive politics, one grounded in a principle of radical diversity and the assumption of heterogeneity inscribed within it. Urrea's subaltern narrative becomes both an announcement and a prefiguration of this possibility. Given these stakes, challenges to the Arizona legislation can no longer be conceived and articulated from within the biopolitical limits of the *recién llegado*. Instead a political agenda informed by and accounting for the sheer heterogeneity of *los que nunca llegarán* obtains now as the only challenge available that critically engages the conditions defining the contemporary at the U.S.-Mexico border.

Notes

Introduction

1. In particular, see Moreiras 2001; Williams 2002; Lund 2006.

2. Most recently, in his book *Less Than Nothing* (2012: 239), Žižek asserts the otherwise productive nature of "negative" critique: "The transcendental standpoint is in a sense irreducible, for one cannot look 'objectively' at oneself and locate oneself in reality; and the task is to think this impossibility itself as an ontological fact, not only as an epistemological limitation. In other words, the task is not to think this impossibility as a limit, but as a positive fact."

Chapter 1: Thresholds of Illiteracy, or the Deadlock of Resistance in Latin America

1. Sanchez Prado's paper from this panel, "Is the Postcolonial South Asian? A Latin American Reply," was later published in his professional blog, accessed January 21, 2012, http://ignaciosanchezprado.blogspot.com/2011/01/is-postcolonial-south-asian-latin.html.

2. See essays by Santiago Castro-Gómez, Eduardo Mendieta, and Walter Mignolo in *Teorías sin disciplina* (Castro-Gómez and Mendieta 1998), as well as in the recently published *Coloniality at Large: Latin America and the Postcolonial Debate* (Moraña, Dussel, and Jáuregui 2008).

3. See Charles Hatfield's excellent critique of this tendency in "The Limits of 'Nuestra America'" (2010).

4. Biopolitics was first introduced as a fully developed concept in Foucault's *The History of Sexuality* (1978). However, Foucault first used the term in lectures at the Collège de France in 1976–79. These lectures have been translated and published in English (2003, 2009, 2010).

5. These include but are not limited to edited volumes by Gugelberger (1996); Rodriguez (2001); Verdesio (2005); as well as works by Mallon (1994, 1995); Beverley (1999); Levinson (2001); Bosteels (2005); Moreiras (2001); Williams (2002).

6. Linda Craft's (1997: 14) articulation provides the most succinct rehearsal of this tendency. Doris Sommer (1999: 20) provides the shortest iteration, while also maintaining the conventional form of the reply I diagnose (yes and no): "The pertinent question is whether the other party can listen." See also Antonio Cornejo Polar's (1994: 202, my translation) brief declaration on the question of subalternity in *Escribir en el aire*: "In the meantime, I will not fall prey to Spivak's elegant sophism, for whom the subaltern, as such, cannot speak; primarily because it is obvious that he speaks, and eloquently, among his own and in his world; and secondly, because in reality what happens is that those non-subalterns do not have the ears to hear him, except only when we transfer his word into our customary decrypting practices." P. Peres (1994: 113) provides further illustration: "Gayatri Spivak's now infamous essay, 'Can the Subaltern Speak,' sparked a critical debate on writings of the Indian Subaltern Group. Spivak's position provoked a host of earnest responses that misread her critique of the essentialist elements of subaltern theory as an attack, instead, on the whole notion of subaltern discourses and spaces. The more important questions, perhaps, were not to be framed around the critique of essentialism, but rather the need to study the ways in which subalterns speak—i.e., whose voices are reproduced and where—and our roles as non-subaltern critics." As well as from Jose Rabasa (1994: 268n1): "Readers of Gayatri Spivak's essay 'Can the Subaltern Speak?' have generally failed to foreground a recommendation to learn to speak to the subaltern, rather than limit the import of her question to an affirmative or negative response. We might all be willing to listen to the subaltern, but how would we know that the subaltern agrees on what we are hearing? The 'learn-to-listen' solution invariably ends up in a we/them structure that betrays an anthropological will to objectify that obviates dialogue."

7. For a more comprehensive and incisive reading of the Founding Statement, see Williams 1996.

8. Compare this passage with a republished version of "El Boom del Subalterno" in *Cuadernos Americanos* only a year later, in which one notes (within the parenthetical) a shift in position from "despite Spivak's objections [a pesar de los reparos de Spivak]" to "as Spivak indicates [como indicaba Spivak]" (Moraña 1998a: 218). This essay was translated for publication in the *Latin American Cultural Studies Reader* (Sarto, Ríos, and Trigo 2004), but it is based on this republished version, which is why, for this quoted passage from the 1997 version, I provided my own translation.

9. One finds ample suggestion of this in his introduction, for instance: "My sense is that deconstruction is yielding diminishing and politically ambiguous returns, and that this has something to do with the way in which both 9/11 and the emergence of the marea rosada have shifted the grounds of theory and criticism in our time" (Beverley 2011: 9). See also Beverley's chapter on Morei-ras's *Exhaustion of Difference* as well as his last chapter "The Subaltern and the State."

10. In addition to other works that I discuss specifically in the following pages, many books and articles have been published in whole or in substance on the question of orality in Latin America. While by no means an exhaustive list, notable examples include *La Voz y su Huella: Escritura y conflicto étnico-social en America Latina* (Lienhard 1991), *La comarca oral: La ficcionalización de la oralidad cultural en la narrativa latinoamericana contemporánea* (Pacheco 1992), *The Darker Side of the Renaissance: Literacy, Territoriality, and Colonization* (Mignolo 1995), *La oralidad escrita: Sobre la reivindicación y re-inscripción del discurso oral* (Marcone 1997), *Coros mestizos del Inca Garcilaso* (Mazzotti 1996), and *Voices from the* fuente viva*: The Effect of Orality in Twentieth-Century Spanish American Narrative* (Millay 2005).

Chapter 2: Other Perus

1. Unless otherwise noted, all translations in this chapter are mine.

2. Mabel Moraña's essay "Indigenismo y Globalización" (1998b: 245) proposes a similar understanding of indigenismo that continues to neglect the critical implications of identity-based thinking and the assumptions of presence in speech, for which deconstruction signifies nothing other than one of a host of "homogenizing and reductive critical gestures."

3. Vargas Llosa's (1969a: 32) praise of Arguedas is noteworthy:

Ambiguity (a distinction of humanity that the primitive novel ignores) also character-izes *Los ríos profundos*, which narrates the story of a boy torn, like his author, like Peru, between a double loyalty to two worlds which war within him. Son of whites, raised by Indians, returned to the white world, the novel's narrator is a privileged witness to evoke the oppositional sides of his being. Although the most faithful, of the new authors, to the forefathers of the primitive novel, Arguedas does not fall into its most obvious defects because he does not intend to photograph the Indian world (which he knows thoroughly): he wishes to place the reader intimately in it. The abstract Indians of indigenismo are transformed, in Arguedas, in real beings, thanks to a style that reconstitutes, in Spanish and in occidental perspective, the most closely held intuitions and devotions of the Quechua world, its magical roots, its collective ani-mism, their philosophy—between resignation and heroism—that has given them the strength to survive centuries of injustice.

4. Vargas Llosa (1996: 23) conceptualizes literature's role as having no explicit social or political function; its function is to re-create reality rather than to depict it in any sort of "realistic" way:

> Because literature doesn't represent it presents: in it obsessions and intuitions are of equal importance to ideas; its truth is not contingent on its semblance with the real world, but of its capacity to construct something distinct from the model that inspires; to actuality it is indifferent, for it exists to the extent that it transcends it and takes root onto something more permanent; its sources come the more spontaneous, foggy, and prohibitive spaces of individual experience rather than from social responsibility. And the service literature provides does not consist in contributing to the propagation of religious or political faith, but rather, to undermine the foundations upon which this faith rests and put rationalist knowledge to the test (to relativize). The insubordinate nature of literature overwhelms any mission to combat government or social structures: it erupts against all dogma and logical exclusivism in the interpretation of life, which is to say, both orthodox and heterodox ideology. *In other words, it is a living, systematic contradiction of all that exists.*

5. Vargas Llosa (1996, 23–24) critiques indigenista authors mainly for their partisanship as it *necessarily* produces weak literary quality:

> Novels and poems often written in haste, under the imperative to change a certain state of things, often with militant passion, pregnant with the willingness to correct some injury, frequently lack that which is indispensable in a work of art: a life of its own, which emerges from the richness of expression and technical skill. Its mainly didactic objective determines that they be simplistic, and its politically affiliated character makes them discursive, if not demagogic. Through their zeal to vindicate what is local, they can be folkloric to such an extent (above all, in their abuse of colloquial language), that they become unintelligible for those who are not familiar with the world they describe. Of many indigenista authors it can be said that to better serve certain political ideals, they sacrificed all that was literary in their vocation.

6. This rhetorical strategy, largely symbolic and empty, of questioning whether or not Arguedas and his work are indeed indigenista, figures prominently in this discussions. William Rowe (2003: 245) rehearses this very gesture: "In summary, not only is Arguedas not an indigenista because of the complex cultural analysis that his novels accomplish, as he himself would argue, but also because of his particular theory of writing."

7. I will be analyzing his theoretical contributions to indigenista narrative as a whole and in its published entirety (Cornejo Polar 1977b, 1978a, 1978b, 1979, 1980a, 1980b, 2005). Much of his literary criticism on Arguedas and Ciro Alegría (see 1967, 1975), which I will be also highlighting and discussing in more detail, has recently been compiled and republished by his foundation, Centro de Estudios Literarios "Antonio Cornejo Polar" (see 2004, 2005). Of further interest are his analyses of Clorinda Matto de Turner's novel *Aves sin*

nido: Novela peruana (1889), which I will not treat here but can be found in "Clorinda Matto de Turner: Para una imagen de la novela peruana del siglo XIX" (1977a) and in the prologue to the Ayacucho publication of *Aves sin Nido* (1994), both of which can now be found under one title (Cornejo Polar 2005). Cornejo Polar's analysis of the indigenista novels of Manuel Scorza (1928–1983) can be found in "Sobre el 'neoindigenismo' y las novelas de Manuel Scorza" (1984).

8. Cornejo Polar enlists the help of the Peruvian cultural critic and founder of the Socialist Party in Peru, José Carlos Mariátegui (1894–1930) to articulate these conditions. I note three quotes from Mariátegui as cited in Cornejo Polar:

> The Quechua-Spanish dualism in Peru, still unresolved, prevents our national literature from being studied with the methods used for literatures that were created and developed without the intervention of the conquest. (in Cornejo Polar 1977b: 40; Mariátegui 1971: 188)

> Socialism orders and defines the demands of the masses, the working class. In Peru the masses—the working class—are four fifths indigenous. Our Socialism would not be, then, Peruvian—nor socialist—if we did not create solidarity, principally, with indigenous demands. No opportunism is found in this attitude, and if one reflects on socialism for more than two minutes, nor would you find any trace of artifice. This is nothing more than socialism. (in Cornejo Polar 1980a: 20; Mariátegui, Sánchez, and Aquézolo Castro 1976: 75)

> A critic could commit no greater injustice than to condemn indigenista literature for its lack of autochthonous integrity or its use of artificial elements in interpretation and expression. Indigenista literature cannot give us a strictly authentic version of the Indian, for it must idealize and stylize him. Nor can it give us his soul. It is still a mestizo literature and as such is called indigenista rather than indigenous. If an indigenous literature finally appears, it will be when the Indians themselves are able to produce it. (in Cornejo Polar 1978b: 51; Mariátegui 1971: 274)

9. He articulates this same idea in many of the aforementioned essays; I note two instances:

> It is evident, at the moment, that every instance of indigenismo's mode of production signals its pertinence to western or the westernized environments of Andean countries: in Peru's case, to the cultural system that is proper to the coast and the metropolitan centers. It is from here, from the cultural and literary values that govern, that indigenismo deviates from its project of revealing the nature and dynamic of the indigenous world, a world that offers, of course, another cultural system and a distinct manner of understanding and realizing literary production. From its initial conception, by privileging the option of writing in Spanish, and not from the orality of Quechua or Aymara, indigenismo demonstrates its cultural affiliation. (1977b: 42)

Here is a later rearticulation of the same idea:

The intellectual and artistic operation of indigenismo presupposes the features of a system that recognizes itself as occidental culture. As is evident, this system's procedures, forms, and values are not the same as those appearing in Quechua culture. It is from this order of things that indigenismo needs to be understood as the mobilization of the attributes of one culture to bestow reason on another. (1980a: 22–23)

10. He notes at the conclusion of *Literatura y sociedad en el Perú: La novela indigenista*:

The indigenista novel (and indigenismo in totality) should not be understood in exclusive relationship with the indigenous world, like a revealing or illumination of that reality, as a vindication of its social interests and revalorization of its culture: rather, it needs to be understood as a cultural exercise, situated in the conflictive intersection between two sociocultural systems, that intends a dialogue that is often polemical, and which expresses, at a certain level, one of the core problems of the Peruvian nation: its dismembered and conflictive constitution. The indigenista novel is not a literary testimony, of more or less veracity, and more or less "internal," to the indigenous world; more than that, although obviously being that in some way, the indigenista novel is the most exact literary representation of Peru's mode of existence. The indigenista novel enunciates its problematic nature at the moment—and in its profundity—it is captured in its form, in its general structure, in its signification. As the most exceptionally clear case to understand in what way literature verbally expresses society's conflicts and tensions, it also embodies and reproduces it in its own formal constitution. The dense and heteroclite multiplicity of the country—the country that Arguedas refers to as "all of the nations"—is present and active in the Peruvian indigenista novel. (1980a: 88–89)

11. Cornejo Polar (1979: 62) notes, "From its inaugural text [*Aves sin Nido*], the indigenista novel signals, then, its most profound feature, its characteristically exteriorized narration, not only because its perspective is such, but, more decisively, because it cannot be otherwise. The exteriorized perspective is the indigenista novel's condition of possibility. Curiously, the history of indigenismo can be explained as the tenacious and ongoing struggle to erase this distinction, either to hide it, or, in some cases, to attempt to transcend it. Indigenista literature, in this case, is a literature that denies its own material conditions, obscuring its heterogeneous base and imagining itself as something it can never become, an indigenous novel."

12. Particularly noteworthy is Cornejo Polar's (1975: 54–55) assessment of the breakdown of narrative perspective in Alegría's *La serpiente de oro*:

It so happens, however, that the fictional consistency of the narrator-character leads to an alley with no exit: within it, as within the narrative of which he is a part, he repeats the same dismemberment. He needs, in sum, to be a speaker of double consistency, and as conflicted as the basic normal speaker. The author here has no other remedy than to abandon the process of narration and accept, in crude but equally real terms, the contradiction underlying the essential design of the novel. This contradiction reproduces one of the most basic contradictions of Peruvian culture and society, its heteroclite plurality, and simultaneously expresses the painful displacement of the writer, who, without any effective possibilities to modify social structures that condition his activity, attempts to reveal some facets of a world that this same structure rejects and marginalizes. At bottom, the writer himself is constitutive of the conflict: he too is foreign to the world he is attempting to authentically represent; because of this, and in order to proceed, he has no other option than to establish—paradoxically—an artifice.

13. See the discussion of this very subject by indigenista authors in Casa de la Cultura de Arequipa (1969), in particular the third debate (233–61).

14. See Escobar, Matos Mar, and Alberti's (1975) discussion of the institutional role of the Quechua language in Peru: its grammatization, as part of educational curriculum, as a sanctioned national language.

15. All translations provided by the 1978 translation, *Deep Rivers*. This and all subsequent citations reference page numbers from the 1978 translation and 1958 editions, respectively.

16. Vargas Llosa (1996: 184) notes, "Is it not symptomatic that the title of *Los ríos profundos* alludes exclusively to the natural order? But this order does not appear, narratologically, as opposed to the human, and is vindicated in that sense. On the contrary: the natural order appears 'humanized' to a point that exceeds simple metaphor, rather, it invades the dominion of the magico-religious. In an instinctive yet obscure fashion, Ernesto attempts to substitute one order for another, to displace himself onto that zone of the world where he cannot be rejected by mankind's privative values."

Chapter 3: Secrets Even to Herself

1. See Jon Beasley-Murray's essay "Thinking Solidarity: Latinamericanist Intellectuals and *Testimonio* (1998). There he examines the implications for testimonio in Latinamericanist study after the publication of *The Real Thing: Testimonio Discourse and Latin America* (Gugelberger 1996).

2. In 2004 Beverley published *Testimonio: The Politics of Truth*, a collection that draws together most of his essays on testimonio since 1989, many of which I consider here. However, when compared to the originally published texts, I have noted significant changes to key passages in at least one essay. Unless otherwise noted, all references to Beverley will refer to their original publications.

3. The 1980s marked the early years of testimonio discourse in the North American academy. Barbara Harlow's *Resistance Literature* (1987) made early reference to the testimonio genre and to *Me llamo Rigoberta Menchú*, but she subsumed them under the rubric of autobiography and situated them within the larger, global context of resistance, not specific to Latin America. *Testimonio y literatura* (1986), edited by René Jara and Hernán Vidal, represents a key

early collection of essays on testimonio in Latin America. Ileana Rodriguez (1982) and Elzbieta Sklodowska (1982) were also making critical entrances on the testimonio form in Latin America.

4. For analyses of how the novel was deployed to consolidate political and/or national communities, see Anderson's *Imagined Communities* (1983) and Sommer's *Foundational Fictions* (1991a). It is not accidental that Beverley is seen here combining elements of political narratology, that is, the "Nation and Narration" thesis primarily associated with the novel, and testimonial discourse, as mutually exclusive yet identically productive processes.

5. Beverley begins to express such doubts as early as his essay "Through All things Modern: Second Thoughts on Testimonio" (1991).

6. Most notably, see Yúdice 1991; Sklodowska 1993; Sommer 1991b.

7. It is important to note Beverley's own participation in this collection, whose essay "What Happens When the Subaltern Speaks" attempts to reframe the entire Stoll debate as ultimately ideological and not empirically based.

8. Unless otherwise noted, all subsequent translations in this chapter are mine.

9. All textual references to Barnet are from his collection of essays, entitled *La fuente viva* (1983a).

10. In a later version of her essay "Rigoberta's Secrets," Doris Sommer (1999: 117) provides an alternative history of the Latin American novelists' break with Cuba, arguing instead that it was due to Cuba's support of the Soviet invasion of Czechoslovakia in 1968: "As a politicized alternative to fiction, testimonials received official literary status in Cuba after that country lost the support of Latin American novelists because Castro defended the Soviet invasion of Czechoslovakia."

11. Translations and even later Spanish editions of *Biografía de un cimarrón* show significant changes to Barnet's original introduction from 1966. As a result I have translated this and subsequent passages myself and include the original passages where appropriate.

12. See also his later, more explicitly nationalist essay, "Testimonio y comunicación: Una vía hacia la identidad" (Barnet 1983b).

13. Recent, particularly noteworthy attempts at reconciling testimonio discourse and criticism are Craft's *Novels of Testimony and Resistance in Central America* (1997) and Saldaña-Portillo's reading of Menchú in *Revolutionary Imagination in the Americas and the Age of Development* (2003).

14. See also Vera León 1992.

15. One of Saldaña-Portillo's main theses is the masculinist tropology of revolutionary discursive forms in Latin America, which ultimately reproduce the subalternization of gendered, indigenous, and peasant forms of praxis.

16. See also Beverley's (1989: 15n8) brief note on Randall.

17. All translations of Burgos's introduction provided by the 1984 translation, *I Rigoberta Menchú*. This and all subsequent citations to the introduction reference page numbers from the translation and original editions, respectively.

18. This essay was subsequently incorporated into Levinson's book *The Ends of Literature* (2001). See also Gordon Brotherston's (1997) response to Levinson's essay as an example of the pervasiveness of the tensions outlined earlier in Beverley and Barnet.

19. All translations of speech attributed to Menchú herself are mine. In this particular example, the significance of the passage lies in its grammatical rendition, an element lost in the English translation.

Chapter 4: Silence, Subalternity, the EZLN, and the Egalitarian Contingency

1. For a transcript of this and all related EZLN documents on the Internet, see http://www.cedoz.org/site/index.php. See also the five-volume compendium of EZLN documentation published by Ediciones Era (*EZLN: Documentos y comunicados*, vols. 1–5, 1994, 1995, 1997, 2003a, 2003b); Díaz Arciniega and López Téllez 1997; various collections of Marcos's writings: *Nuestra arma es nuestra palabra* and *Our Word Is Our Weapon* (Marcos 2001a, 2001b), *El sueño Zapatista* (Marcos, Lebot, and Najman 1997), *Ya Basta!* (Marcos and Vodovnik 2004), and *Conversations with Durito* (Marcos 2005).

2. Most recently a communiqué was issued on December 2, 2012, weighing in on the recent return of the Institutional Revolutionary Party to the Mexican presidency with their candidate, Enrique Peña Nieto.

3. This chapter was previously published in *Review Fernand Braudel Center for the Study of Economies, Historical Systems, and Civilizations* (2002).

4. Later in the essay Mignolo (2011: 234, my italics) also suggests that Subcomandante Marcos equally expresses himself within Tojolabal grammatical logic: "Subcomandante Marcos's definition *follows* Tojolabal logic while it is *expressed* in Spanish syntax and semantics."

Chapter 5: Hinging on Exclusion and Exception

1. U.S.-based border theory in this critique includes Gloria Anzaldúa's *Borderlands/La Frontera* (1987), Harry Polkinhorn, Gabriel Trujillo Muñoz, and Rogelio Reyes's *La línea* (*The Line*; 1987), Héctor Calderón and José David Saldívar's *Criticism in the Borderlands* (1991), Saldívar's *Dialectics of Our America* and *Border Matters* (1991, 1997), Emily Hicks's *Border Writing* (1991), and Claire Fox's *The Fence and the River* (1999). See also Tabuenca Córdoba's

previous iterations of this very argument (1995, 1995–96) and Santiago Vaquera-Vásquez's "Wandering in the Borderlands" (1998).

2. Latinamericanist thought suffers from the same problem. This is not accidental, but rather constituent of the legacy of mestizaje as sociocultural paradigm and populist rationality. I discuss Joshua Lund's (2006) excellent study on the notion of hybridity in Latin America in chapter 1.

3. From this group no deaths were reported. Brady McCombs, "Border Agents Catch Group of 105 Crossers Southwest of Tucson," *Arizona Daily Star*, April 29, 2010.

4. For a sustained historical examination of this inscription of race and of the violence this has wrought in the U.S. Southwest, see Guidotti-Hernandez, *Unspeakable Violence* (2011).

Afterword

1. The Support Our Law Enforcement and Safe Neighborhoods Act, Arizona SB1070 (passed April 13, 2010); Arizona HB2281 (Arizona Revised Statutes, Sections 15–111 and 15–112, passed April 11, 2010). It is important to mention that Native American studies and studies related to the teaching of the Holocaust are excluded from HB2281. From the bill itself one clause in particular stands out for its profoundly willful misrecognition: "Nothing in this section shall be construed to restrict or prohibit the instruction of the Holocaust, any other instance of genocide, or the historical oppression of a particular group of people based on ethnicity, race, or class" (HB2281, Sec. 1, F).

2. The federal government's response to SB1070 came on July 6, 2010, in a lawsuit requesting an injunction to enjoin Arizona from enforcing the law until the Supreme Court can make a final determination on its constitutionality. On July 28, 2010, just one day before SB1070 was to go into effect, a ruling by Federal Judge Susan Bolton struck down major aspects of the law and granted the temporary injunction. HB2281, on the other hand, went into effect on December 31, 2010. On January 3, 2011, State Superintendent Tom Horne (now Arizona's attorney general) declared the Tucson Unified School District (TUSD) in violation of HB2281. On January 10, 2012, the TUSD Board voted to cut the program. Several lawsuits against HB2281, including those from the ACLU and from eleven TUSD ethnic studies teachers, are still pending.

Works Cited

Achugar, Hugo. 1997. "Leones, cazadores e historiadores, a propósito de las políticas de la memoria y del conocimiento." *Revista Iberoamericana* 63 (180): 379–87.

Adorno, Rolena. 1993. "Colonial Discourse for Sixteenth- and Seventeenth-Century Spanish America." *Latin American Research Review* 28 (3): 135–45.

Agamben, Giorgio. 1998. *Homo Sacer: Sovereign Power and Bare Life.* Translated by D. Heller-Roazen. Stanford: Stanford University Press.

Alegría, Ciro. 1943. *The Golden Serpent.* New York: Signet.

———. 1993. *La serpiente de oro.* Lima: Editorial Mantaro. Original edition, 1935.

Anderson, Benedict. 1983. *Imagined Communities: Reflections on the Origin and Spread of Nationalism.* London: Verso.

Anzaldúa, Gloria. 1987. *Borderlands/La Frontera.* San Francisco: Aunt Lute Books.

Arguedas, José María. 1958. *Los ríos profundos.* Buenos Aires: Editorial Losada.

———. 1967. *Los ríos profundos.* Santiago: Editorial Universitaria.

———. 1974. *El sexto.* Barcelona: Editorial Laia.

———. 1978. *Deep Rivers.* Austin: University of Texas Press.

Arias, Arturo, ed. 2001. *The Rigoberta Menchú Controversy.* Minneapolis: Minnesota University Press.

Bakhtin, Mikhail. 1981. *The Dialogic Imagination: Four Essays.* Edited by M.

Holquist. *University of Texas Press Slavic, series 1*. Austin: University of Texas Press.

Barnet, Miguel. 1969. *La canción de Rachel*. Havana: Instituto del Libro.

———. 1983a. *La fuente viva*. Havana: Editorial Letras Cubanas.

———. 1983b. "Testimonio y comunicación: Una vía hacia la identidad." In *La Fuente Viva*. Havana: Editorial Letras Cubanas.

Barrios de Chungara, Domitila, and Moema Viezzer. 1978. *Let Me Speak! Testimony of Domitila, a Woman of the Bolivian Mines*. New York: Monthly Review Press.

Bartra, Roger. 2002. *Blood, Ink and Culture: Miseries and Splendors of the Post-Mexican Condition*. Translated by M. A. Healey. Durham, NC: Duke University Press.

Beasley-Murray, Jon. 1998. "Thinking Solidarity: Latinamericanist Intellectuals and Testimonio." *Journal of Latin American Cultural Studies* 7 (1): 121–29.

———. 2000. "Hacia unos estudios impopulares: La perspectiva de la multitud." In *Nuevas perspectivas desde/sobre América Latina: El desafío de los estudios culturales*, edited by M. Moraña. Providencia, Santiago: Editorial Cuarto Propio, Instituto Internacional de Literatura Iberoamericana.

———. 2010. *Posthegemony: Political Theory and Latin America*. Minnesota: University of Minnesota Press.

Beverley, John. 1987. "Anatomia del testimonio." In *Del Lazarillo al Sandinismo: Estudios sobre la función ideológica de la literatura española e hispanoamericana*. Minneapolis: Prisma.

———. 1989. "The Margin at the Center: On Testimonio (Testimonial Narrative)." *Modern Fiction Studies* 35 (1): 11–28.

———. 1991. "Through All things Modern: Second Thoughts on Testimonio." *boundary 2* 18 (2): 1–21.

———. 1996. "The Real Thing." In *The Real Thing: Testimonial Discourse and Latin America*, edited by G. Gugelberger. Durham, NC: Duke University Press.

———. 1999. *Subalternity and Representation: Arguments in Cultural Theory*. Durham, NC: Duke University Press.

———. 2004. *Testimonio: On the Politics of Truth*. Minneapolis: University of Minnesota Press.

———. 2008. "The Neoconservative Turn in Latin American Literary and Cultural Criticism." *Journal of Latin American Cultural Studies* 17 (1): 65–83.

————. 2011. *Latinamericanism after 9/11*. Durham, NC: Duke University Press.

Beverley, John, Michael Aronna, and José Oviedo. 1995. *The Postmodernism Debate in Latin America*. Durham, NC: Duke University Press.

Bhabha, Homi K. 1994. *The Location of Culture*. New York: Routledge.

Bolaños, Alvaro Félix, and Gustavo Verdesio. 2002. *Colonialism Past and Present: Reading and Writing about Colonial Latin America Today*. Albany: State University of New York Press.

Bosteels, Bruno. 2005. "Theses on Antagonism, Hybridity, and the Subaltern in Latin America." *Dispositio/n (American Journal of Cultural Histories and Theories)* 25 (52): 147–58.

Brady, Mary Pat. 2002. *Extinct Lands, Temporal Geographies: Chicana Literature and the Urgency of Space*. Durham, NC: Duke University Press.

Brokaw, Galen. 2010. "Indigenous American Polygraphy and the Dialogic Model of Media." *Ethnohistory* 57 (1): 117–33.

Brotherston, Gordon. 1997. "Regarding the Evidence in *Me llamo Rigoberta Menchú*." *Journal of Latin American Cultural Studies* 6 (1): 93–103.

Calderón, Hectór, and José David Saldívar. 1991. *Criticism in the Borderlands: Studies in Chicano Literature, Culture, and Ideology*. Durham, NC: Duke University Press.

Carpentier, Alejo. 1949. *El reino de este mundo, relato*. Mexico City: Edición y Distribución Ibero Americana de Publicaciones.

Casa de la Cultura de Arequipa. 1969. *Primer encuentro de Narradores Peruanos, Arequipa, 1965*. Lima: Casa de la Cultura del Perú.

Castillo, Debra A., and María Socorro Tabuenca Córdoba. 2002. *Border Women: Writing from* La Frontera. Minneapolis: University of Minnesota Press.

Castro-Gómez, Santiago, and Eduardo Mendieta, eds. 1998. *Teorías sin disciplina (latinoamericanismo, poscolonialidad y globalización en debate)*. Mexico City: Miguel Ángel Porrúa.

Collier, George Allen, and Elizabeth Lowery Quaratiello. 1994. *Basta! Land and the Zapatista Rebellion in Chiapas*. Oakland, CA: Food First, Institute for Food and Development Policy.

Cornejo Polar, Antonio. 1967. "La estructura del acontecimiento de 'Los perros hambrientos.'" *Letras: Organo de la Facultad de Letras y Ciencias Humanas de la Universidad Nacional Mayor de San Marcos* 78–79: 5–25.

――――. 1973. *Los universos narrativos de Jose Maria Arguedas.* Buenos Aires: Losada.

――――. 1975. "La imagen del mundo en 'La serpiente de oro.'" *Revista de Crítica Literaria Latinoamericana* 1 (2): 51–62.

――――. 1977a. "Clorinda Matto de Turner: Para una imagen de la novela peruana del siglo XIX." *Escritura: Teoria y Critica Literarias* 3: 91–107.

――――. 1977b. "Para una interpretacion de la novela indigenista." *Casa de las Americas* 100: 40–48.

――――. 1978a. "Interés social y forma literaria en el indigenismo." *Prismal/Cabral: Revista de Literatura Hispanica/Caderno Afro-Brasileiro Asiatico Lusitano* 2: 5–15.

――――. 1978b. "Sobre el modo de producción de la literatura indigenista." In *Historia, problema y promesa: Homenaje a Jorge Basadre,* edited by F. Miró Quesada. Lima: Pontificia Universidad Católica del Perú, Fondo Editorial.

――――. 1979. "La novela indigenista: Un genero contradictorio." *Texto Critico* 14: 58–70.

――――. 1980a. *Literatura y sociedad en el Perú: La novela indigenista, Biblioteca de cultura andina. 1.* Lima: Lasontay.

――――. 1980b. "La novela indigenista: Una desgarrada conciencia de la historia." *Lexis: Revista de Linguistica y Literatura* 4 (1): 77–89.

――――. 1984. "Sobre el 'neoindigenismo' y las novelas de Manuel Scorza." *Revista Iberoamericana* 50 (127): 549–57.

――――. 1994. *Escribir en el aire: Ensayo sobre la heterogeneidad socio-cultural en las literaturas andinas.* Lima: Editorial Horizonte.

――――. 2004. *La "trilogía novelística clásica" de Ciro Alegría.* Lima: Centro de Estudios Literarios "Antonio Cornejo Polar," Latinoamericana Editores.

――――. 2005. *Literatura y sociedad en el Perú: La novela indigenista y Clorinda Matto de Turner, novelista.* Lima: Centro de Estudios Literarios "Antonio Cornejo Polar" Latinoamericana.

Coronado, Jorge. 2009. *The Andes Imagined: Indigenismo, Society, and Modernity.* Pittsburgh: University of Pittsburgh Press.

Craft, Linda. 1997. *Novels of Testimony and Resistance from Central America.* Gainesville: University Press of Florida.

de la Cadena, Marisol. 2005. "Are 'Mestizos' Hybrids? The Conceptual Politics of Andean Identities." *Journal of Latin American Studies* 37 (2): 259–84.

Derrida, Jacques. 1976. *Of Grammatology*. Baltimore: Johns Hopkins University Press.

Díaz Arciniega, Víctor, and Adriana López Téllez, eds. 1997. *Chiapas para la historia: ntología hemerográfica, 10 de enero de 1994 al 10 de abril de 1995*. 3 vols. Mexico City: Universidad Autónoma Metropolitana-Azcapotzalco.

Earle, Rebecca. 2007. *The Return of the Native: Indians and Myth-making in Spanish America, 1810–1930*. Durham, NC: Duke University Press.

Edwards, Jorge. 1974. *Persona non grata*. Barcelona: Barral Editores.

Ejército Zapatista de Liberación Nacional. 1994. *EZLN: Documentos y comunicados*. Vol. 1: *10 de enero–8 de agosto de 1994*. Mexico City: Ediciones Era.

———. 1995. *EZLN: Documentos y comunicados*. Vol. 2: *15 de agosto de 1994–29 de septiembre de 1995*. Mexico City: Ediciones Era.

———. 1997. *EZLN: Documentos y comunicados*. Vol. 3: *2 de octubre de 1995–24 de enero de 1997*. Mexico City: Ediciones Era.

———. 1998. "Quinta Declaración de la Selva Lacandona." http://www.cedoz. org/site/content.php?doc=564&cat=10. Accessed July 11, 2013.

———. 2003a. *EZLN: Documentos y comunicados*. Vol. 4: *14 de febrero de 1997–2 de diciembre de 2000, Colección Problemas de México*. Mexico City: Ediciones Era.

———. 2003b. *EZLN: Documentos y comunicados*. Vol. 5: *2 de diciembre de 2000–4 de abril de 2001, Colección Problemas de México*. Mexico City: Ediciones Era.

———. 2005. "Sexta Declaración de la Selva Lacandona." http://www.cedoz.org/site/content.php?doc=19&cat=10. Accessed July 11, 2013.

Escobar, Alberto, José Matos Mar, and Giorgio Alberti. 1975. *Perú, ¿país bilingüe?* Perú problema 13. Lima: Instituto de Estudios Peruanos.

Flores, Roberto. 1996. "A Semiotics of Identity: The Letters of Sub-commander Marcos to the Press." In *Semiotics 1995*, edited by C. W. Spinks and J. Deely. New York: Peter Lang.

Foucault, Michel. 1978. *The History of Sexuality*. Translated by R. Hurley. New York: Pantheon.

———. 2003. *"Society Must Be Defended": Lectures at the Collège de France, 1975–1976*. Translated by D. Macey. New York: Picador.

———. 2009. *Security, Territory, Population: Lectures at the Collège de France 1977–1978*. Translated by G. Burchell. New York: Picador.

———. 2010. *The Birth of Biopolitics: Lectures at the Collège de France, 1978–1979*. Translated by G. Burchell. New York: Picador.

Fox, Claire F. 1999. *The Fence and the River: Culture and Politics at the U.S.-Mexico Border*. Minneapolis: University of Minnesota Press.

García, María Elena. 2005. *Making Indigenous Citizens: Identities, Education, and Multicultural Development in Peru*. Stanford: Stanford University Press.

Gollnick, Brian. 2008. *Reinventing the Lacandón: Subaltern Representations in the Rain Forest of Chiapas*. Tucson: University of Arizona Press.

Goody, Jack. 1977. *The Domestication of the Savage Mind*. Cambridge, UK: Cambridge University Press.

————. 1987. *The Interface between the Written and the Oral*. Cambridge, UK: Cambridge University Press.

Gugelberger, Georg M., ed. 1996. *The Real Thing: Testimonial Discourse and Latin America*. Durham, NC: Duke University Press.

Guha, Ranajit, and Gayatri Chakravorty Spivak. 1988. *Selected Subaltern studies*. New York: Oxford University Press.

Guidotti-Hernández, Nicole Marie. 2011. *Unspeakable Violence: Remapping U.S.. and Mexican National Imaginaries*. Durham, NC: Duke University Press.

Harlow, Barbara. 1987. *Resistance Literature*. New York: Methuen.

Harvey, Neil. 1998. *Chiapas Rebellion: The Struggle for Land and Democracy*. Durham, NC: Duke University Press.

Hatfield, Charles. 2010. "The Limits of 'Nuestra América.'" *Revista Hispánica Moderna* 63 (2): 193–202.

Havelock, Eric A. 1986. *The Muse Learns to Write: Reflections on Orality and Literacy from Antiquity to the Present*. New Haven: Yale University Press.

Herlinghaus, Hermann. 2005. "Subcomandante Marcos: Narrative Policy and Epistemological Project." *Journal of Latin American Cultural Studies* 14 (1): 53–74.

Hicks, D. Emily. 1991. *Border Writing: The Multidimensional Text*. Minneapolis: University of Minnesota Press.

Higgins, Nicholas P. 2001. "Mexico's Stalled Peace Process: Prospects and Challenges." *International Affairs* 77 (4): 885–903.

————. 2004. *Understanding the Chiapas Rebellion: Modernist Visions and the Invisible Indian*. Austin: University of Texas Press.

Holloway, John. 1993. "Dignity's Revolt." In *Zapatisa! Reinventing Revolution in Mexico*, edited by J. Holloway and E. Peláez. London: Pluto Press.

————. 2002. *Change the World without Taking Power*. London: Pluto Press.

Holloway, John, and Eloína Peláez, eds. 1998. *Zapatista! Reinventing Revolution in Mexico*. London: Pluto Press.

Inda, Jonathan Xavier. 2006. *Targeting Immigrants: Government, Technology, and Ethics*. Oxford: Blackwell.

Irr, Caren. 2003. "All Published Literature Is World Bank Literature; or, the Zapatistas' Storybook." In *World Bank Literature*, edited by A. Kumar, J. Berger, and B. Robbins. Minneapolis: University of Minnesota Press.

Jara, René, and Hernán Vidal, eds. 1986. *Testimonio y literatura*. Monographic series of the Society for the Study of Contemporary Hispanic and Lusophone Revolutionary Literatures, no. 3. Minneapolis: Institute for the Study of Ideologies and Literature.

Klor de Alva, J. Jorge. 1992. "Colonialism and Postcolonialism as (Latin) American Mirages." *Colonial Latin American Review* 1 (1–2): 3–23.

Láscar, Amado J. 2004. "La teoría zapatista: Una huella en la selva o un camino en la resistencia anti-neoliberal?" *ALPHA: Revista de Artes, Letras y Filosofía* 20: 181–200.

Latin American Subaltern Studies Group. 1994. "Founding Statement." *Dispositio/n (American Journal of Cultural Histories and Theories)* 19 (46): 1–12.

Levinson, Brett. 1996. "Neopatriarchy and After: *I, Rigoberta Menchú* as Allegory of Death." *Journal of Latin American Cultural Studies* 5 (1): 33–50.

———. 2001. *The Ends of Literature: The Latin American "Boom" in the Neoliberal Marketplace*. Stanford: Stanford University Press.

———. 2007. "Globalizing Paradigms, or, The Delayed State of Latin American Theory." *South Atlantic Quarterly* 106 (1): 61–83.

Lienhard, Martín. 1991. *La voz y su huella: Escritura y conflicto étnico-social en América Latina, 1492–1988*. Hanover, NH: Ediciones del Norte.

Lund, Joshua. 2006. *The Impure Imagination: Toward a Critical Hybridity in Latin American Writing*. Minneapolis: University of Minnesota Press.

Mallon, Florencia E. 1994. "The Promise and Dilemma of Subaltern Studies: Perspectives from Latin American History." *American Historical Review* 99 (5): 1491–515.

———. 1995. *Peasant and Nation: The Making of Postcolonial Mexico and Peru*. Berkeley: University of California Press.

Marcone, Jorge. 1997. *La oralidad escrita: Sobre la reivindicación y re-inscripción del discurso oral*. Lima: Fondo Editorial de la Pontificia Universidad Católica.

Marcos, Subcomandante Insurgente. 2001a. *Nuestra arma es nuestra palabra: Escritos selectos*. Edited by J. Ponce de León. New York: Siete Ensayos Editorial.

———. 2001b. *Our Word Is Our Weapon: Selected Writings*. Edited by J. Ponce de Léon. New York: Seven Stories Press.

———. 2005. *Conversations with Durito: Stories of the Zapatistas and Neoliberalism*. Edited by AZE Collective. New York: Autonomedia.

Marcos, Subcomandante Insurgente, Yvon Lebot, and Maurice Najman. 1997. *El sueño zapatista: Entrevistas con el subcomandante Marcos, el mayor Moisés y el comandante Tacho, del Ejército Zapatista de Liberación Nacional*. Barcelona: Plaza y Janés.

Marcos, Subcomandante Insurgente, and Ziga Vodovnik. 2004. *Ya basta! Ten Years of the Zapatista Uprising: Writings of Subcomandante Insurgente Marcos*. Oakland, CA: AK Press.

Mariátegui, José Carlos. 1928. *Siete ensayos de interpretación de la realidad peruana*. Lima: Biblioteca Amauta.

———. 1971. *Seven Interpretive Essays on Peruvian Reality*. Austin: University of Texas Press.

Mariátegui, José Carlos, Luis Alberto Sánchez, and Manuel Aquézolo Castro. 1976. *La Polémica del indigenismo*. 2nd ed. Lima: Mosca Azul Editores.

Martí, José. 1977. "Nuestra América." In *Nuestra América*. Caracas: Biblioteca Ayacucho.

Matto de Turner, Clorinda. 1889. *Aves sin Nido: Novela Peruana*. Lima: Imprenta del Universo de Carlos Prince.

Matto de Turner, Clorinda, and Antonio Cornejo Polar. 1994. *Aves sin nido*. Caracas: Biblioteca Ayacucho.

Mazzotti, José Antonio. 1996. *Coros mestizos del Inca Garcilaso*. Mexico City: Fondo de Cultura Económica.

Menchú, Rigoberta, and Elisabeth Burgos-Debray. 1983. *Me llamo Rigoberta Menchú y así me nació la conciencia*. Havana: Casa de las Américas.

Menchú, Rigoberta, and Elisabeth Burgos-Debray. 1984. *I, Rigoberta Menchú: An Indian Woman in Guatemala*. Translated by A. Wright. London: Verso.

Michaelsen, Scott, and David E. Johnson, eds. 1997. *Border Theory: The Limits of Cultural Politics*. Minneapolis: University of Minnesota Press.

Michaelsen, Scott, and Scott Cutler Shershow. 2007. "Rethinking Border Thinking." *South Atlantic Quarterly* 106 (1): 39–60.

Mignolo, Walter. 1993. "Colonial and Postcolonial Discourse: Cultural Critique or Academic Colonialism." *Latin American Research Review* 28 (3): 120–34.

———. 1995. *The Darker Side of the Renaissance: Literacy, Territoriality, and Colonization*. Ann Arbor: University of Michigan Press.

————. 2002. "The Zapatista's Theoretical Revolution: Its Historical, Ethical and Political Consequences." *Review Fernand Braudel Center for the Study of Economies, Historical Systems, and Civilizations* 25 (3): 245–75.

————. 2011. *The Darker Side of Western Modernity: Global Futures, Decolonial Options*. Durham, NC: Duke University Press.

Millay, Amy Nauss. 2005. *Voices from the* fuente viva: *The Effect of Orality in Twentieth-Century Spanish American Narrative*: Lewisburg, PA : Bucknell University Press.

Montejo, Esteban, and Miguel Barnet. 1966. *Biografía de un cimarrón*. Havana: Instituto de Ethnología y Folklore.

Montemayor, Carlos. 1997. *Chiapas: La rebelión indígena de México*. Mexico City: J. Mortiz.

Mora, Mariana. 2003. "The Imagination to Listen: Reflections on a Decade of Zapatista Struggle." *Social Justice* 30 (3): 17–31.

Morales, Mario Roberto. 2008. "Peripheral Modernity and Differential *Mestizaje* in Latin America: Outside Subalternist Postcolonialism." In *Coloniality at Large: Latin America and the Postcolonial Debate*, edited by M. Moraña, E. Dussel, and C. Jauregui. Durham, NC: Duke University Press.

Moraña, Mabel. 1997. "El Boom del Subalterno." *Revista de Critica Cultural* 15: 48–53.

————. 1998a. "El Boom del Subalterno." *Cuadernos Americanos* 67: 214–22.

————. 1998b. "Indigenismo y globalización." In *Indigenismo hacia el fin del milenio: Homenaje a Antonio Conejo-Polar*. Pittsburgh: Instituto Internacional de Literatura Iberoamericana.

Moraña, Mabel, Enrique D. Dussel, and Carlos A. Jáuregui. 2008. *Coloniality at Large: Latin America and the Postcolonial Debate*. Durham, NC: Duke University Press.

Moreiras, Alberto. 2001. *The Exhaustion of Difference: The Politics of Latin American Cultural Studies*. Durham, NC: Duke University Press.

Olesen, Thomas. 2005. *International Zapatismo: The Construction of Solidarity in the Age of Globalization*. New York: Zed Books.

Ong, Walter J. 1982. *Orality and Literacy: The Technologizing of the Word*. London: Methuen.

Ortiz Pérez, Luisa. 2003. "Marcos: El icono desconocido. El uso del mito como herramienta política del EZLN mexicano." *Brújula: Revista Interdisciplinaria Sobre Estudios Latinoamericanos* 2 (1): 72–86.

Pacheco, Carlos. 1992. *La comarca oral: La ficcionalización de la oralidad cultural en la narrativa latinoamericana contemporánea.* Caracas: Ediciones La Casa de Bello.

Padilla, Heberto. 1968. *Fuera del juego.* Havana: La Habana Unión de Escritores y Artistas de Cuba.

Peres, P. 1994. "Subaltern Spaces in Brazil." *Dispositio/n (American Journal of Cultural Histories and Theories)* 19 (46): 113–26.

Pérez, Alberto Julián. 1999. "El postcolonialismo y la inmadurez de los pensadores Hispanoamericanos." In *El debate de la postcolonialidad en Latinoamérica,* edited by A. D. Toro and F. D. Toro. Madrid: Vervuert, Iberoamericana.

Polkinhorn, Harry, Gabriel Trujillo Muñoz, and Rogelio Reyes. 1987. *La Línea: Ensayos sobre literatura fronteriza méxico-norteamericana (The Line: Essays on Mexican/American Border Literature).* Mexicali, Mexico: Universidad Autónoma de Baja California, San Diego State University.

Prakash, Gyan. 2000. "The Impossibility of Subaltern History." *Nepantla: Views from South* 1 (2): 287–94.

Rabasa, José. 1994. "Pre-Columbian Pasts and Indian Presents in Mexican History." *Dispositio/n (American Journal of Cultural Histories and Theories)* 19 (46): 245–70.

———. 1997. "Of Zapatismo: Reflections on the Folkloric and the Impossible in a Subaltern Insurrection." In *The Politics of Culture in the Shadow of Capital,* edited by L. Lowe and D. Lloyd. Durham, NC: Duke University Press.

———. 2005. "Negri by Zapata: Constituent Power and the Limits of Autonomy." In *Resistance in Practice: The Philosophy of Antonio Negri,* edited by T. S. Murphy and A.-K. Mustapha. London: Pluto Press.

———. 2010. *Without History: Subaltern Studies, the Zapatista Insurgency, and the Specter of History.* Pittsburgh: University of Pittsburgh Press.

Rama, Angel. 1984. *La ciudad letrada.* Hanover, NH: Ediciones del Norte.

———. 1996. *The Lettered City.* Translated by J. C. Chasteen. Durham, NC: Duke University Press.

Ramos, Julio. 2001. *Divergent Modernities: Culture and Politics in Nineteenth Century Latin America.* Translated by J. D. Blanco. Durham, NC: Duke University Press.

Rancière, Jacques. 1999. *Disagreement: Politics and Philosophy.* Minneapolis: University of Minnesota Press.

Randall, Margaret. 1983. *Testimonios.* San José, Costa Rica: Centro de Estudios y Publicaciones Alforja.

Rodó, José Enrique. 1900. *Ariel.* Montevideo: Impr. de Dornaleche y Reyes.

Rodríguez, Ileana. 1982. "Organizaciones Populares y literatura testimonial: Los años treinte en Nicaragua y El Salvador." in *Literatures in Transition: The Many Voices of the Caribbean Area,* edited by R. Minc. Gaithersburg, MD: Montclair State College, Hispamérica.

———. 2001. *The Latin American Subaltern Studies Reader.* Durham, NC: Duke University Press.

Rowe, William. 2003. "Sobre la heterogeneidad de la letra en Los ríos profundos: Una crítica a la oposición polar escritura/oralidad." in *Heterogeneidad y literatura en el Perú,* edited by J. Higgins. Lima: Centro de Estudios Literarios "Antonio Cornejo Polar."

Rubio-Goldsmith, Raquel, M. Melissa McCormick, Daniel Martinez, and Inez Magdalena Duarte. 2006. *The "Funnel Effect" and Recovered Bodies of Unauthorized Migrants Processed by the Pima County Office of the Medical Examiner, 1990–2005 (Report Submitted to the Pima County Board of Supervisors).* Tucson: Binational Migration Institute, Mexican-American Studies and Research Center at the University of Arizona.

Saldaña-Portillo, María Josefina. 2003. *Revolutionary Imagination in the Americas and the Age of Development.* Durham, NC: Duke University Press.

Saldívar, José David. 1991. *The Dialectics of Our America: Genealogy, Cultural Critique, and Literary History.* Durham, NC: Duke University Press.

———. 1997. *Border Matters: Remapping American Cultural Studies.* Berkeley: University of California Press.

Sarto, Ana del, Alicia Ríos, and Abril Trigo. 2004. *The Latin American Cultural Studies Reader.* Durham, NC: Duke University Press.

Seed, Patricia. 1991. "Colonial and Postcolonial Discourse." *Latin American Research Review* 26 (3): 181–200.

———. 1993. "More Colonial and Postcolonial Discourses." *Latin American Research Review* 28 (3): 146–52.

Sinnigen, John H. 1999. "Narrativa de diversas guerras: Los comunicados zapatistas." *Universidad de La Habana* 250: 152–64.

Sklodowska, Elzbieta. 1982. "La forma testimonial y la novelística de Miguel Barnet." *Revista/Review Interamericana* 12 (3): 375–84.

———. 1992. *Testimonio hispanoamericano: Historia, teoría, poética.* New York: Peter Lang.

———. 1993. "Testimonio mediatizado: Ventriloquia o heteroglosia? (Barnet/ Montejo; Burgos/Menchú)." *Revista de Crítica Literaria Latinoamericana* 19 (38): 81–90.

Sommer, Doris. 1991a. *Foundational Fictions: The National Romances of Latin America.* Berkeley: University of California Press.

———. 1991b. "Rigoberta's Secrets." *Latin American Perspectives* 18 (3): 32–50.

———. 1992. "Sin Secretos." *Revista de Crítica Literaria Latinoamericana* 18 (36): 135–54.

———. 1999. *Proceed with Caution, When Engaged by Minority Writing in the Americas.* Cambridge, MA: Harvard University Press.

Spivak, Gayatri Chakravorty. 1988a. "Can the Subaltern Speak?" In *Marxism and the Interpretation of Culture*, edited by L. Grossberg and C. Nelson. Urbana: University of Illinois Press.

———. 1988b. "Subaltern Studies: Deconstructing Historiography." In *Selected Subaltern Studies*, edited by R. Guha and G. C. Spivak. New York: Oxford University Press.

Steele, Cynthia, Ignacio Corona, and Beth E. Jörgensen. 2002. "The Rainforest Chronicles of Subcomandante Marcos." In *The Contemporary Mexican Chronicle: Theoretical Perspectives on the Liminal Genre*, edited by I. Corona and B. E. Jörgensen. Albany: State University of New York Press.

Stoll, David. 1999. *Rigoberta Menchú and the Story of All Poor Guatemalans.* Boulder, CO: Westview Press.

Tabuenca, María Socorro. 1995. "Reflexiones sobre la literatura de la frontera." *Puente Libre* 4: 8–12.

Tabuenca Córdoba, María Socorro. 1995–96. "Viewing the Border: Perspectives from 'the Open Wound.'" *Discourse: Journal for Theoretical Studies in Media and Culture* 18 (1–2): 146–68.

Tarica, Estelle. 2008. *The Inner Life of Mestizo Nationalism.* Minneapolis: University of Minnesota Press.

Taylor, Analisa. 2009. *Indigeneity in the Mexican Cultural Imagination: Thresholds of Belonging.* Tucson: University of Arizona Press.

Tello Díaz, Carlos. 2000. *La rebelión de las Cañadas: Origen y ascenso del EZLN.* 11th ed. Mexico City: Aguilar, León y Cal Editores.

Tormey, Simon. 2006. "'Not in My Name': Deleuze, Zapatismo and the Critique of Representation." *Parliamentary Affairs* 59 (1): 138–54.

Toro, Alfonso de, and Fernando de Toro. 1999. *El debate de la postcoloniali-dad en Latinoamérica. Teoría y crítica de la cultura y literatura.* Madrid: Iberoamericana, Vervuert.

Urrea, Luis Alberto. 2004. *The Devil's Highway: A True Story.* New York: Back Bay Books.

Vanden Berghe, Kristine. 2005. *Narrativa de la rebelión zapatista: Los relatos del Subcomandante Marcos:* Madrid: Iberoamericana, Vervuert.

Vaquera-Vásquez, Santiago. 1998. "Wandering in the Borderlands: Mapping an Imaginative Geography of the Border." *Latin American Issues* 14(6), http://sites.allegheny.edu/latinamericanstudies/latin-american-issues/volume-14/. Accessed July 11, 2013.

Vargas Llosa, Mario. 1969a. "Novela primitiva y la novela de creación en America Latina." *Revista de la universidad de Mexico* 23 (10): 29–36.

———. 1969b. "Tres notas sobre Arguedas." In *Nueva novela Latinamericana,* edited by L. Jorge. Buenos Aires: Editorial Paidós.

———. 1996. *La utopia arcaica: José María Arguedas y las ficciones del indigenismo.* Mexico City: Fondo de Cultura Económica.

Vera León, Antonio. 1992. "Hacer Hablar: La transcripción testimonial." *Revista de Crítica Literaria Latinoamericana* 36 (2): 183–202.

Verdesio, Gustavo, ed. 2005. "Latin American Subaltern Studies Revisited." Special issue of *Dispositio/n (American Journal of Cultural Histories and Theories)* 25.

Vidal, Hernán. 1993. "The Concept of Colonial and Postcolonial Discourse: A Perspective from Literary Criticism." *Latin American Research Review* 28 (3): 113–19.

Vila, Pablo. 2000. *Crossing Borders, Reinforcing Borders: Social Categories, Metaphors, and Narrative Identities on the U.S.-Mexico Frontier.* Austin: University of Texas Press.

Wagner, Valeria, and Alejandro Moreira. 2003. "Toward a Quixotic Pragmatism: The Case of the Zapatista Insurgence." *Boundary 2: An International Journal of Literature and Culture* 30 (3): 185–212.

Williams, Gareth. 1993. "Translation and Mourning: The Cultural Challenge of Latin American Testimonial Autobiography." *Latin American Literary Review* 21 (41): 79–99.

———. 1996. "The Fantasies of Cultural Exchange in Latin American Subaltern Studies." In *The Real Thing: Testimonial Discourse and Latin America,* edited by G. M. Gugelberger. Durham, NC: Duke University Press.

———. 2002. *The Other Side of the Popular: Neoliberalism and Subalternity in Latin America.* Durham, NC: Duke University Press.

———. 2007. "The Mexican Exception and the 'Other Campaign.'" *SAQ* 106 (1): 129–51.

———. 2011. *The Mexican Exception: Sovereignty, Police, and Democracy.* New York: Palgrave Macmillan.

Yúdice, George. 1991. "Testimonio and Postmodernism." *Latin American Perspectives* 18 (3): 15–31.

Žižek, Slavoj. 2006. *The Parallax View.* Cambridge, MA: MIT Press.

———. 2012. *Less Than Nothing: Hegel and the Shadow of Dialectical Materialism.* New York: Verso.

Index

just ideas

Roger Berkowitz, *The Gift of Science: Leibniz and the Modern Legal Tradition*

Jean-Luc Nancy, translated by Pascale-Anne Brault and Michael Naas, *The Truth of Democracy*

Drucilla Cornell and Kenneth Michael Panfilio, *Symbolic Forms for a New Humanity: Cultural and Racial Reconfigurations of Critical Theory*

Karl Shoemaker, *Sanctuary and Crime in the Middle Ages, 400–1500*

Michael J. Monahan, *The Creolizing Subject: Race, Reason, and the Politics of Purity*

Drucilla Cornell and Nyoko Muvangua (eds.), *uBuntu and the Law: African Ideals and Postapartheid Jurisprudence*

Drucilla Cornell, Stu Woolman, Sam Fuller, Jason Brickhill, Michael Bishop, and Diana Dunbar (eds.), *The Dignity Jurisprudence of the Constitutional Court of South Africa: Cases and Materials, Volumes I & II*

Nicholas Tampio, Kantian Courage: *Advancing the Enlightenment in Contemporary Political Theory*

Carroll Clarkson, *Drawing the Line: Toward an Aesthetics of Transitional Justice*

Jane Anna Gordon, *Creolizing Political Theory: Reading Rousseau through Fanon*

Jimmy Casas Klausen, *Fugitive Rousseau: Slavery, Primitivism, and Political Freedom*

Drucilla Cornell, *Law and Revolution in South Africa: uBuntu, Dignity, and the Struggle for Constitutional Transformation*

Abraham Acosta, *Thresholds of Illiteracy: Theory, Latin America, and the Crisis of Resistance*